Women's careers.

DATE			

© THE BAKER & TAYLOR CO.

Women's Careers

Women's Careers

PATHWAYS AND PITFALLS

EDITED BY

Suzanna Rose

AND

Laurie Larwood

New York
Westport, Connecticut
London

Library of Congress Cataloging-in-Publication Data

Women's careers.

Bibliography: p.
Includes index.
1. Women—Employment. 2. Women executives.
3. Women—Employment—United States. 4. Women—
Employment—Canada. 5. Sex discrimination in
employment—United States. 6. Sex discrimination
in employment—Canada. I. Rose, Suzanna. II. Larwood,
Laurie. III. Title.
HD6053.W668   1988   331.4'0973   88-2344
ISBN 0-275-92724-5 (alk. paper)

Library of Congress Catalog Card Number: 88-2344

ISBN: 0-275-92724-5

First published in 1988

Praeger Publishers, One Madison Avenue, New York, NY 10010
A division of Greenwood Press, Inc.

Printed in the United States of America

∞

˙ The paper used in this book complies with the
Permanent Paper Standard issued by the National
Information Standards Organization (Z39.48-1984).

10   9   8   7   6   5   4   3   2   1

Contents

Preface

A growing interest in women's careers has spread to personal, academic, and organizational life. The proliferation and quality of research on women and work that we saw as program chairs of the 1986 International Conference on Women and Organizations inspired us to edit this book. That highly successful conference was the source of several chapters included here.

Our goal was to select timely topics that had immediate relevance to career women, students, and scholars of women and work. Part I of the book begins with an introduction by the editors which highlights five major issues that affect working women and what has been learned about those issues in the 1980s. Other chapters are ordered thematically. In Part II, "Personal Career Planning," the themes touch on pathways and pitfalls confronting women as they plan their career strategies. In Chapters 2, 3, and 4, Shapiro and Farrow discuss the merits of mentors, Case analyzes women's speech, and Ely explores women's leadership styles, respectively; with an eye to how women can apply the information to their own work situation. Family relationships also have been shown to affect women's careers. In Chapter 5, "Husbands' Job Satisfaction and Wives' Income," and Chapter 6, "Have Women's Career and Family Values Changed?" questions are raised concerning the relationship between marriage, family, and careers. In Chapter 7, Chao and Malik present a career planning model which ties together individual, organizational, and societal constraints and facilitators of professional development.

Part III, "The Challenge of the Workplace," deals with broader issues related to the context of work. Stella Nkomo, in Chapter 8, presents the unique problems black women face that have not been addressed adequately in the past. The commonalities between token women in organizations and token women in academe are explored by Dyer and Devine in Chapter 9. The impact of affirmative action programs nationally is assessed by Cullen, Nakamura, and Nakamura in Chapter 10 by comparing the United States with Canada, which has no comparable programs. Clarke, in Chapter 11, and Hisrich and Brush in Chapter 12, examine the more personal issues of sexual harassment and getting established as an entrepreneur, and suggest avenues for coping with negative experiences.

Each chapter opens with a *preview*. In it, authors give first person accounts of what motivated them to write their chapters and how they think you, the reader, will be able to apply what they have written to your own career. In addition, although each chapter has its own bibliography, a list of general references is included at the end of the book. These references were selected to represent only the more significant and current work in the field.

We are pleased to acknowledge the support of those who helped us complete this book. We give special thanks to Victoria Sork, who generously devoted many hours to the preparation of the final manuscript and who provided encouragement throughout the project. We also extend thanks to Lynda L. Moore and V. Jean Ramsey, executive directors of the Institute for Women and Organizations and sponsors of the 1986 conference.

PART I
INTRODUCTION

1

Charting Women's Careers: Current Issues and Research

Suzanna Rose
Laurie Larwood

PREVIEW

A vast amount of information on women and work is available today. In writing this chapter, we decided to focus on only a few of the most relevant issues confronting professional women. Our emphasis was on women who have made a clear commitment to their career. Issues related to working women in general were brought in only where they affected the status of the woman professional. What we present here represents a very selective look at the contemporary career woman— her opportunities, goals, personality, relationships, and family life.

The importance of careers in the plans and lives of women continues to grow as people become aware that the working woman now has replaced the housewife as the norm in the United States. The absolute number of women in the workforce currently exceeds that of men (U.S. Department of Labor Statistics 1986). By 1990, 70–75 percent of all women aged 18–64 are expected to be in the labor force, compared to 63 percent for 1984. "Having it all" is the goal of a majority of young women who plan to work all or most of their lives and have a family, too (Betz and Fitzgerald 1987).

Striking changes in how women's careers are viewed have accompanied their increased occupational involvement. Early models of career development aimed at men failed to account for the many factors that uniquely affect women's careers, including cultural and organizational barriers to women's advancement, sex role training, and competing work and family roles. Interest in women's careers has burgeoned in the past decade, however, producing a flood of research about women and work and culminating in the "career psychology of women" as a field of its own (Betz and Fitzgerald 1987).

In this chapter, a selective review of research since 1980 will be presented to illustrate the present status of women's careers. A profile of five major issues concerning women's careers will be drawn, including the nature of sex discrimination, leadership strategies for women, the interface between the professional and personal at work, the impact of race, and balancing career and family roles.

UNDERSTANDING SEX DISCRIMINATION

Women's career progress has not been commensurate with our increased participation in the workforce and work commitment. About 45 percent of women are full-time, year-round workers, compared to 65 percent of men, yet we earn from 24 percent to 45 percent less than men, depending on the type of job we hold (Blau and Ferber 1985). Professional level jobs offer no exception to the wage inequity rule. Women MBAs average less in earnings than men within a few years of graduation (Olson and Frieze 1987), women civil servants are concentrated in the lower paying grades, and only 10 percent of full professorships in academe are held by women (Blau and Ferber 1985).

Why do women earn less than men? Three approaches have been used to answer this question. The first has been to identify patterns and changes in occupational sex segregation to determine if they can explain wage differences. A substantial degree of occupational sex segregation continues to be the norm, with women comprising about 81 percent and 73 percent, respectively, of employees in low paying clerical and service jobs, while men predominate in better paying managerial and blue collar supervisory, labor, and farm jobs (Blau and Ferber 1985). Recent figures indicate that three out of five workers of one sex would have to change jobs to duplicate the distribution of workers of the opposite sex. However, some slight changes have been documented that might have an impact on occupational sex segregation. The number of black women employed in domestic service has decreased rapidly since 1970 and there has been a large increase in the number of women earning degrees in predominantly male fields (Blau and Ferber 1985; Jacobs 1985). Whether the change in occupational distribution will result in a concomitant change in the wage gap is of great future interest.

A second approach focuses on teasing out the factors that might account for salary inequities or hierarchical segregation, such as work experience or prejudice. This research has conclusively demonstrated that sex differences in productivity cannot explain the major part of the wage differential between women and men. Variables such as number of hours worked, amount of past work experience, type of occupation or industry, and race, account for only about half of the observed sex-wage differential (Madden 1985)—and even these beg further explanation. Treiman and Roos (1983), in a wide scale study of salary structures in the United States and eight other nations, demonstrated that the sex-wage differential could not be explained by differential investments by women and men in their careers, by women's family responsibilities, or by differences in jobs. Olson, Good, and Frieze (1985) reported that job area, job level, type of job, and type of prior work experience could explain only $700 of the $2900 gender difference in starting salaries for MBA (Masters of Business Administration) alumni of one university. Thus, economists' "human capital" argument that men's higher wages reflect greater levels of worth—education, training, and time in the market—is not supported.

Mounting evidence indicates that continued discrimination against women in terms of unequal pay for equal work is responsible for much of the wage gap (Blau and Ferber 1985). Crosby (1982), in an investigation of high and low status employed women and men in the Boston suburbs, found that even women who were equal to men in terms of job relevant characteristics (e.g., occupational prestige, education, years of training) and job-related attitudes (e.g., job commitment) still earned $8000 less than men, on average. Similarly, women engineers with educational backgrounds and work experience equivalent to men's earn less (Jagacinski 1987). Discrimination might even be underestimated in some cases. For instance, Olson and Frieze (1987) found that women MBAs came from higher socioeconomic backgrounds than men MBAs, a factor predictive of higher earnings, yet they earned less than men.

As evidence for sex discrimination accumulates, what causes it and how it might be changed have made up a third significant research area. Two factors that have been explored recently are organizational climate (affirmative action programs) and cognitive factors (attitudes). For instance, Rosenbaum (1985) documented the positive effect of affirmative action on pay inequalities in a large corporation from 1962 to 1975. In 1969, women's earnings were 46 percent lower than men's. After 1975, with an affirmative action program in place, the wage gap dropped to 23 percent. Women also had promotion rates as high or higher than men, compared to lower promotion rates prior to 1969. However, other research indicates that affirmative action has had little effect on sex segregation of jobs, one major source of wage inequity. Even after two decades of affirmative action, occupational sex segregation in the United States does not differ from that of Canada, which has had no similar programs (Cullen, Nakamura, and Nakamura 1988). This research suggests that gains some women have made have not yet translated into improvements for women overall.

Cognitive biases are also germane to understanding sex discrimination. Most people today have favorable attitudes toward women as workers. In 1970, only 45 percent of men and 55 percent of women in a public opinion poll agreed that "women could run a business as well as men." By 1982, 91 percent of men and 92 percent of women agreed (Kahn and Crosby 1985). Similarly, most adults profess to believe in equal pay for equal work. Yet these beliefs have not resulted in economic equity for women. Why? Two of the many answers to this question emphasize the role of context in people's decisions to discriminate or not.

Rational bias theory argues that "rational," self-interested managers make decisions in the context of the organization and take into account the attitudes and preferences of powerful others (Larwood, Gutek, and Gattiker 1984). The rational manager prefers to hire and keep the best subordinates, including women and minorities, but might engage in discrimination if it were thought to be expected or preferred by superiors or major clients. Research on the attitudes of management consulting clients and management students has supported the theory. Larwood and Gattiker (1985) reported that client attitudes supported discrimination against women management consultants by management. Likewise, management students who perceived that business norms favored discrimination were more likely to discriminate against white women, black men, and black women when asked to select one of two subordinates for a hypothetical job (Larwood, Szwajkowski, and Rose 1987).

Alternatively, Kahn and Crosby (1985) contend that discrimination is the result of cumulative discrete individual decisions favoring men, which are not identified singly as discriminatory acts. In a laboratory test of this hypothesis, Crosby, Clayton, Alksnis, and Hamker (1986) found that men were more likely to view discrimination as having occurred if presented with complete descriptions of ten hirings and promotions involving women than if presented with the same ten cases one at a time. These results might also explain why women do not always perceive they are being discriminated against. Job experiences of token women are more comparable to the single case than to the total picture format.

In summary, women are far from having achieved economic equality, but the gap is very slowly closing. Research on sex discrimination has contributed to a clear understanding of the depth of the problem and possible causes and solutions. Other clues concerning how and when women achieve leadership roles can provide additional insight into women's current economic status.

LEADERSHIP STRATEGIES FOR WOMEN

Do women have the leadership skills necessary to obtain top positions? A wealth of research, trade books, and popular articles have addressed this question. Many people tend to equate leadership skills with masculine traits. For instance, "successful managers" are described as competitive, self-confident, objective, aggressive, forceful, and desiring of responsibility—traits that are more often used to describe men than women (Arkkelin and Simmons 1985; Powell and Butterfield 1984; Schein 1973). Consequently, for women to be seen as successful, they must either redefine notions of what a good leader is or conform to these traits.

The assumption that masculine traits and values are superior has been challenged in recent years, as efforts to redefine leadership in less sex-typed terms have become more common. For example, the six abilities of change masters (business people who know how to lead change productively and positively) identified by Kanter (1986) include the ability to create new patterns from old information, communicate visions, be persistent, build coalitions, work through teams to carry out ideas, and share credit. These skills and labels avoid the use of terms that are inherently masculine. Other redefinitions have emphasized the importance of feminine traits such as compassion and cooperation in effective management or the utility of women's and men's "separate strengths" (Case 1988; Kasten 1986). These new views of leadership may reflect changes in workplace values resulting from women's increasing economic role. Perhaps eventually they will compete successfully with current views of leadership. At present, however, masculine norms define the work world and shape the template against which women's fit or lack of fit is judged.

If women must conform to masculine stereotypes in order to be recognized as leaders, it becomes important to determine, first, what specific sex differences exist in work-related attitudes and behaviors and second, what are the professional, interpersonal, and personal consequences of conformity with the masculine stereotype? There is a great deal of speculation and much less evidence concerning whether women and men have different leadership styles. Women's socialization into more expressive family roles and their lack of experience at boys' games are the most often cited explanations for assumed sex differences (see, e.g., Harragan 1977; Kessler-Harris 1985; Landau and Amoss 1986).

Dexter (1985) and Greenhalgh and Gilkey (1986) provide recent examples of this approach. Dexter has attributed women's difficulty in achieving managerial positions in large organizations to the long resocialization necessary for women to make the transition from ascribed to achieved status. Men learn, primarily from other men, that they must achieve their status. However, women's status is ascribed, that is, determined at birth, based on the unchanging characteristic of sex. Based on ascribed status, women are socialized into family roles that subordinate them to men. Consequently, once on the job, women must learn what male managerial candidates already know, including how to acquire and exercise organizational power, treat people with the same status equally, and share the cultural (male) values of the organization.

According to Greenhalgh and Gilkey (1986), women are at a disadvantage in the business world because their pattern of negotiation is not based on the values of competitive games. Like the games boys learn, in business the objective is to beat one's opponent. Each victory or loss is viewed as a single episode. In contrast, girls learn that relationships should not be sacrificed in order to win. As a result, women are more cooperative and compromising than competitive, which gives men the edge in strategic negotiations.

Sex differences in a wide range of work-related attitudes have been explored and some evidence for arguments like the ones presented above have been found (e.g., Gomez-Mejia 1983; Greenhalgh and Gilkey 1986; Stratham 1987). However, it is difficult to determine whether these perceived sex differences reflect actual ones because little research using objective measures has been done. In a 1981 review, Nieva and Gutek reported that no sex difference in *behavior* had yet been uncovered. In addition, situational factors have not usually been assessed in studies showing women to be perceived as less competent than men (Riger and Galligan 1980). When these factors, including age, organizational level, experience, and status, are evaluated, they often are related to reported sex differences. For instance, Liden (1985) found that women subordinates in the banking business preferred men managers, but that the men managers had significantly more managerial experience than the women. Thus, experience could as easily account for subordinates' preferences as managers' gender.

If sex differences in organizational behavior are proven eventually, they might effectively explain why the stereotypic feminine woman will not become a leader after the male model. However, they will *not* be able to explain why women pioneers, indistinguishable in many ways from men, nonetheless find a ceiling on their careers beyond which top positions of power are not obtainable. Women pathbreakers into primarily men's fields differ significantly from conventional women. Lemkau (1983) reported that women in atypical professions (at least 75 percent male) were more likely to be tough-minded realists, assertive, happy-go-lucky, and masculine than women in sex typical professions. Williams and McCullers (1983) also found higher masculinity scores and preference for sports among highly successful women in atypical fields than among women in lower status, sex-typed jobs. The personalities of 25 black and 25 white women identified as extraordinary achievers were characterized by high achievement motivation, an internal locus of control, a reward orientation (an emphasis on benefits to be gained in risk taking rather than costs to be accrued), and constructive defenses against stress (Boardman, Harrington, and Horowitz 1987).

Profiles of high achieving women typically more strongly resemble those of men in the same profession than of average women. More Type A personalities—aggressive, competitive, hostile—have been found among groups of executive women than in the general population of women (Lipton 1986). Women managers have higher needs for achievement and power and similar needs for affiliation compared to men managers (Chusmir 1985). Masculine features in women might be preferred even in terms of body type and coloring. According to Wolff and Tarrand (in Lipton 1986), women in traditionally male jobs tend to be taller and thinner than average and to have short, dark hair. Furthermore, many successful women in male-dominated fields—like men—do not bear children. Professional women are much more likely than other women to be single or, if married, to have no children (Betz and Fitzgerald 1987).

Arguments that women do not have the personality traits necessary to achieve in male-defined arenas are refuted by these data. Expected rewards for fitting the male template are not realized, however. The rungs at the tops of women's career ladders are missing, whereas men's are evenly spaced and sturdy. Larwood and Gattiker (1987) found that successful men in 17 major corporations had followed a clearly identified career path, starting with high-level positions in a department, moving to line positions, and then becoming a professional. No similar consistently successful route was found for women. Nor does the ladder reach as high. The numbers of women in corporate America remain constant because top-level women often leave to develop their own businesses once they realize women can go no higher in the organization (Kasten 1986). It took women MBAs studied by Landau and Amoss (1986) only eight to ten years to reach the invisible ceiling on their careers. Within five years of graduation, with equivalent work experience, type of degree, and type of employment, 60 percent of women earned less than $30,000 compared to 40 percent of the men. Fourteen percent of the men earned over $50,000; only 5 percent of women were in that income bracket.

Women experience additional interpersonal and personal costs associated with their short career ladders. High performing women in male-dominated fields report stress associated with having to confront prejudice, discrimination, and isolation (Lipton 1986). Black women even more than white women are likely to lose friends and community (Boardman et al. 1987). Not surprisingly, women often are less satisfied with their advancement opportunities than men and more pessimistic about their future (Jagacinski 1987; Zanna, Crosby, and Loewenstein 1987).

There is some cause for optimism, however, that women will burst through the ceiling artificially limiting them as the rate of women entering the ranks of middle management and male fields accelerates. Attitudinal and behavioral change might accompany the change in sex ratios. For example, young men's attitudes toward women in the U.S. Coast Guard have been shown to improve over time as a result of working with women cadets (Stevens and Gardner 1987). A recent study of undergraduates in leadership roles indicated that authoritarian women leaders were as accepted as men authoritarians (Linimon, Barron, and Falbo 1984). Furthermore, husbands' support of women's rights have been found to increase as a function of wives' labor force involvement; husbands with wives working full-time are the most liberal (Smith 1985). The impact of these and other changes on the workplace might not be felt for another generation.

Certain organizational characteristics favorable to women have also been identified. For instance, Dexter (1985), in a review of research, reported that industrial firms had more sex-equitable occupational distributions than nonindustrial firms and that women were more likely to reach middle management in large companies. High growth rate communities also were seen as offering better career opportunities for women. Organizational climates which are explicitly egalitarian reduce discrimination (Katz 1987; Larwood et al. 1987). Conversely, more discrimination was observed in firms with plants in suburbs or small towns, those having government contracts with nondefense agencies, and those with little or no civil rights or labor litigation.

In conclusion, many women have the leadership skills as defined by the male template to obtain top positions. External barriers to their advancement prevent them from fulfilling their potential. Equal opportunity has not been achieved, but the ranks of women at the middle levels are swelling and the wage gap is closing. The forecast for the future? Steady change due to a pressure system caused by a rising mass of competent women.

THE PERSONAL-PROFESSIONAL INTERFACE

An exciting new body of research has been developing that explores the relationship between work and intimacy. These two areas frequently are treated as separate domains. The extensive overlap between personal and professional life is typically denied, ignored, or viewed as inappropriate. Yet people consistently self-disclose at work about their personal lives, including children, sexual adventures, and relationships. Professionals often must maintain social connections with colleagues. Working together also increases opportunities for friendship and attraction between coworkers to grow. The importance of the personal-professional interface is just beginning to be recognized. Mentoring, networking, and sexual harassment have received the most attention to date. A few other promising new research directions have emerged lately, including workplace romance, women's relationships with women, and the consequences of public disclosure of a lesbian identity at work.

Mentoring and networking were among the first workplace relationships to capture the public eye. For a time, having a mentor was believed to be a necessary and sufficient condition for career growth; networking was considered an alternate route to success (Rose 1986). Both strategies recognized the crucial impact of the informal context of work on careers. Current views of mentors and networks are more tempered, but both still are regarded as having a significant effect on advancement.

The positive benefits of same-sex mentors as role models is the most clearly established finding. Having women role models is associated with greater achievement for women. Subjectively, Gilbert (1985) found two aspects of same-sex models to be more salient for women graduate students than men. First, the women with women faculty models rated the relationship as significantly more important to their development than men with men models did. Second, women viewed the model's life-style and values as more important than men did. Both results could be due to women students' need for affirmation of their competence and role conflict in a male-dominated environment.

Women mentors might be preferable for professional women, then, but few women have enough status and power to fill this role at the top levels of organizations. Consequently, women seeking a mentor most often must depend on men. However, Dexter (1985) has warned against the female protégée–male mentor model, because it affirms women's ascriptive status. Promotion is based only on the male superior's endorsement; like women's family roles, this places her under male authority. This type of mentorship also acts as a form of social control, promoting only the careers of approved candidates.

The usefulness and necessity of a continuous one-to-one relationship with a mentor has been challenged by recent research. Keele (1986) argued that dependency on a mentor may lead to social isolation if it weakens other network ties. Other helpers often are overlooked as significant sources of support. An overwhelming majority of professionals described relationships with other helpers (colleagues, friends, and bosses) as being just as (or more) important to their careers as mentors (Keele 1986; Shapiro and Farrow 1988).

The studies reported above point to the need to differentiate the relative merits of strong and weak ties (Keele 1986). Protégée–mentor relationships involve strong ties, networks, weak ties. They anchor two endpoints of a continuum of work relationships. Weak ties, like networks, can provide sources of information and support that are very helpful professionally, if they are not pursued to the exclusion of other relationships on the continuum. Keeping a balance of both types of relationships is probably the best career strategy. Women faculty reported by Rose (1985) had networks that fit this pattern. They were comprised of a combination of "important colleagues" that included at least one higher-status woman, one or more higher-status man, and several other women and men peers. More will be learned if future research examines social networks at work instead of only one end of the continuum.

Sexual harassment has probably been focused on more than other forms of work relationships or sexual behavior because of its legal consequences (Gutek and Dunwoody 1987) and its implications for the efficiency and well-being of women workers. About 53 percent of working women will experience sexual harassment sometime in their working lives (Gutek 1985). Young, single, and educated women are more likely to be victims, particularly if they work in nontraditional jobs or have a male supervisor. Some evidence indicates that women over 30 might also be targets (Coles 1986). The effects of sexual harassment on women ranges from being forced to quit, to lower productivity, to self-blame (Gutek and Dunwoody 1987). Often the victim is fired (Coles 1986). Laws have granted some protection to women and Coles (1986) asserts that it pays to complain. In a study of 88 cases of sexual harassment submitted during 1979–1983 in a California county, she found that 42 suits were settled within three months. Complaints for which there were witnesses were more successful.

Sexual harassment recently has been examined within the broader context of sexual behavior at work (Gutek 1985). Estimates of nonharassing sexual behavior at work are quite high. Anywhere from 55 to 76 percent of women and 47 to 55 percent of men report being the recipient of at least one sexual overture that was meant to be complimentary (Gutek and Dunwoody 1987). Combined with estimates of sexual harassment, sex appears to permeate work.

Explorations of the consequences of workplace sexuality and intimacy are only beginning. Issues that have been raised include how to manage workplace romances (Spelman, Crary, Kram, and Clawson 1986), the organizational and personal factors associated with the incidence of romance (Haavio-Mannila 1988), and the consequences of nonharassing sexual behavior for women (Gutek and Dunwoody 1987). Research on sex at work reveals an interesting paradox. "At work, women are perceived as using sex to their advantage, yet in practice, they are hurt by sex at work. On the other hand, men who are perceived as concerned with business display more sexual behavior than women at work and may benefit from it" (Gutek and Dunwoody 1987, p. 250). Even when sexual behavior is mutual, an office affair will have more negative effect on a woman's career than a man's. Given the unequal impact of the personal-professional interface on women's careers, further research in this area is urgently needed.

Interest in women's relationships with other women as a research area has been heightened by the increase in the number of working women and the developments in feminist theory. The emphasis has been on predicting whether woman boss–woman employee relationships will be productive or unproductive and identifying what factors (age, personality) are likely to affect the relationships (see, e.g., Henderson and Marple 1986; O'Leary 1988). Will women bosses be more willing to facilitate a woman subordinate's career than a man boss would, or will women bosses be fearful of losing their authority if they are more responsive to women employees? One empirical study by Statham (1987) indicated the former was true. Statham interviewed 22 women and 18 men managers from a financial institution, a manufacturing firm, and a technical institute, and their women secretaries. The secretaries rated the women managers as being both task- and person-oriented (men were rated as neither), as more willing to give the secretaries responsibility and to help advance their careers, and as providing more structure for the job than men. The men managers and the two women managers who behaved more like the men were not liked by the secretaries as well as the other women managers. Additional research could be aimed at determining if the experience of working with a woman could change previously documented preferences among women for men bosses.

A final personal-professional interface issue that has been addressed is the consequences of public disclosure of a sexual identity at work. Schneider (1986) surveyed a national sample of 228 lesbians between the ages of 21 and 58, most of whom were professionally employed. Sixteen percent reported they were totally open about their sexuality at work, 55 percent were open with some coworkers, and 29 percent were not open at all. Open lesbians were more likely to have lower incomes, work with adults, and to be employed in small, female-dominated, human service settings. The lesbians least likely to "come out" were those in professional as opposed to working-class jobs, those with higher income, and those in male-dominated fields. Disclosure also was inhibited if the lesbian worked with children or in a large workplace, or if she had previously lost a job because of her sexuality.

Schneider's research indicates that lesbians may be burdened by stress due to isolation and prejudice even more than is generally true for professional women. The fear of harassment for disclosure is likely to affect the type of interpersonal contacts lesbians seek and their opportunities for promotion. Given the current public concern over AIDS and its effect on coworker relationships, the risks associated with being open might become greater. The labeling of AIDS as a "homosexual disease" by the media has obscured the fact that lesbians are less likely than even heterosexuals are to get AIDS. Lesbians who do come out will have to contend with both homophobia and fear of AIDS. Additional research on the linkage between work and intimacy as it affects lesbians would help to identify other problems and solutions.

In summary, the interface between the personal and professional is a newly emerging area within the field of women and work. A broad range of issues is being investigated that should begin to delineate the impact of work relationships on careers and of careers on relationships.

THE IMPACT OF RACE

Black women are in a unique situation in the 1980s. Black women now earn 84 percent of what white women earn, on the average. The job status of younger black women has improved almost to the level of white women. However, women of both races lag behind white and black men in terms of pay and status. Not only are black women concentrated within sex-typical professions, but they are further racially segregated within very few jobs. Black women comprised 5 percent of the labor force in 1985, but made up 25 percent of nursing aides and orderlies, 24 percent of maids, 19 percent of licensed practical nurses, and 17 percent of typists. The primary professional level jobs available for black women include teaching, social work, and nursing. Many of these jobs are vulnerable to cuts in government spending for education, health and social services, increased competition for human service and teaching jobs, and the professionalization of technical jobs like increased education requirements for practical nurses. Therefore, while the occupational position of black women has improved, their unemployment rate has increased and new job areas have not opened to them. Indeed, black women are now "between a rock and a hard place," according to Malveaux (1988).

These special employment problems confronting black women often are overlooked in favor of an emphasis on commonalities with either white women or black men. When speaking of women and minorities, black women as a separate group are rendered invisible. Yet a growing body of evidence is beginning to clarify the additional barriers to success black women face due to a confluence of race and sex discrimination. Young black women begin with high career aspirations—higher, in fact, than either white women or black men—but during college their aspirations decline until they are below those of black men (Betz and Fitzgerald, 1987). The causes and consequences of this decline have not been explored, but perhaps it reflects an awareness of diminished job opportunities and unequal treatment for black women.

Research on black women in management provides a closer look at what happens to those few who aspire to nontraditional professional level jobs. About 6 percent of black women hold executive, managerial, and administrative jobs, compared to 7 percent of black men, 10 percent of white women, and 14 percent of white men (U.S. Department of Labor 1986). Recent figures on salaries for these groups is not available, but earlier work by Brown and Ford (1977) indicated that the starting and current salaries of black women MBAs were substantially below those of their black male counterparts, which in turn, were much lower than those of white men. Business students in a laboratory study who had to choose a subordinate to work with a client most often preferred a white man, followed by a black man, white woman, and black woman in order of descending preference (Larwood, Swajkowski, and Rose 1988). These data dispel a harmful myth that black women "have it made" because they fulfill two affirmative action criteria by being black and female. Quite the contrary, black women encounter limits on their mobility due to both race and sex (Nkomo 1988).

Professional black women who do manage to pole vault or circumvent obstacles provide an exceptional opportunity to understand how success is achieved in the face of negative expectations. Several background factors have been identified which seem to propel pioneering black women. Black women who chose nontraditional college majors like engineering, physical sciences, and economics had mothers who were better educated and more frequently employed in nontraditional work than were the mothers of black women with traditional majors (Burlew 1982). The nontraditional black women also were less sex-typed, more confident about reaching their goals, had more work experience, and expected to have fewer female friends because of their ambition than the traditional women. Thus, as for white women, maternal success and a less feminine sex role identity are related to atypical career choices.

Other research by Boardman et al. (1987) examined the backgrounds and personalities of a group of white and black women who were "negative prediction defiers" (NPDs). Negative prediction defiers were women from low socioeconomic families whose parents had not finished high school, yet who had achieved extraordinary success. Both black and white NPDs had a high need for achievement and a very high internal locus of control, that is, they assumed personal responsibility for how their lives turned out. However, the black women NPDs were less reward-oriented than the white women, perceiving there to be more potential costs associated with taking risks than potential rewards. In addition, black NPDs reported twice as many costs as accompanying their success, including loss of friends and community and stress on family. However, their experience had made them more altruistic than bitter—the black women were significantly more willing to help others than the white NPDs. These results suggest that black women who achieve success must not only be prepared to face economic discrimination, but must have the internal resources to withstand personal isolation and loss.

Three new directions concerning black women's careers have been stimulated by the issues raised above. One has been a heightened interest in pinpointing survival strategies black women can use. Advice-oriented articles like those by Banks (1986) and Barnes (1986) detail the problems black women Ph.Ds are likely to confront, including lack of credibility, intense visibility, discrimination, and isolation, and present suggestions on how to cope. A second direction is aimed at future research: What questions should be asked next? Nkomo (1988) raises several topics that warrant further exploration, including how black women professionals perceive their experience, how mentoring is affected by race, and how white managers view black women. Lastly, our knowledge of the effect of race largely has been limited to research on black women. A third avenue for research would be to investigate the careers of other ethnic minority women. Clearly, we have been able to see only the tip of the iceberg concerning the impact of race and sex on women's careers. Much more awaits discovery.

BALANCING CAREER AND FAMILY ROLES

As the phenomenon of the dual career couple has become more commonplace, women have sought new ways of balancing work and family roles. The responsibilities of marriage and family generally have been regarded as detracting from women's professional commitment, even as they are viewed as enhancing men's. Many career women avoid the double duty of an eight-hour or more workday followed by housework and childcare by eliminating the roles of wife and mother. Women in high status jobs, especially those of manager, are more likely to be widowed, divorced, or separated or, if married, to be childless or have fewer children than women in lower status jobs (Valdez and Gutek 1987). Others struggle to do the housework that continues to fall disproportionately on their shoulders. Working women spend twice as much time as husbands and almost as much time as full-time housewives on maintaining the household (Nieva 1985).

Both positive and negative effects of juggling both roles have been found. On the positive side, married working women have higher self-esteem and marital satisfaction than unemployed wives. Husbands of working women also benefit in terms of better physical and mental health and happier marriages (Nieva 1985). Negative effects are more numerous, however. One drawback for women in terms of career development is their decreased job mobility. Markham (1987) concluded that migration does enhance careers and that men are more likely than women to move for their own advancement. Furthermore, not only do women move less for their own benefit, but when they do move for husbands' jobs, their own careers are often set back or interrupted. The underemployment of women in dual-career marriages is a familiar event. Research on husband-wife members of the same professions (psychology and sociology) indicated that wives often are unemployed, employed part-time and have the lowest incomes compared to husbands, single men, and single women in the same fields. Their husbands fared much better—they were fully employed, were more likely to have full professor rank, and were more productive than the other groups (reviewed in Betz and Fitzgerald 1987).

The extensive pattern of career subordination among middle-class women to marital and family roles briefly described above has led some couples to create novel arrangements to maintain the delicate balance of career and family. The commuter marriage is one such form. In a study of 50 commuter couples, the precipitating causes of this life-style were poor job opportunities available for the wife and a strong commitment from both spouses to the wife's career aspirations (Gerstel and Gross 1984).

Individual strategies used to respond to the demands placed on married women or mothers include trying to change the objective situation by managing one's time better. However, this solution does not change the basic nature of the problem. Women are still held (and perhaps hold themselves) responsible for a majority of household work and childcare. Short of convincing husbands of the intrinsic satisfactions associated with such tasks, women's balancing act will not be ended until organizations step in to help the dual career family. Beutell and Greenhaus (1986) propose some suggestions organizations could utilize to ease the strain, including giving employees realistic information concerning the amount of commitment and stress involved in different career paths, flex-time arrangements, the establishment of support systems through company seminars on stress management, and help with meeting childcare needs. In the meantime, "having it all" is likely to continue to mean "doing it all," as career women and researchers search for other solutions.

CONCLUSIONS

The intent in the present chapter was to demonstrate where career women stand in the 1980s with regard to five crucial issues—sex discrimination, leadership, personal-professional interfaces, race, and dual career and family roles. The overall picture shows that women have made significant gains in most areas, but substantial barriers to our career development still exist. Research on women and work has made substantial inroads into identifying sources of problems in each area and specific solutions. Full details on the chart of women's careers are not yet available, but our visibility of what lies ahead is improving.

REFERENCES

Arkkelin, D., and R. Simmons. 1985. "The "good manager": Sex-typed, androgynous, or likable? *Sex Roles, 12:* 1187–1198.

Banks, M.E. 1986. Black women clinicians: Survival against the odds. In S. Rose (Ed.), *Career guide for women scholars.* (pp. 108–114). New York: Springer.

Barnes, D.R. 1986. Transitions and stress for black female scholars. In S. Rose (Ed.), *Career guide for women scholars*. (pp. 68–80). New York: Springer.

Betz, N.E., and L.F. Fitzgerald. 1987. *The career psychology of women*. Orlando, FL: Academic Press.

Beutell, N., and J. Greenhaus. 1986. Balancing acts: Work-family conflict and the dual-career couple. In L. Moore (Ed.), *Not as far as you think: The realities of working women*. (pp. 163–180). Lexington, MA: D. C. Heath.

Blau, F.D., and M.A. Ferber. 1985. Women in the labor market: The last twenty years. In L. Larwood, A.H. Stromberg and B.A. Gutek (Eds.), *Women and work: An annual review*. (Vol. 1, pp. 19–49). Beverly Hills, CA: Sage.

Boardman, S.K., C.C. Harrington, and S.V. Horowitz. 1987. Successful women: A psychological investigation of family class and education origins. In B.A. Gutek and L. Larwood (Eds.), *Women's career development*. (pp. 66–86). Newbury Park, CA: Sage.

Brown, H.A. and D.L. Ford, Jr. 1977. An exploratory analysis of discrimination in the employment of black MBA graduates. *Journal of Applied Psychology, 62,* 50–56.

Burlew, A.K. 1982. The experience of black females in traditional and nontraditional professions. *Psychology of Women Quarterly, 6,* 312–326.

Case, S.S. 1988. Cultural differences, not deficiencies: An analysis of managerial women's language. In S. Rose and L. Larwood (Eds.), *Women's careers: Pathways and pitfalls*. New York: Praeger.

Chusmir, L.H. 1985. Dimensions of need for power: Personalized vs. socialized power in female and male managers. *Sex Roles, 11,* 759–769.

Coles, F.S. 1986. Forced to quit: Sexual harassment complaints and agency response. *Sex Roles, 14,* 81–95.

Crosby, F. 1982. *Relative deprivation and working women*. New York: Oxford University Press.

Crosby, F., S. Clayton, O. Alksnis, and K. Hemker. 1986. Cognitive biases in the perception of discrimination: The importance of format. *Sex Roles, 14,* 637–646.

Cullen, D., A. Nakamura, and M. Nakamura. 1988. Occupational sex segregation in Canada and the United States: Does affirmative action make a difference? In S. Rose and L. Larwood (Eds.), *Women's careers: Pathways and pitfalls*. New York: Praeger.

Dexter, C.R. 1985. Women and the exercise of power in organizations: From ascribed to achieved status. In L. Larwood, A.H. Stromberg, and B.A. Gutek (Eds.), *Women and work: An annual review*. (Vol. 1, pp. 239–258). Beverly Hills, CA: Sage.

Gerstel, N., and H. Gross. 1984. *Commuter marriage*. New York: The Guilford Press.

Gilbert, L. 1985. Dimensions of same-gender student-faculty role-model relationships. *Sex Roles, 12,* 111–123.

Gomez-Mejia, L.R. 1983. Sex differences during occupational socialization. *American Management Journal, 26,* 492–499.

Greenhalgh, L. and R.W. Gilkey. 1986. Our game, your rules: Developing effective negotiating approaches. In L. Moore (Ed.), *Not as far as you think: The realities of working women*. (pp. 135–148). Lexington, MA: D. C. Heath.

Gutek, B. 1985. *Sex and the workplace: The impact of sexual behavior and harassment on women, men, and organizations*. San Francisco: Jossey-Bass.

Gutek, B.A. and V. Dunwoody. 1987. Understanding sex in the workplace. In A.H. Stromberg, L. Larwood, and B.A. Gutek (Eds.), *Women and work: An annual review*. (Vol. 2, pp. 249–269). Beverly Hills, CA: Sage.

Haavio-Mannila, E. In press. Sex structure of the workplace, informal interaction, and sentiments of liking between women and men at work. In B. Gutek, A.H. Stromberg, and L. Larwood (Eds.), *Women and work: An annual review*. (Vol. 3). Newbury Park, CA: Sage.

Harragan, B. 1977. *Games mother never taught you*. New York: Warner Books.

Henderson, J. and B.L. Marple. 1987. When older women work for younger women. In L. Moore (Ed.), *Not as far as you think: The realities of working women*. (pp. 107–120). Lexington, MA: D.C. Heath.

Jacobs, J.A. 1985. Sex segregation in American higher education. In L. Larwood, A.H. Stromberg, and B.A. Gutek (Eds.), *Women and work: An annual review*. (Vol. 1, pp. 191–214). Beverly Hills, CA: Sage.

Jagacinski, C.M. 1987. Engineering careers: Women in a male-dominated field. *Psychology of Women Quarterly, 11*, 97–110.

Kahn, W.A., and F. Crosby. 1985. Discriminating between attitudes and discriminatory behaviors: Change and stasis. In L. Larwood, A.H. Stromberg, and B.A. Gutek (Eds.), *Women and work: An annual review*. (Vol. 1, pp. 215–238). Beverly Hills, CA: Sage.

Kanter, R.M. 1986. Mastering change: The skills we need. In L. Moore (Ed.), *Not as far as you think: The realities of working women*. (pp. 181–194). Lexington, MA: D. C. Heath.

Kasten, B.R. 1986. Separate strengths: How men and women manage conflict and competition. In L. Moore (Ed.), *Not as far as you think: The realities of working women*. (pp. 121–134). Lexington, MA: D. C. Heath.

Katz, D. 1987. Sex discrimination in hiring: The influence of organizational climate and need for approval on decision-making behavior. *Psychology of Women Quarterly, 11*, 11–20.

Keele, R. 1986. Mentoring or networking? Strong and weak ties in career development. In L. Moore (Ed.), *Not as far as you think: The realities of working women*. (pp. 53–68). Lexington, MA: D. C. Heath.

Kessler-Harris, A. 1985. The debate over equality in the workplace: Recognizing differences. In L. Larwood, A.H. Stromberg, and B.A. Gutek (Eds.), *Women and work: An annual review*. (Vol. 1, pp. 141–161). Beverly Hills, CA: Sage.

Landau, J., and L. Amoss. 1986. Myths, dreams and disappointments: Preparing women for the future. In L. Moore (Ed.), *Not as far as you think: The realities of working women*. (pp. 13–24). Lexington, MA: D. C. Heath.

Larwood, L., and U.E. Gattiker. 1985. Rational bias and interorganizational power in the employment of management consultants. *Group and Organization Studies, 10*, 3–18.

Larwood, L., and U.E. Gattiker. 1987. A comparison of the career paths used by successful women and men. In B. Gutek and L. Larwood (Eds.), *Women's career development*. (pp. 129–156). Newbury Park, CA: Sage.

Larwood, L., B. Gutek, and U.E. Gattiker. 1984. Perspectives on institutional discrimination and resistance to change. *Group and Organization Studies, 9*, 333–352.

Larwood, L., E. Szwajkowski, and S. Rose. 1988. Sex and race discrimination resulting from manager-client relationships: Applying the rational bias theory of managerial discrimination. *Sex Roles, 18,* 9–29.

Lemkau, J.P. 1983. Women in male-dominated professions: Distinguishing personality and background characteristics. *Psychology of Women Quarterly, 8*(2), 144–165.

Liden, R.C. 1985. Female perceptions of female and male managerial behavior. *Sex Roles, 12*(3/4), 421–432.

Linimon, D., W.L. Barron, and T. Falbo. 1984. Gender differences in perceptions of leadership. *Sex Roles, 11,* 1075–1089.

Lipton, M. 1986. Successful women in a man's world: The myth of managerial androgyny. In L. Moore (Ed.), *Not as far as you think: The realities of working women.* (pp. 13–24). Lexington, MA: D. C. Heath.

Madden, J.F. 1985. The persistence of pay differentials: The economics of sex discrimination. In L. Larwood, A.H. Stromberg, and B.A. Gutek (Eds.), *Women and work: An annual review.* (Vol. 1, pp. 76–114). Beverly Hills, CA: Sage.

Malveaux, J. In press. Between a rock and a hard place: Integration, structural change, and the status of black women in typically female professions. In B. Gutek, A.H. Stromberg, and L. Larwood (Eds.), *Women and work: An annual review.* (Vol. 3). Beverly Hills, CA: Sage.

Markham, W.T. 1987. Sex, relocation, and occupational advancement: The "real cruncher" for women. In A.H. Stromberg, L. Larwood, and B.A. Gutek (Eds.), *Women and work: An annual review.* (Vol. 2, pp. 207–232). Newbury Park, CA: Sage.

Nkomo, S. 1988. Race and sex: The forgotten case of the black female manager. In S. Rose and L. Larwood (Eds.), *Women's careers: Pathways and pitfalls.* New York: Praeger.

Nieva, V.F. 1985. Work and family linkages. In L. Larwood, A.H. Stromberg, and B.A. Gutek (Eds.), *Women and work: An annual review.* (Vol. 1, pp. 162–190). Beverly Hills, CA: Sage.

Nieva, V.F., and B.A. Gutek. 1981. *Women and work: A psychological perspective.* New York: Praeger.

O'Leary, V. In press. Women's relationships with women in the workplace. In B. Gutek, A.H. Stromberg, and L. Larwood (Eds.), *Women and work: An annual review.* (Vol. 3). Newbury Park, CA: Sage.

Olson, J.E., D. Cain, and I.H. Frieze. August 1985. Income differentials of male and female MBA's: The effects of job type and industry. Paper presented at the Academy of Management, San Diego, CA.

Olson, J.E., and I.H. Frieze. 1987. Income determinants for women in business. In A.H. Stromberg, L. Larwood and B.A. Gutek (Eds.), *Women and work: An annual review.* (Vol. 2, 173–206). Beverly Hills, CA: Sage.

Powell, G.N., and D.A. Butterfield. 1984. If "good managers" are masculine, what are "bad managers"? *Sex Roles, 10,* 477–484.

Riger, S. and P. Galligan. 1980. Women in management. An exploration of competing paradigms. *American Psychology, 35,* 902–920.

Rose, S. 1985. Professional networks of junior faculty in psychology. *Psychology of Women Quarterly, 9*(4), 533–547.

Rose, S. 1986. Building a professional network. In S. Rose (Ed.), *Career guide for women scholars.* (pp. 46–56). New York: Springer Verlag.

Rosenbaum, J.E. 1985. Persistence and change in pay inequalities: Implications for job evaluation and comparable worth. In L. Larwood, A.H. Stromberg, and B.A. Gutek (Eds.), *Women and work: An annual review.* (Vol. 1, pp. 115-140). Beverly Hills, CA: Sage.

Schein, V.E. 1973. The relationship between sex role stereotypes and requisite management characteristics. *Journal of Vocational Behavior, 22,* 95-100.

Schneider, B. 1986. Coming out at work: Bridging the private/public gap. *Work and Occupation, 13*(4), 463-487.

Shapiro, G. and D. Farrow. 1988. Mentors and others in career development. In S. Rose and L. Larwood (Eds.), *Women's careers: Pathways and pitfalls.* New York: Praeger.

Smith, T.W. 1985. Working wives and women's rights: The connection between the employment status of wives and the feminist attitudes of husbands. *Sex Roles, 12,* 501-508.

Spelman, D., M. Crary, K.E. Kram, and J.G. Clawson. 1986. Sexual attraction at work: Managing the heart. In L. Moore (Ed.), *Not as far as you think: The realities of working women.* (pp. 181-194). Lexington, MA: D. C. Heath.

Statham, A. 1987. The gender model revisited: Differences in the management styles of men and women. *Sex Roles, 16,* 409-429.

Stevens, G., and S. Gardner. 1987. But can she command a ship? Acceptance of women by peers at the Coast Guard Academy. *Sex Roles, 16,* 181-188.

Treiman, D.J., and P.A. Roos. 1983. Sex and earnings in industrial society: A nine-nation comparison. *American Journal of Sociology, 89,* 612-650.

U.S. Department of Labor, Bureau of Labor Statistics 1986.

Valdez, R.A., and B.A. Gutek. 1987. Family roles: A help or a hindrance for working women? In B.A. Gutek and L. Larwood (Eds.), *Women's career development.* (pp. 157-169). Newbury Park, CA: Sage.

Williams, S.W., and J.C. McCullers. 1983. Personal factors related to typicalness of career and success in active professional women. *Psychology of Women Quarterly, 7,* 343-359.

Zanna, M., F. Crosby, and G. Loewenstein. 1987. Male reference groups and discontent among female professionals. In B. Gutek and L. Larwood (Eds.), *Women's career development.* (pp. 28-41). Newbury Park: Sage.

PART II
PERSONAL CAREER PLANNING

2

Mentors and Others in Career Development

Gloria L. Shapiro
Dana L. Farrow

PREVIEW

In this chapter, we offer some guidance in your search for help in career development/advancement. Although based on research, the career implications and our advice to you is written (we trust!) in clear, non-technical language. First, it is important to recognize that career help is available outside as well as within the work environment. We, therefore, encourage you to seek career assistance closer to home—more specifically, from family and friends. Next, we believe that a continuous one-to-one relationship with an individual throughout your career development may result in problems that will hinder your advancement. Some potential problems associated with a single relationship during one's career development are described in this chapter. Consequently, from this and our empirical study, we suggest it may be more advantageous to seek help from a variety of sources rather than from only one person. In addition, we offer reasons why your immediate superior should not necessarily be sought after as a helper. In conclusion, we identify two characteristics of effective helpers of career development/advancement: (1) exhibiting a personal interest and commitment to the relationship, and (2) having the ability to influence your career.

MENTORS AND OTHERS IN CAREER DEVELOPMENT

Is a mentor a necessary ingredient for success? May the functions performed by a mentor be performed by other "helpers?" Can this help be obtained from outside as well as within the organization? What characteristics should the aspiring manager look for in a helper? Since most people require some form of assistance during their career and mentors are difficult to obtain (Kram 1985), the answers to these questions are important for those embarking on the pathways of their career. In this chapter we seek to find the answers to the above questions.

A mentor, per se, may not be necessary if the same kinds of help are available and obtainable from a variety of sources. We first will show, based upon an empirical study, that important sources of career help may be overlooked if one focuses solely upon helpers within the organization. In this chapter we reveal where and from whom one may get help. Second, the characteristics of helpers will be examined to determine how those considered to be mentors differ from others who provide help. That is, we will focus on what characteristics helpers should possess in order to provide worthwhile and valuable assistance to those embarking on the pathway of their careers.

Before describing our study, let us briefly review some controversial questions concerning mentors.

Are Mentors Necessary to Career Success?

During the 1970s much discussion focused on the importance of having a mentor to further career development/advancement. In fact, it was viewed by many as a necessary ingredient for success. This is suggested by articles such as "Everyone Who Makes It Has a Mentor" (Collins and Scott 1978) and "Mentors Held Vital to Women" ("Mentors Held Vital" 1983). Articles such as these sent many individuals scurrying in search of a mentor, and as a result more articles appeared on how to get one (e.g., "Picking the Right Person for Your Mentor," Bushardt, Moore, and Debnath 1982; Odiorne 1985). However, even with this advice and assistance, many individuals discovered that it was extremely difficult to find a suitable mentor (Kram 1985). Organizations then began to establish both formal and informal mentoring programs.

Later research indicated that mentoring is *not* essential to career success (Clawson 1985), although such help can facilitate the attainment of career objectives (Lea and Leibowitz 1983). According to Clawson (1985) most learning about management occurs from one's immediate superior. He concludes that young individuals should focus on learning from their supervisors, and look for a mentor later in their careers, when they need an advocate within the organization. However, Burke (1984) found that the mentors of his sample respondents provided early career development and acted as role models. Thus, there is far from universal agreement on the value of having a mentor, particularly in the early years of a person's career. Although Levinson (1978) suggests that all men need a mentor, he points out that "mentoring relationships are more the exception than the rule for both workers and managers" (p. 334).

Lea and Leibowitz (1983) assert that in seeking a mentor, young managers may find that *several* relationships are necessary for different mentoring behaviors. Kram (1985) suggests young people seek peer relationships, since the mentor-protégé relationship is unavailable to most people. Women in top management often point to strong and inspiring fathers as having provided them with the most career motivation and support (Adams 1979; Hennig and Jardim 1976).

All this raises the possibility that assistance in one's career may be obtained from a variety of sources; that is, from *helpers* who do not serve as a person's sole mentor but who collectively provide the assistance traditionally received from a mentor. According to Speizer (1981), there is little foundation for the belief that men and women need a mentor.

Are Mentors Harmful to Career Advancement?

During the early 1980s, articles and books questioning the value of having a mentor emerged on both the academic and popular market (e.g., Blotnick 1984; Myers and Humphreys 1985). Some writers began to offer evidence that having a mentor could be detrimental to one's career. Blotnick (1984) listed a number of problems that occur in a mentor-protégé relationship: especially harsh treatment when the protégé makes a mistake, the mentor's unwelcome interference in projects, and the mentor's resentment when the protégé's corporate status threatens to equal or exceed the mentor's. Myers and Humphreys (1985) emphasized the process problems of the protégé's being assigned "busy-work" or being used as a substitute for clerical workers, protégé work overload, sexual harassment in cross-sex mentoring relationships, and mentors who are tyrannical, poor role models, or selfish. Some mentors may not "let go," thereby preventing the growth that comes through assuming more challenging work assignments. Since protégés become identified with their mentor, the protégé's career progression may halt if the mentor's career falters.

Because mentoring can be such an intense personal relationship, Bowen (1985) asked whether women should have male mentors. It is possible that the potential for stress and disaster offsets any potential benefit to the protégé. In a study with 32 mentor-protégé pairs in which all protégés were female but the mentors were about equally divided between the sexes, sex-related problems were reported in cross-sex mentoring which affected relationships at work and at home. The largest single problem was the resentment by co-workers. However, both protégés and mentors believed the benefits of the relationship outweighed any problems.

In addition to sexual problems, Hennecke (1983) noted resentment from other employees regarding the mentor-protégé relationship and the potential of receiving conflicting advice from one's mentor and one's supervisor. Of the 520 executives in the Columbia University Executive Program studied by Reich (1985), one-third believed that others in their organizations identified them too strongly with their mentors, and one-quarter said the relationship caused some degree of stress. Because of all these problems, Blotnick (1984) and Myers and Humphreys (1985) suggested that other avenues for help such as peer relationships be explored.

Who Is a Mentor?

There is no universal agreement as to who or what a mentor is. Kram (1985) defines a mentor as an experienced, productive manager who relates well to a less experienced person and is willing to help that person develop within and for the benefit of the organization. Burke (1984) defines mentoring as a one-to-one relationship between a more experienced person and an inexperienced person. Protégés most frequently describe their mentors as older professionals in their career field, often immediate supervisors or division/department heads in their organization (Michael and Hunt 1981; Roche 1979). Despite these differing perspectives, most agree that a mentor is a person who has a close relationship with the protégé and acts as a teacher, coach, counselor, guide, protector, sponsor, etc. From these definitions it appears that a protégé can have only one mentor at any one point in time.

There is even disagreement concerning whether or not successful people had a mentor. For example, Misserian (1982) interviewed several successful women who claimed they did not have a mentor. However, on the basis of their responses to specific questions, Misserian concluded that they did in fact have mentors. Henderson (1985) concluded that only the recipient of the career assistance can determine whether it was received from a "mentor."

What Are the Characteristics of Helpers?

A number of authors have investigated the characteristics of helpers, mainly in the context of mentors. Collins (1983) suggests five necessary criteria: the person must be higher up on the organizational ladder, an authority in his/her field, influential, interested in the protégé's growth and development, and willing to commit time and emotion to the relationship. Zey (1984) suggests that a sponsor, the highest in his/her hierarchy of mentoring, takes the most risk in that he/she provides the protégé with upward mobility. Kram (1985) suggests two types of mentoring functions: (1) career functions, which enhance career advancement, and (2) psychosocial functions, which enhance a sense of competence, identity, and effectiveness in a professional role.

Waesche and Zabalaoui (1986) consider a high standard of integrity to be the main criterion for a mentor. Odiorne (1985) says a protégé must choose a mentor who will cheer one on and encourage one's growth. In addition, good mentors are successful people themselves, are superior performers, realize they set an example, are supportive, good delegators, and arrange feedback. Reich (1985) notes that mentors offer concrete help in the early transfer to more challenging positions, and open up new positions and assignments to special projects. In turn, this concrete help results in increased chances for the protégé to develop abilities, be innovative, make difficult decisions, and become more self-confident. According to Farren, Grey, and Kaye (1984), mentors help with networking and with introducing the protégé to key organizational personnel. Mentors function as teachers who create learning opportunities, serve as devil's advocates, and coach by reacting to the protégé's decisions and by sharing their own career histories.

Berry (1983) indicates that a mentor should be at or near the executive level and still be moving upward in the organization. Ross (1984) says mentors advise on career planning; instruct in social, technical, and managerial skills; counsel on work related and personal problems; and encourage the young manager to take risks. Characteristics of a good mentor include a successful record of achievement, credibility, trust, and a commitment to the mentoring process. According to Kram (1985), characteristics of successful mentors include being personally secure, being capable of genuine interest in the protégé's growth and development, and feeling good about their own accomplishments.

PURPOSE OF THE STUDY

Almost all of the above writers are concerned with the career help provided by mentors and mentor characteristics. This chapter focuses on part of a larger study designed to determine the functions of those who helped in the career development of managers (Shapiro 1985). We feel it is important to identify *all* the people (mentors and nonmentors) who actually provide career help, and to determine the characteristics they possess. Investigation of this will assist aspiring young managers who seek help in career development. The above writers offer much speculation concerning helper functions and characteristics, but there is little empirical research to verify their conclusions. Notable exceptions are the work of Kram (1985) investigating the career and psychosocial functions and Reich's (1985) study of concrete help offered.

Therefore, the two goals of this study were (1) to identify the people offering career help to aspiring managers, and (2) to investigate the characteristics of these helpers. We were also interested in determining whether men and women managers differ in their perception of helpers as mentors.

The *identities* of the helpers were investigated using the following questions:

1. Who are the people most likely to provide help in career development? Which of these people are considered to be mentors?
2. Are the more important helpers perceived primarily as mentors?
3. Are business or nonbusiness people considered to be the most important source of help?
4. Do men and women differ in their perceptions of whether or not they consider their helpers to be mentors?

The *characteristics* of helpers were explored using the following questions:

1. How do the specific characteristics of mentors and nonmentors compare? What specific characteristics distinguish mentors from nonmentors?
2. Can the specific characteristics of helpers be reduced to a lesser number of more general helper functions?

METHOD

Subjects

We sampled a wide range of organizations in order to make the results as generalizable as possible. Top level executives (i.e., presidents, vice-presidents, and directors of personnel) in banking, insurance, health care, retailing, transportation, education, and city and metropolitan county government distributed the questionnaires among their top and middle level managers. Responses were confidential and were returned directly to the authors using stamped, self-addressed envelopes supplied with the survey. One hundred forty useable responses were obtained from 20 corporations in a large metropolitan area in South Florida. Seventy-three men and 67 women participated in the study. Sixteen of the men (21.9 percent) and 19 of the women (28.4 percent) indicated they were in top level management positions. The average age of men was 40.11 years and the average for women was 39.11 years. Almost 80 percent of the men were married compared to only 47 percent of the women. Although there was a significant difference in marital status ($p < .01$), there was no significant difference between men and women on age or years of education.

Measures

A questionnaire was developed in which subjects were asked to select up to four people who most significantly helped them in their career development/advancement. Selections were made from a list of 11 categories. These were:

1. Friend
2. Professor/teacher
3. Colleague/peer
4. Immediate superior
5. Person higher ranking than immediate superior
6. Parent
7. Brother/sister
8. Husband/wife
9. Lover
10. Other relative
11. Other (specify) _____

Subjects were asked to indicate the importance of each selected person in their career development/advancement. Ratings were performed using a seven-point Likert scale where "1" indicated "not at all important" and "7" indicated "extremely important."

In order to investigate the characteristics of helpers, subjects were then asked to rate, using a seven-point scale (7 = very much), the degree to which each of the identified helpers was described by the following statements:

Is (was) a recognized authority in his or her field.

Is (was) an influential leader.

Is (was) present during crisis periods or turning points in your career.

Is (was) interested in your growth and development.

Is (was) willing to commit time and emotion to the relationship.

Is (was) willing to take risks for you.

Provided you with upward mobility.

Finally, subjects were asked to indicate whether or not they considered each selected person to be a mentor. They then specified the number of mentors across their careers.

Table 2.1
Frequency Distribution of Mentors and Nonmentors
in Career Development of Managers

Person	Mentors		Non-Mentors		Total	
	Frequency	Percent[a]	Frequency	Percent	Frequency	Percent
Friend	6	2.9	26	7.6	32	5.9
Professor/Teacher	12	5.8	23	6.7	35	6.4
Colleague/Peer	18	8.8	45	13.2	63	11.5
Immediate Superior	90	43.9	70	20.6	160	29.3
Higher Rank than Immediate Superior	42	20.5	43	12.6	85	15.6
Parent	12	5.8	61	17.9	73	13.4
Brother/Sister	3	1.5	5	1.8	8	1.5
Husband/Wife	16	7.8	53	15.6	69	12.7
Lover	3	1.5	7	2.0	10	1.8
Other Relative	2	1.0	6	1.7	8	1.5
Other	1	0.5	1	0.3	2	0.4
TOTAL	205	37.6[b]	340	62.4[c]	545	100.0

[a]Percentage in each column total 100 (i.e., 2.9% of 205 perceived mentors were friends).
[b]37.6% represents the proportion of total sample considered to be mentors.
[c]62.4% represents the proportion of total sample considered to be non-mentors.

RESULTS

Who Are the Helpers?

Question 1 asked "Who are the people most likely to provide help in career development? Which of these people are considered to be mentors?" Table 2.1 indicates that subjects most frequently cited an immediate supervisor as providing help in career development/advancement, followed by higher ranking persons than immediate supervisor—then parent, spouse, and colleague/peer. Table 2.1 also indicates that helpers who were immediate supervisors were more likely to be considered mentors than nonmentors. Parents and spouses were more likely to be considered nonmentors than mentors. Persons higher ranking than immediate supervisors were just as likely to be considered mentors as nonmentors.

Table 2.2
Point-Biserial Correlations Between Degree of Importance
and Persons Considered to Be Mentors

Person	r	N
Overall Correlation	.42***	536
Friend	.34[a]	31
Professor/Teacher	.40*	35
Colleague/Peer	.42**	60
Immediate Superior	.50***	158
Higher Rank than Immediate Superior	.43***	83
Parent	.26*	73
Husband/Wife	.14	69

[a] $\underline{p} < .06$
* $\underline{p} < .05$
** $\underline{p} < .01$
*** $\underline{p} < .001$

NOTE: Brother/sister, lover, and other sample sizes were too small and therefore omitted from subgroup analysis. Thus subgroup sample sizes do not total to 536.

Upon looking at the results in Table 2.1, we were curious as to whether there is a relation between the *degree* of importance of *all* helpers selected by respondents and whether they are considered to be mentors. Using a point-biserial correlation on *all* selected helpers, we found a significant relationship ($r = .42$, $p < .001$). That is, the more important the helper was rated in providing career help, the more likely that person was considered to be a mentor.

We then wanted to see if the same held true for *specific* persons designated as helpers. Further point-biserial correlations were performed on each of the selected persons with the exception of brother/sister, lover, and others. These were omitted because the sample sizes were too small. The results showed all but spouse and friend were significantly related (see Table 2.2).

The above results led us to wonder what would happen if we looked at only those selected helpers who were rated 5 or higher on the Likert scale (i.e., considerably to extremely important). Would these more important helpers be primarily mentors? This led to investigation of the next question.

Question 2 asked "Are the *more important* of these helpers perceived primarily as mentors?" To answer this, only those helpers who were rated from "considerably" to "extremely" important were included in the analysis. Of the 376 persons in this group, 193, or 51.3 percent, were not considered mentors and 183, or 48.6 percent, were considered mentors. This indicated that, in general, the most important helpers were just as likely to be considered nonmentors as mentors.

Question 3 asked whether business or nonbusiness people were considered to be the most important source of help. Again, only those helpers who were rated "considerably" or more important were included in the analysis. Helpers were grouped into business (i.e., immediate supervisor, higher ranking than immediate supervisor, colleague/peer) and nonbusiness (i.e., parent, spouse, relatives, friends) categories. Of the helpers perceived as *nonmentors*, 50.8 percent were business-related and 49.2 percent were not. Obviously, it made no difference to the managers whether *nonmentors* were business persons. On the other hand, 74.9 percent of those helpers perceived as *mentors* were business-related and 25.1 percent were nonbusiness people, a statistically significant difference ($z = 6.74$, $p < .001$). Thus, persons in the business environment who played an important role in career development were more likely to be considered mentors than family and friends who made equally significant career contributions.

Question 4 asked whether men and women differ in their perceptions of their helpers being mentors? In answer, there was no significant difference between men and women in terms of whom they were likely to select as helpers (e.g., immediate supervisor, person higher ranking than immediate supervisor). However, a somewhat greater proportion of female than male managers considered family and friends to be mentors ($z = 1.91$, $p < .06$).

What Are the Characteristics of the Helpers?

The *first question* in this part of the investigation asked "How do the specific characteristics of mentors and nonmentors compare? What specific characteristics distinguish mentors from nonmentors?" We performed a Hotelling T^2 test to search for differences between mentors and nonmentors on all seven helper characteristics (e.g., "Was a recognized authority in his/her field," "Was interested in your growth and development"). Table 2.3 shows that mentors were rated significantly higher than nonmentors on all characteristics ($T^2 = 162.21$, $F(7,531) = 22.91$, $p < .0001$).

We used a two group stepwise discriminant function analysis to determine which characteristics distinguish mentors from nonmentors. Of the seven variables submitted, three were statistically selected for inclusion. "Provided upward mobility" was the best discriminating variable. This

Table 2.3
Mentor Versus Nonmentor Characteristics

Characteristics	Mentors (N = 246)		Non-Mentors (N = 277)		
	Mean	SD	Mean	SD	t
Was a recognized authority in his/her field	5.48	(1.49)	4.48	(1.90)	6.57*
Was an influential leader[a]	5.52	(1.46)	4.25	(1.88)	8.12*
Was present during crisis or turning points in your career	5.64	(1.56)	4.65	(2.03)	5.81*
Was interested in your growth and development	6.14	(1.14)	5.37	(1.61)	5.79*
Was willing to commit time and emotion to the relationship[a]	5.80	(1.27)	5.05	(1.70)	5.46*
Was willing to take risks for you	5.32	(1.63)	4.37	(1.94)	5.73*
Provided you with upward mobility[a]	5.27	(2.00)	3.40	(2.05)	10.48*

Overall Hotelling T^2 = 162.21, $\underline{F}$(7, 531) = 22.91, $\underline{p}$ < .0001

* $\underline{p}$ < .0001

[a]Variables selected for inclusion.

was followed by "willing to commit time and emotion to the relationship" and "is an influential leader." Overall, 72.3 percent of the responses were correctly classified into mentors and nonmentors, indicating the above three variables were good discriminators.

The *second question* of this part of the study asked "Can the seven specific characteristics of helpers be reduced to a lesser number of more general helper functions?" A principal components factor analysis with varimax rotation was performed on the seven helper characteristics for all helpers, both mentors and nonmentors. Two meaningful factors emerged. Using a factor loading of .50 or higher to determine to which factor a characteristic belonged, we defined Factor 1 as describing the helper's demonstrating a *Personal Interest/Commitment to Relationship*, and Factor 2 as describing the helper's *Ability to Influence Career*.

Helpers who demonstrate *Personal Interest/Commitment to Relationship* are (1) present during a crisis period or turning point in the subjects' careers, (2) interested in their growth and development, (3) willing to commit time and emotion to the relationship, and (4) willing to take risks for them. Helpers who demonstrate the *Ability to Influence Career* function are (1) recognized authorities in their fields, (2) influential leaders, and (3) provide subjects with upward mobility.

Additional factor analyses were performed for both men and women separately and by mentor status of the helper (i.e., for helpers who were considered to be mentors, and for helpers who were not). All results were essentially the same. That is, whether or not the helper was considered a mentor, and whether or not the manager is a man or a woman, the characteristics of our generalized functions remain the same as described above.

SUMMARY AND CONCLUSIONS

Although immediate superior, person higher ranking than immediate superior, parent, and spouse were the four most frequent persons cited as having the most important impact on the manager's career, in general only those outside the circle of family and friends were considered to be mentors. One possible explanation for this is that the concept of the term *mentor* is generally associated with persons in the business environment.

However, when the *most* important helpers were analyzed, it was found that these helpers were just as likely to be nonmentors as mentors. This shows that aspiring managers may do well to obtain help from people other than mentors. In fact, for our sample, the chances were about 50-50 that the most important helpers were *not* "mentors."

The implications of the above are obvious—a person need not have a traditional mentor to receive career assistance. Indeed, many people may be ignoring or overlooking important sources of career help from nontraditional (i.e., nonmentoring) sources.

In addition, our results clearly demonstrate that career help need not come from only one person or mentor but instead does come from *many* different people. Aspiring young managers may do well to seek career assistance from a number of helpers, both *within* the organizational environment and from sources such as parents and spouses *outside* the organization.

It is interesting to note that although 83 percent of the subjects indicated they had mentors, 40 percent of them did not list one or more of their mentors as one of the four most significant people who helped them in their career development. Of course, it is possible that helpers selected had a major impact at a particular point in the managers' careers, but were not considered mentors. It is also possible that the mentor relationship had a negative effect on the protégé.

Although there was no difference between business and nonbusiness people in their importance to the managers' career development, helpers in the business environment were more likely to be considered mentors than equally important family and friends. This verifies our conclusion that aspiring managers may be overlooking sources of career help by concentrating on higher ranking persons within their organizations.

A greater proportion of women than men considered family and friends to be mentors. Women have fewer role models and correspondingly find it more difficult than men to find a mentor. Thus, there is a greater necessity for women to seek help outside the business environment. This represents another pathway for women to obtain the assistance necessary to advance their careers.

Having multiple helpers from both within and outside the organization may also be a way for women to avoid some of the pitfalls to career advancement. The authors discussed at the beginning of this chapter a number of pitfalls to career advancement, particularly when cross-sex mentoring is involved. Some of the problems mentioned with having a mentor were sexual harassment, dealing with sexual innuendos about the relationship, resentment of other employees regarding the relationship, becoming too identified with the mentor, becoming too dependent on the mentor, and having a tyrannical mentor. The young career woman can reduce the severity of each of these problems, if not eliminate them altogether, if at any one time she does *not* have a single mentor, but instead has relationships with a *number* of helpers from inside and outside the organization.

Having several helpers would reduce the chances of becoming too dependent upon any one of them. It would be easier to simply walk away from a tyrannical or harassing helper if one knew there were others one could go to for advice. To the extent that one has many helpers, the less the chances one would become too identified with any one of them. Thus, the young manager's career advancement is less likely to be harmed if any one helper's career becomes sidetracked in the organization. The young employee's spending less time with any one helper should reduce the amount of sexual gossip about the relationship, and the helper's spending less time with any one employee should reduce resentment from other employees.

Similarly, having helpers outside the organization eliminates some of these problems. Coworkers are less likely to know about outside relationships. Thus, the identification, sexual innuendo, and employee resentment problems may be prevented from arising. Having one's career advancement jeopardized by the faltering career of a helper is also eliminated by having helpers from outside the organization.

The results of the helper characteristics analysis are especially intriguing. Our two empirically derived general helper functions of *Personal Interest/Commitment to Relationship* and *Ability to Influence Career* seem to complement the two broad categories of helper functions summarized by Kram (1985) from the studies of others. Her "career functions" category was described as serving primarily to aid advancement up the hierarchy of an organization and included sponsorship, exposure and visibility, coaching, protection, and challenging assignments. Such functions could be carried out best by someone high on our *Ability to Influence Career* function; in other words, someone who is a recognized authority in her/his field, is an influential leader, and who provides upward mobility. Similarly, Kram's "psychosocial functions" category was described as affecting each individual on a personal level by building self-worth both inside and outside the organization. This function included role modeling, acceptance and confirmation, counseling, and friendship. These functions could be carried out best by someone high on our *Personal Interest/Commitment to Relationship* function; that is, someone who is present during crisis periods in one's career, is interested in one's growth and development, is willing to commit time and emotion to the relationship, and is willing to take risks on one's behalf.

In summary, our study adds to current knowledge by demonstrating that help in career advancement is available from a number of sources, some considered to be mentors and some not. We also have shown that whether or not they are perceived as mentors, helpers exhibit *personal interest and commitment to the relationship* and have the *ability to influence the young manager's career.* Together, these results suggest both sources of help and characteristics to look for along the pathway to career success. What is important to remember is that career help is available and should be obtained, no matter what the organizational or nonorganizational status of the helper.

REFERENCES

Adams, J. 1979. *Women on top.* New York: Berkeley Publishing Corporation.

Berry, P. 1983. Mentors for women managers: Fast-track to corporate success? *Supervisory Management, 28*(8), 36–40.

Blotnick, S.R. 1984. With friends like these . . . *Savvy,* October.

Bowen, D.D. 1985. Were men meant to be mentors? *Training & Development Journal, 39*(2), 30–34.

Burke, R.J. 1984. Mentors in organizations. *Group & Organization Studies, 9*(3), 353–372.

Bushardt, S.C., R.N. Moore, and S.C. Debnath. 1981. Picking the right person for your mentor. *S.A.M. Advanced Management Journal* (Summer), 46–51.

Clawson, J.G. 1985. Is mentoring necessary? *Training & Development Journal, 39*(4), 36–39.

Collins, E., and P. Scott. 1978. Everyone who makes it has a mentor. *Harvard Business Review,* July–August, 89–101.

Collins, N.W. 1983. *Professional women and their managers.* Englewood Cliffs, NJ: Prentice-Hall.

Farren, C., J.D. Grey, and B. Kaye. 1984. Mentoring: A boon to career development. *Personnel, 61*(6), 20–24.

Henderson, D.W. 1985. Enlightened mentoring: A characteristic of public management professionalism. *Public Administration Review,* November/December, 857–863.

Hennecke, M.J. 1983. Mentors and protégés: How to build relationships that work. *Training, 20*(7), 36–41.

Hennig, M., and A. Jardim. 1976. *The managerial woman.* New York: Pocket Books, Doubleday.

Kram, K.E. 1985. *Mentoring at work: Developmental relationships in organizational life.* Glenview, IL: Scott, Foresman.

Lea, D., and Z.B. Leibowitz. 1983. A mentor: Would you know one if you saw one? *Supervisory Management, 28*(4), 32–35.

Levinson, D.J. 1978. *The seasons of a man's life.* New York: Alfred A. Knopf.

Mentors held vital to women. 1983. *New York Times Service,* 6.

Michael, C.M., and D.M. Hunt. 1981. *Women and organizations: A study of mentorship.* Unpublished manuscript. Miami University, Oxford, OH.

Missirian, A.K. 1982. *The corporate connection: Why executive women need mentors to help them reach the top.* Englewood Cliffs, NJ: Prentice-Hall.

Myers, D.W., and N.J. Humphreys. 1985. The caveats in mentorship. *Business Horizons, 28*(4), 9–14.

Ordiorne, G.S. 1985. Mentoring—An American management innovation. *Personnel Administrator, 30*(5), 63–70.

Reich, M.H. 1985. Executive views from both sides of mentoring. *Personnel, 62*(3), 42–46.

Roche, G.R. 1979. Much ado about mentors. *Harvard Business Review, 10,* 14–28.

Ross, A. 1984. The mentor's role in developing new leaders. *Hospital & Health Services Administration, 29*(5), 21–29.

Shapiro, G. August, 1985. Sex differences in mentoring functions received and valued by managers. Paper presented at the 45th Annual Meeting of the Academy of Management, San Diego, CA.

Speizer, J.J. 1981. Role models, mentors, and sponsors: The elusive concepts. *Signs* (Summer), 692–712.

Waesche, D.R., and J.C. Zabalaoui. 1986. From trainee to business partner. *Life Association News, 81*(4), 137–144.

Zey, M.G. 1984. *The mentor connection.* Homewood, IL: Dow Jones-Irwin.

3

Cultural Differences, Not Deficiencies: An Analysis of Managerial Women's Language

Susan Schick Case

PREVIEW

So often I've sat in managerial meetings, struck by how differently men and women managers describe and frame problems. As I've thought about this, I've had to say, "Why is it so surprising that men and women would have different perceptions, beliefs, and ways of describing their experiences?" After all, because of their gender, they had different experiences growing up. Given that language use tells us how people see their world, and given that so much of managerial behavior occurs through linguistic activity, I wanted to find out if there were typical male and female speech styles used in natural conversational groups of managers. I found two predominant styles of speech: a facilitative/personal style, used mostly by women, which appears to be more relational and integrative; and an assertive/authoritative style, used mostly by men, which appears to be more directive, depersonalized, and commanding.

Even though my research describes clear differences in male and female speech styles, I claim that these *differences* do not involve *deficiencies*. By reading this chapter, I hope that more women will begin to reject the idea that effectiveness in management means talking and acting like a man. No form of speech is intrinsically strong or weak. Rather than try to change speech patterns, I suggest that women capitalize on the strengths of some of the differences that emerge from their feminine heritage. For example, based on current organizational realities, such as multicultural organizations, global competition, deregulation, and the heavy legal context in which businesses must operate, certain features of women's speech (indirectness, mitigation of criticism, solicitation of others' ideas) are useful organizational functions. These vital features influence the performance and goal attainment of the organization as a whole, as well as help in the development of complex and novel decisions that require pulling together perspectives and information from many different groups. The results of this study suggest that women's speech IS compatible with leadership activity. Both styles of speech have strengths that benefit an organization. By including both voices in organizational decision making, problems will be seen in new ways.

Women and men managers, because of their gender, have had different life experiences and participated in different activities growing up. Thus, it would not be surprising that they would have different perceptions, beliefs, and categories for describing experiences (Alderfer 1977; Alderfer and Smith 1982; Miller 1983). Much of managerial behavior occurs through linguistic activity, yet organizational analysis of behavior has paid almost no attention to how people actually speak (Mintzberg 1973; Gronn 1983; Levine et al. 1984). Since the language people use and the associations they make reveal how they see and interact with their world, the experiences of women, and their increasing presence in the work force, mandate understanding their cultural perspective and respecting their differences where they exist.

Unfortunately, when behavioral differences between the sexes are believed to exist or are found, women's behavior often is labeled "deficient," not "different." For instance, women's language is believed to reflect uncertainty and weakness, men's rationality (Rubin 1976), although there is little evidence to support this view. Yet the belief in women's speech "deficiency" has led to the proliferation of numerous "assertiveness" training programs in the past decade aimed at changing women's tone of voice, sentence structure, and other speech style traits so that they are less feminine (Lakoff 1975; Stone and Bachner 1977; Eakins and Eakins 1978; Kramarae 1982; Thorne, Kramarae and Henley 1983).

In our research we were interested in how men and women managers talked when they interacted with one another. We suspected that some gender differences would be revealed in the language used by men and women in problem-solving and decision-making settings that involved leadership and influence, partly as a function of their different equations of power. This work is one piece in a larger body of studies about language use within which diversity of speech repertoires, ways of speaking, and choices among them find a natural place.

Research on men's and women's language styles primarily has been based on two types of studies. One approach has been to measure people's perceptions of the kinds of language men and women use (Thorne and Henley 1975; Lakoff 1973, 1975; Key 1975; Baird 1976; Rubin 1976; Kramer 1977; Fisher 1980; Kramarae 1980, 1981, 1982; and Bonanno 1982). Most of this research has been done through informants, anecdotes, and structured observation, all methods highly susceptible to influence by preconceptions.

For example, in work situations, women are often expected to be nurturant, emotional, and expressive, just as they are responsible for providing emotional support to family members, whereas men are expected to be rational and ignore feelings (Rubin 1976). Perceptions of the language of the sexes seems shaped to be consistent with generalized sex role images. Since women are thought to be emotional, indecisive, submissive, supportive, and interpersonally oriented (Key 1975; Baird 1976), their speech is rated likewise. Similarly, since men are seen as behaving aggressively, instrumentally, bluntly, and decisively (Key 1975; Baird 1976), their speech is also rated consistent with that role image.

Conclusions based on these studies contain all of the problems of subjectivity and selectivity inherent in any investigation of people's opinions of a topic. In some cases, empirical findings actually invert the stereotypes (e.g., women are said to be more talkative than men, but when men and women talk together in groups, the finding has consistently been reversed: men talk more than women [Strodtbeck, James and Hawkins 1957; Doherty 1974; Aries 1976]).

A second class of studies addressing gender differences in language has involved empirical linguistic description of certain isolated speech elements in actual conversations (Shuy et al. 1967; Fasold 1968; Barron 1971; Labov 1972; Trudgill 1972; Mitchell-Kernan 1972; Kramer 1974; Bodine 1975; Swacker 1975; Aries 1976; Gilbert 1976a, b; Fishman 1978; and Bonanno 1982). Three generalizations of sex-based language are most consistently validated. These include:

1. Men more often assume task roles when communicating and women more often assume expressive socioemotional roles;
2. The speech of women is more likely to be correct in terms of pronunciation; and
3. In mixed-sex interaction, men engage in more interaction than women.

But many results from studies contradict each other. For example, Lakoff (1975) conjectured that women used more tag questions ("Sally stayed in school, didn't she?"), which made their language sound uncertain. McMillan et al. (1977), studying mixed-sex discussion groups of college students, and Fishman (1980), studying heterosexual couples talking at home, also found evidence for Lakoff's conjecture that women used more tags in their speech to elicit responses from uncommunicative male conversational partners. On the other hand, Baumann (1976) found no differences in tag use by gender in a classroom setting. In contrast, men used more tags in informal conversation (Lapadat and Seesahai 1977), at a professional conference among participants (Dubois and

Crouch 1977), and when in a leadership role, as a device to sustain inter-action (Johnson 1980). In the examples above, the same feature appears to be used differently depending on the gender composition of the group and the situation, leading to questions about language function and use (McConnell-Ginet 1980).

The results of empirical studies of the past few years encourage cau-tion before making sweeping generalizations about extensive gender dif-ferences in speech. Basically, descriptions of linguistic gender differentia-tion is uneven and incomplete. Methodological problems in all these studies include the analysis of only small segments of conversation or the examination of only a few traits. In addition, some conclude that women and men are different when different scales were used to evalu-ate each sex, thereby ensuring these differences. Usually, snippets of conversation took place in contrived situations rather than in natural settings where one can examine the give-and-take flow of actual conver-sation between men and women in formal and informal organizational groups and simultaneously think about the effects that the setting, topic, or roles might have as they interact with gender. Furthermore, the groups and contexts selected vary from study to study.

The much-publicized data regarding the difference between male and female speech is over-reported, polarizing gender stereotypes, and has yet to be empirically demonstrated in a systematic, comprehensive, and thorough way. There is a need for descriptive, exploratory studies of language differences within the context of the give-and-take of actual talk (Berryman and Eman 1980; Fishman 1983). Measuring many vari-ables of speech with the same speakers also would enable more general claims to be made about sex differences in talk, at least for that group (Thorne 1986).

Our study improves on previous methodology by using a natural setting, lengthy conversational interactions, and comprehensive analy-sis of the language interaction in a managerial context. We asked the question, "What are the characteristics of typical male and female speech?" The natural conversation of women and men as they worked together in a group over time was empirically analyzed and quantified, with a speech profile for each gender developed, enabling women and men to be compared on 34 speech traits. Based on the differing expe-riences of men and women in our culture, two predominant styles of speech were expected: a facilitative/personal style, used mostly by women, appears to be more relational and integrative; and an asser-tive/authoritative style, used mostly by men, appears to be more direc-tive and commanding. Gender-related speech was also expected to correspond with influence in the group, with the masculine style speech being regarded as more influential.

METHOD

The study was conducted in a ten-person group (five women, five men) at a leading Eastern management school. The group of managers worked together in an unstructured setting, observing and attempting to understand their own leadership and influencing behavior as it occurred, and coming face to face with issues of power, uncertainty, and normlessness. Group members were of comparable age (29–40), status (high, middle management), social class (upper middle), and ethnicity (Caucasian), which should decrease linguistic variation. Since the group formed naturally, the fact that we were able to exclude many potential linguistic determinants due to race or social class was serendipitous. It meant there was little variation that would be expected in language except that due to gender differences.

Audiotaped, 45-minute sessions completed over 15 weeks were made from group formation until termination. All tapes were transcribed by the experimenter, who recorded as accurately as possible everything that was said without altering the grammar or verbal form of speech. A man and women from the group were used to help fill in sections of the transcripts, because of a confidentiality contract among group members that allowed only group members to listen to the tapes. Reliabilities were calculated for the transcript process. There was a 96 percent agreement for words, and 93 percent for utterance boundaries (where one speaker began and ended). Reliability is slightly lower for the latter because it is harder to establish when one speaker ends when more than one person speaks at the same time. Numbers were substituted for names so that analysis of data could be done without regard to the sex of participants.

Participant observation of group sessions occurred simultaneously, supplementing verbatim transcripts and empirical scoring schemas to record language interactions and comments on the social life of the group. Without the participant observation, the complexity, and dynamic nature of what occurs in conversational interactions is lost.

Analysis of Transcripts

Four randomly selected tapes were analyzed. Each was drawn from a different four-week calendar block to eliminate differences in speech that might have occurred as the result of group development over time (Bales 1953; Bennis and Shepard 1956; Schutz 1958; Bion 1961; Alderfer 1980).

Phonological, morphological, semantic, and structural analyses of each member's speech were completed. Overall 34 different language traits were examined. The phonological variables included differences in pronunciation, intensifiers (such as *so* or *such* used in an expressive way), and discourse length. Morphological variables included (a) the smallest

Table 3.1
Influence Measures

Area		Indicator
Who talks	1.	Frequency of initiation
How much	2.	Mean utterance length
	3.	Percentage of total words spoken
To whom	4.	Frequency of being talked to
	5.	Number of persons talked to per session
	6.	Frequency of talking to group as a whole
About what	7.	Frequency of being talked about
	8.	Frequency of ideas being talked about
In what way	9.	Proportion of fillers and qualifiers

meaningful units of language, and (b) syntactic usage (conjunctions, interjections, qualification, and type of sentence construction). The semantic variables related to the meaning of what was said, including pronoun choices, proof strategies referring to outside experts or personal experiences, and conversational topics and themes. The structural variables included communication patterns of language organization and arrangement in interaction, such as turn taking, patterns of interruption, topic changes, who talks to whom about what, and messages of inclusion and exclusion.

A ranking and weighting schema for establishing influence behavior at each stage and for influence in the group as a whole was used (Case 1985). Nine indicators of influence were employed, corresponding to five general measures: who talks, how much, to whom, about what, and in what way (Bales 1950, 1968; Borgatta and Bales 1953; Bales and Cohen 1979; Hare 1972) (see Table 3.1).

Procedure for Establishing Speech Styles

Frequency of occurrence for each of the 34 traits was counted for each person. Proportion of usage of the trait also was calculated for each individual. Then individual language profiles were drawn. The extent to which an individual consistently employed certain linguistic features and patterns determined his or her predominant communication style. Reliability was obtained independently by a colleague who did not know the purpose of the study but who took the transcripts and did the same tasks with influence and scoring categories. Reliability on influence measures ranged from 93 to 100 percent and from 88 to 100 percent on each speech style scoring category for each individual.

RESULTS

Three speech styles were thus identified. In this chapter, we report on two of them: a predominantly feminine style (N = 5) and a predominantly masculine style (N = 5). We also found a wide verbal repertoire style used by two men and one woman, which still maintained gender appropriate patterns. See Case (1985, 1987) for a description of this speech style. Figure 3.1 is a speech profile for each gender group. It includes all traits examined by each linguistic area with percentage of occurrence of each. To arrive at the percentage of occurrence for each variable, individual frequencies were counted by gender, a group and gender total were obtained on the variable, and the percentage of usage of that form of speech by men and by women was calculated. The figure also draws attention to those that were statistically significant by use of an asterisk preceding the variable.

Two separate profiles, one for men's speech and one for women's speech, emerged. Within each variable (phonological, morphological, semantic, and structural) traits were ordered from high-to-low usage for men and low-to-high usage for women. The greater the contrast between percentage of occurrences of the variables for men and women, the more likely the importance of the variable as a distinguishing characteristic.

The graph illustrates two discrete profiles of gender-based speech. In spite of the fact that our group consisted of well-educated men and women, who should be more similar in their speech (Maccoby 1966), there were 23 traits that occurred more than two-thirds of the time in only one gender group, and of these all but five were statistically significant (p < .05). Of the five that were not, all were so close to significance (p < .1) that with the small population (N = 10) and gender samples (N = 5), each was suggestive of further examination. The results included below are of the traits that were significant.

The phonological and morphological areas both had some of the most extreme gender contrasts on traits. Phonologically, the group was not an exception to the usual predicted patterns. Women used more refined enunciation, sounding more polite in their speech than the men, whereas men sounded more challenging with their informal pronunciation. Women also varied the tone of their speech more through the use of intensifiers.

In the morphological area, the group also was not an exception to the usual predicted patterns. The women used tag questions (a shortened question added to a declarative sentence such as "The idea is good, don't

Figure 3.1
Proportional Profiles of Male and Female Speech

Variable	Frequency	Proportional Use by Gender	
Phonological:			
•Informal pronunciation	75	90.7	9.3
•Intensifiers	26	84.6	15.4
a Varied discourse length	a		
Morphological:			
•Imperative construction	24	91.7	8.3
•Active agreement	59	74.6	25.4
•Interjections topic shifts	77	72.2	27.3
Exact words	126	66.7	33.3
•Compound-complex sentences	90	53.3	46.7
Incomplete sentences	90	53.3	46.7
Compound sentences	73	56.2	43.8
Approximation/qualifiers	224	60.3	39.7
•Modal construction	245	66.5	33.5
•Conjunction topic shift	18	77.8	22.2
•Tag questions	32	96.9	3.1
•Passive agreement	8	100	

48

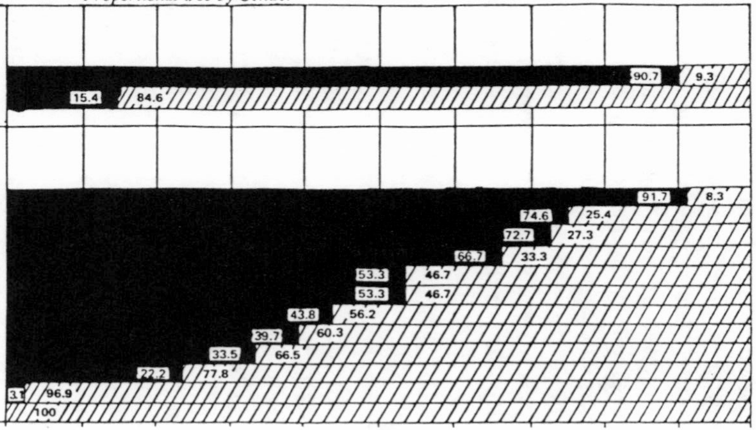

Semantic:

Category	n
*Swears	8
*Slang	128
*Proof authority	23
*Jokes	13
*Talks competition/aggression	195
Hyperbole	24
*Third person/depersonalizes	797
First person/personalizes	1005
Talks relations/responsibility	440
*Proof personal experience	84

Structural:

Category	n
*Disallows interruptions	8
*Interruptions	22
*Changes topic	98
Confronts/attacks	74
b Talks more	b
Builds on utterances	145
Asks questions	162
Answers questions	62
Allows interruptions	14

Bar chart values (% of occurrence):

Semantic:
- Swears: 100 / 6.2
- Slang: 93.8 / 8.7
- Proof authority: 91.3 / 15.4
- Jokes: 84.6 / 21.5
- Talks competition/aggression: 78.5 / 29.2
- Hyperbole: 70.8 / 30.2
- Third person/depersonalizes: 69.8 / 43.2
- First person/personalizes: 56.8
- Talks relations/responsibility: 29.3 / 70.7
- Proof personal experience: 10.7 / 89.3

Structural:
- Disallows interruptions: 75 / 25
- Interruptions: 72.7 / 27.3
- Changes topic: 70.4 / 29.6
- Confronts/attacks: 63.5 / 36.5
- Talks more: 60.7 / 39.1
- Builds on utterances: 60.7 / 39.3
- Asks questions: 54.3 / 45.7
- Answers questions: 51.6 / 48.4
- Allows interruptions: 21.4 / 78.6

% of occurrence

10 20 30 40 50 60 70 80 90 100

Note. * statistically significant difference p ≤.1 by t test or Mann-Whitney U.

a M variation calculated.

b Indicators of variable include percent of words spoken and percent of initiation. Added average percent of indicators over sessions, then divided by two. Speakers on .4% of tapes not identifiable.

Male ■ Female ▨

49

Table 3.2
Gender-Speech Congruity Contrast by Linguistic Areas

Speech Traits Ascribed to Gender	Percent of Utterances		Ratio*
	Men	Women	
	Phonological		
Masculine	90.7	9.3	9.8:1.0
Feminine	15.4	84.6	1.0:5.5
	Morphological		
Masculine	71.8	28.2	2.6:1.0
Feminine	27.9	72.0	1.0:2.6
	Semantic		
Masculine	84.3	15.7	5.4:1.0
Feminine	27.7	72.3	1.0:2.6
	Structural		
Masculine	65.1	34.9	1.9:1.0
Feminine	45.5	54.5	1.0:1.2

*Note.   The ratio given for both men and women is their proportion of
usage of more typical masculine to more typical feminine speech.

you think?"), conjunctions rather than interjections to introduce topic
shifts, and "mm-hmm" as passive agreement, all adding to a sense of the
women being more uncertain in their speech. Yet their manner of speaking seemed more socially facilitative. The men's speech included statistically significant differences in such traits as imperative construction
(a form of commanding, implying obedience), interjections for topic
shifts, and active agreement like "right" or "yeah," all assertive, direct,
authoritative forms of speaking.

A major contrast centered around semantic variables, with a different set
of themes and styles of speaking utilized by each group. The data of this
study demonstrates that the substance of male and female messages may
be quite different. Five-sixths of the utterances counted as indicators of
male traits were made by men, whereas only three-fourths of those labeled
female were made by women. (See the ratios in Table 3.2 and the semantic
variable in Figure 3.1). Female themes included responsibility, affiliation,
fairness, understanding, and commitment to the group, with use of words
implying feeling, emotion, and personal references to their own experiences as their talk involved extensive self-disclosure. Women almost exclusively used personal experiences rather than authority, as proof to convince others of their point of view. The responsibility, affiliation theme of
female talk is illustrated by the following comment, "I think we pushed
Linda outside. We're going to lose her." The themes used in our group by
the women support Gilligan's (1982) notions of a different voice.

Semantically, there were significant differences in male use of swearing, slang, depersonalization and third person usage, and competitive/aggressive talk about violence, victimization, one-upmanship, taking charge, control, superior status, and fear of self-disclosure. A man said, "I'm waiting for a leader to establish himself so I can go for his throat." Another male group member said, "I don't feel particularly like that much of a civilized adult, and I guess I don't trust anyone else in the group to be that much of a civilized adult. If I stick my neck out, someone will take out a razor blade and knock my head off." In contrast to women's use of personal experience as proof, men used proof from authoritative sources, appealing to objectivity.

A significant contrast was expected between gender groups in the structure of speech interactions, including patterns of language organization and arrangement, such as changing topics, interrupting, and disallowing interruptions. But the contrast did not occur. Although men were almost twice as assertive in the group as females, including interrupting women ($p < 0.1$), which was expected, females did *not* follow the expected conversational behavior of being significantly less talkative or more supportive in their language. Men also were different from what was predicted: answering questions, asking questions, and building on utterances. Women and men were the most similar in the structural area, as can be seen by the ratios in Table 3.2. Some of the women in the group had learned to hold their own among the men, not allowing interruptions, changing the topic, and asking questions. Yet what they all chose to focus on thematically, and how they chose to express their ideas morphologically, was different.

In general, men were more mixed than women in their speech, using the traits that had been more frequently identified by previous research as male traits in a 3:1 ratio to those which had been more frequently thought to be female traits. In contrast, women had less variation in their speech with a more extreme 7:1 ratio of female to male traits (See Figure 3.2).

All confirmed female traits were expressive in function, contributing to a facilitative, personalized style. All confirmed male traits were authoritative in function, contributing to a take-charge, depersonalized, emphatic speech style (Case 1985).

In addressing the nature of the difference between masculine and feminine speech styles, it is clear that men attempted to assert status and establish dominance in interpersonal situations. They were more direct, informational, and action-oriented. This included extensive use of the imperative form in making demands, commands, and requests. The masculine speech style was an assertively aggressive one that proposed, opposed, competed, and used proof from other sources. It was a style

Figure 3.2
Ratio of Gender-Speech Congruity of Individuals

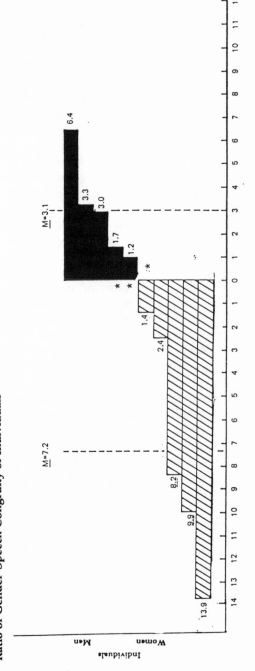

Note.

1. Female ratios given are the proportion of typical feminine to typical masculine speech: male ratios are the proportion of typical masculine to typical feminine speech.

2. * Those individuals who were also called wide-verbal-repertoire

3. ▨ = women
   ■ = men

that pressed compliance on a listener, or led to an argument. It was also a style that withheld personal information, a strategy Sattel (1983) argues helps men exercise and maintain power over others. In general, the masculine style, with verbal gestures of dominance through use of words like *confront* and *attack*, and patterns of conversational assertiveness and control, was action-oriented in its use of imperative construction, and exploitative in its themes of competition and aggression, with little personal information revealed.

It is also clear that the feminine style was slightly more accommodating, with conversation heavily revolving around intimacy through self-revelation, and concern with internal states and behavior. Female talk seemed to attempt to manage relations with others. But it was not done by the expected use of supportive speech. Through their speech style, information was provided to the listener in forms of placating the listener or proof from personal experience about how the speaker thought and felt, including emotional needs, hopes, wishes, likes, and dislikes. Even when the women were angry, they tended to talk about "manipulation" and "control" in terms of *feeling manipulated* or *feeling controlled*. By providing such information, the woman speaker seemed to hope the listener would respond with the desired behavior. Her concern was expressed more passively, yet it expressed the effects of conflict and feelings of victimization. As a style, feminine speech was more polite and indirect, employing many softening devices, such as tags and modal construction, to avoid imposing beliefs or agreement on others through strong statements or commands. In general, the feminine style was collaborative in its drawing out of other speakers, sharing of emotions and personal knowledge, and respecting other's conversational space.

The research described above points to clear differences in men and women's speech styles. But my main claim is that these *differences* do not involve *deficiencies*. The two most influential members of the group were a man and a woman. We had expected that masculine style speech would correspond with influence in the group. Yet, in the case of these influential members, both used speech which combined masculine and feminine characteristics in differing frequencies and proportions. They had the lowest proportions of masculine to feminine speech traits ([Man 1.2:1, woman 1:1.4]. See Figure 3.2). Yet, the woman's speech was predominantly feminine (particularly in the semantic area) and the man's speech was predominantly masculine. The diversity of speech repertoires used by these individuals, which included action and ambition, as well as gentleness and sensitivity, was not in opposition to their leadership activities. Thus, neither the masculine style nor, in particular, the feminine style hindered their leadership activity. Both used both sets of speech traits. We turn to a more detailed discussion of differences without deficiencies in the next section.

IMPLICATIONS

The results we found clearly supported our hypothesis that conjectured a masculine speech style spoken predominantly by men and a feminine speech style spoken predominantly by women. It was clear that the different sexes used certain characteristics of speech more frequently and in sharply distinctive ways, although the speech of all women and all men was not homogeneous. A more accurate representation would be that there exist gender-based distributions with variably occurring differences and similarities in the frequency with which women and men use specific features of a shared language depending on the context of linguistic interactions. For example, we would expect some variation in individual speech used by men and women depending on their role in a group and the issues being discussed, when working in single-sex work groups, in mixed-sex work groups, and as they work in a group over time. Yet in general, there was a more feminine and a more masculine style.

It is a pitfall to believe that a given speech form is intrinsically strong or weak, and that for women in management to be effective they must talk and act like a man (Bennis 1984; Case 1985). In fact, there may be organizational and personal costs to attempts to shape all female managers into imitators of traditional organizational males, honing in on the rational, analytic, and competitive, at the expense of traditional female relation-oriented skills such as understanding, listening, awareness of others' feelings, and collaboration. Men and women have sufficiently different cultural histories that may be responsible for their different modes of communication, different skills, and different ways of personal presentation.

The intergroup framework we use to understand the problem of gender contrasts in speech style usage suggests that groups automatically teach their members about their own and other groups. Even very educated, achievement-oriented women who indicated a desire for power, prestige and money spoke differently than similar male counterparts along a variety of dimensions. This polarization was sufficiently unexpected to suggest further research to understand persistence of the different voice. We suspect that both men and women learn to speak like others in their identity groups very early in life.

One cannot dispose of prejudice or discrimination by eliminating or ignoring such group differences. Intergroup theory recognizes the differences. Differences often lead to defining problems in different ways. How problems are defined frequently provides the solution. Therefore, if females view things in different ways and use a different voice (Gilligan 1984), they may then define problems differently and generate different solutions. Intergroup theory attempts to find ways to negotiate among groups with minimal damage to either the group or to individual interests (Alderfer 1986; Alderfer and Smith 1982).

IMPLICATIONS FOR WOMEN

Many feminists believed that women's language reflected too much uncertainty and nonassertiveness (Lakoff 1973, 1975; Eakins and Eakins 1978; Kramarae 1982; Miller 1983). They argued that women in the professions should adopt the "stronger" forms of the male communication style and consciously work at eliminating their more female-like speech characteristics through assertiveness training, so they would not be perceived as lacking confidence and unable to take on leadership positions.

Some women did adopt the "stronger" masculine take-charge style believing that if they spoke the language of power, they too would be powerful. But women who adopted this strategy were not treated equally. Self-confident, assertive masculine speech, when used by women, was often perceived as overly aggressive or overbearing (Johnson and Goodchild 1976; and Fulmer 1977). Men resented assertive, unemotional women for acting like men, but they also judged women who were passive and emotional as unsuited to management (Kanter 1977). Researchers have also found numerous other cases of similar male/female speech being perceived and evaluated differently (Condry and Condry 1976; Macke et al. 1980; McConnell-Ginet 1983; Bradley (in press).

Others disagree that the speech characteristics more frequently used by many men should be taken as the norm of desirable speech. Bennis (1984:330) states:

There's a mythology of competence going around that says the way for a woman to succeed is to act like a man. . . . What we see today are all kinds of workshops and seminars where women undergo a metaphorical sex change, where they acquire a tough-talking, no-nonsense, sink-or-swim macho philosophy. They're told to take on traits just the opposite of those Harvard psychoanalyst Dr. Helen H. Tartakoff assigns to women; 'endowments which include the capacity for mutuality as well as maternity . . . for creativity as well as receptivity.' In short, she sums up, 'women's feminine heritage, as caretaker and peacemaker, contains the potential for improving the human condition.'

The women we studied in our research were not unassertive in their speech. They spoke up. Yet, they did not monopolize conversation or frequently interrupt others. Even though they spoke up, their speech was very different from the more "masculine" style. This type of difference typically has been interpreted as indicating that the way most women talk is intrinsically weak. The major difference in their speech was in the values expressed through their themes, which showed different perceptions, beliefs, and categories for how they saw and interacted with their world. Thus, even if these women tried to copy a more direct, combative style of speaking, it is likely that the substance of the messages would still differ. It was interesting to us that these women seemed to have resisted the pressure to adopt the more masculine sytle.

Changing language, if possible, assumes that issues of women in management are at the individual level rather than focusing attention on transforming the organizational system. Making one group attempt to shift language styles (the "sex role" school of thought), is an attempt to retrain women to be like men. This wastes potentially valuable organizational resources. Also, work on the psychological structure of women, or sex-role stereotypes, makes no sense if the existing barriers to advancement are at the organizational and institutional levels.

Women's speech has strengths that men might benefit from sharing and that women might benefit from valuing (Aries 1976; Kalcik 1975; Goodwin 1980; Thorne, Kramarae, and Henley 1983). For example, in general, women in our study used language in a way that was more relative, more descriptive, more indirect, and more structured by the desire to include others in the solicitation of ideas than to assert their own ideas. Based on current organizational realities such as multicultural organizations, global competition, deregulation, and the heavy legal context in which businesses must operate, it is very plausible that features of women's speech (indirection, mitigation of criticism, solicitation of others' ideas) are useful organizational functions.

We certainly found in our results a personal, context-bound orientation in how our women talked, with abundant use of softening devices in speech, like tags and qualifiers, which allowed alternative ideas to be easily expressed. This could be especially helpful in the management of conflict or potential conflict among groups that influence the performance and goal attainment of the organization as a whole, as well as in developing complex and novel decisions which require pulling together perspectives and information from many different groups. This style was in contrast to the impersonal, authority-oriented speech style used by men, with its use of competitive and confrontational devices like imperative construction, proof from authority, and interruptions to get one's point heard.

Our position is that it is better for women to utilize their own style of speech, realizing that what they possess is unique. It is especially important to women's careers that they recognize and value the diversity of speech repertoires used by people, and for women whose speech may be different from the more typical organizational speech style to value precisely their own differences and what these differences can contribute to organizational effectiveness.

Since beliefs about differences in language use and its perceived impact are so important, how groups react to these differences becomes an important part of organizational life. However, it is true that if men retain real power, women's style may still not be valued and accepted as valid, since masculine speech embodies the stereotyped images of competence, intelligence, and leadership because of its association with those who have power (Miller 1983). It might be that a *few* distinctions in speech of men and women cause those rendering perceptions to attribute more differences to a message than are actually present in the message. This explanation is consistent with stereotyping, which implies selective perception and attribution by categorization. Where some differences do exist, it is the negative perception of these differences that may lead to problems in power relationships and career development. Yet women most likely will be no worse off using their own speech style than those who copy men, and will at least have preserved their integrity. Hopefully, ways will be found to enable those who make career advancement decisions to expand their images of competence. Intergroup theory helps focus our attention on the many factors that color our interpretation of the language used by women and men. An awareness of how our group memberships affect what we see, hear, and know can help us consider and incorporate alternative points of view.

For example, the propensity for executives and owners to promote those most like themselves reduces the anxiety of filling a position with someone different, who thus may be less understandable and therefore more unpredictable. The root of the fear is in trust and power. One way to expand a manager's image of competence is through managerial communication workshops whose purpose is to reduce mistrust between women and men and explore the fear, hostilities and discomforts they have working with each other and to help build collegial relationships. Such workshops can begin the process of disentangling perceptions and beliefs of feminine qualities and styles from perceptions of competence and value.

ıMPLICATIONS FOR MANAGEMENT

A major function of management is to sense what is going on so the manager can detect potential problems and respond before they become major problems. Good listening is an active process of making sense out of what is heard, although to many people it is an unrecognized process. The women we studied were better active listeners than their male counterparts.

They were the ones to rephrase ideas, ask for clarification, and use qualifiers and modal constructions in idea generation. It is far more common in an interaction to let one's mind wander, to think about what to say next, and when to jump in with an idea, thus missing what is being said. Men in the group showed the latter characteristic by cutting off others to make their points and by changing the topic of conversation.

In our group women's speech permitted the examination of differing value positions through supportive listening, sensitivity to others' needs, and mutual sharing of emotions and personal knowledge. It seemed to be a style driven by a vision of end values, not by a particular method and means to get there. It would appear to be an appropriate style when response to change is needed, when coping with ambiguous situations, when problems require a long-range perspective, and when a variety of values need to be understood or goals may be needed. The speech used by women in our group helped consensus to be reached by competing groups, increased the interaction and the empowerment of others, and was generally a cooperative style which fostered participation and communication rather than domination. The results of this study do suggest that such behavior is compatible with leadership activity.

This style is in contrast to the more impersonal, authority-oriented, dominating and controlling style used by most of our male group members. Women's language is not being adopted by men, because it is not valued as a competent, articulate leadership style (Zimmerman and West 1975; Jakubowski-Spector 1973). Yet, ironically, managerial men are being encouraged to shed some of the same masculine characteristics that women are trying to imitate through sensitivity training programs (Bennis 1984).

Women themselves, now in leadership positions and perhaps out of fear of softness or stereotypical labeling, may help perpetuate the stigma attached to the feminine style. Yet few women can develop enough of the qualities valued by the dominant male culture in a way that eliminates the effect of their gender. For example, assertiveness training may help a woman learn to hold the floor, disallow interruptions, and actively agree in decision-making groups. But it does not focus on the semantic substantive content of feminine speech, which is the area that most reflects the different voice. The type of value orientations that women have learned in our culture are most reflected in this area of speech.

It is not suggested that the women's different voice is a "better voice." But it is much better to have both represented than omitted. If both voices are included in organizational decision making, conversation is transformed and problems can be seen in different ways.

IMPLICATIONS FOR
MANAGEMENT OF CULTURAL DIFFERENCES

Multicultural organizations are a major feature in modern society, raising new issues about what constitutes effective management of human beings in organizations. In a study of a multinational organization with offices in over 40 countries, Hofstede (1984) confirmed that generally masculine norms pervade U.S. management techniques: individualism, tolerance of uncertainty, and achievement striving. He pointed out that these norms do not work well in cultures such as those of Israel, Mexico, and Taiwan, that value the collective over the individual, or ones like Thailand or Scandinavian countries that emphasize feminine values such as nurturance and support. Management practices not only need to be adjusted to cross-cultural management in other nations, but also need to be adjusted for day-to-day work relations with those people who identify with different subcultures within the United States, whether these are based on sex, race, age, religion, or education.

The experiences and knowledge of both women and minorities, and their increasing presence in the work force, mandate understanding their cultural perspective, respecting their differences, refining one's notion of it as more than merely exceptions, and addressing the blind spot in all areas of knowledge that segregate to avoid what has been defined as irrelevant. Organizations are too complicated to have only one set of rules, behavior, and skills that apply to women or men in their attempts to succeed.

Futurologists have predicted that the values of our urbanized society will center on cooperation, de-emphasize competitiveness, and foster an increased need for alternative styles of speaking and for pluralistic management in which many voices can be heard (Rosener and Schwartz 1980; Toffler 1980; Naisbitt 1984). The new leader will need to be a facilitator, not an order giver (Naisbitt 1984). The growth of information in our society involves increased interaction and communication. Having both the feminine and masculine style represented in administrative roles could help increase organizational effectiveness. By including both voices in organizational decision making, problems will be seen in new ways. The differences, then, would be assets, not deficiencies.

This research is important in making clear the powerful masking effects of style. Individual language styles themselves each have unique and positive attributes which can contribute to organizational effectiveness. By understanding the differences in speech style, and not focusing on perceptions of deficiency, we may be able to transcend them so that individuals can be judged on their organizational contributions rather than through the "veil of style" that they use. Further research is needed to help generalize the results.

ACKNOWLEDGMENTS

I am indebted to the following individuals who provided insightful comments on earlier versions of this chapter: Barry Thorne, Cheris Krammarae, William J. Rapaport, Mike Milstein, Kathy Stoudt, Karl Weick, and George Huber.

REFERENCES

Alderfer, C.P. 1977. Improving organizational communication through long-term intergroup intervention. *Journal of Applied Behavioral Sciences, 3*, 193–210.

Alderfer, C.P. 1980. Consulting to underbounded systems. In C.P. Alderfer and C.L. Cooper (Eds.), *Advances in experimental social processes: Vol. 2* (pp. 267–295). London: Wiley.

Alderfer, C.P. 1987. An intergroup perspective on group dynamics. In J.W. Lorsch (Ed.), *Handbook of organizational behavior* (pp. 190–222). Englewood Cliffs, NJ: Prentice-Hall.

Alderfer, C.P., and K. Smith. 1982. Studying intergroup relations in organizations. *Administrative Science Quarterly, 27*, 35–65.

Aries, E. 1976. Interaction patterns and themes of male, female, and mixed groups. *Small Group Behavior, 7*(1), 7–18.

Baird, J.E., Jr. 1976. Sex differences in group communication: A review of relevant research. *The Quarterly Journal of Speech, 62*, 179–192.

Bales, R.F. 1950. *Interaction process analysis: A method for the study of small groups.* Reading, MA: Addison-Wesley.

Bales, R.F. 1953. The equilibrium problem in small groups. In T. Parsons, R.F. Bales, and E.A. Shils (Eds.), *Working papers in the theory of action* (pp. 111–161). New York: Free Press.

Bales, R.F. 1968. Interaction process analysis. In D.L. Sills (Ed.), *International encyclopedia of the social sciences: Vol. 7* (pp. 465–471). New York: Macmillan & Free Press.

Bales, R.F., and S.T. Cohen. 1979. *SYMLOG: A system for the multiple level observation of groups.* London: Free Press.

Barron, N. 1971. Sex-typing language: The production of grammatical cases. *Acta Sociologica, 14*(1–2), 24–72.

Baumann, M. 1976. Two features of "women's speech." In B.L. DuBois and I. Crouch (Eds.), *The sociology of the languages of American women* (pp. 33–40). San Antonio, TX: Trinity University.

Bennis, W.G. 1984. False grit. In D. Kolb, I. Rubin, and J. McIntyre (Eds.), *Organizational psychology: Readings on human behavior in organizations* (pp. 330–334). Englewood Cliffs, NJ: Prentice-Hall.

Bennis, W.G., and Shepard, H. 1956. A theory of group development. *Human Relations, 9*, 415–437.

Berryman, C.L., and Eman, V. 1980. *Communication, language, and sex: Proceedings of the first annual conference.* Rowley, MA: Newbury House.

Bion, W.R. 1961. *Experiences in groups.* New York: Basic Books.

Bodine, A. 1975. Sex differentiation in language. In B. Thorne and N. Henley (Eds.), *Language and sex: Difference and dominance* (pp. 130–151). Rowley, MA: Newbury House.

Bonanno, M. 1982. Women's language in the medical interview. In di Pietro (Ed.), *Linguistics and the professions* (pp. 27–38). Norwood, NJ: Ablex Publishing Co.

Borgatta, E.F., and R.F. Bales. 1980. Interaction of individuals in reconstituted groups. *Sociometry, 16*, 302–320.

Bradley, P. In press. The folklinguistics of women's speech: An empirical examination. *Communication Monographs.*

Case, S.S. 1985. *A sociolinguistic analysis of the language of gender relations, deviance and influence in managerial groups*. Unpublished doctoral dissertation, State University of New York at Buffalo.

Case, S.S. In press. Communication styles in management: Recognition of wide-verbal-repertoire speech. *Proceedings of First Texas Conference on Organizations*.

Condry, J., and S. Condry. 1976. Sex differences: A study of the eye of the beholder. *Child Development, 47*, 812-819.

Doherty, E.G. 1974. Therapeutic community meetings: A study of communication patterns, sex, status, and staff attendance. *Small group behavior, 5*, 244-256.

Dubois, B.L., and I. Crouch. 1977. The question of tag questions in women's speech: They don't really use more of them, do they? *Language in Society, 4*, 289-294.

Eakins, B. 1978. *Sex differences in human communication*. Boston, MA: Houghton Mifflin.

Eakins, B., and G. Eakins. 1976. Verbal turn-taking and exchanges in faculty dialogue. In B.L. DuBois and I. Crouch (Eds.), *Papers in Southwest English IV: Proceedings of the conference on the sociology of the languages of American women* (pp. 53-62). San Antonio, TX: Trinity University.

Fasold, R.W. 1968. *A sociological study of the pronunciation of three vowels in Detroit speech*. Unpublished manuscript. Washington, DC: Center for Applied Linguistics.

Fisher, A.B. 1980. *Group decision making: Communication and the group process* (2nd ed.). New York: McGraw-Hill.

Fisherman, P.M. 1980. Conversational insecurity. In H. Giles, W.P. Robinson, and P.M. Smith (Eds.), *Language: Social psychological perspectives* (pp. 127-132). New York: Pergamon Press.

Fisherman, P.M. 1983. Interaction: The work women do. In B. Thorne, C. Kramarae, and N. Henley (Eds.), *Language Gender, & Society*, (pp. 89-102). Rowley, MA: Newbury House.

Fishman, P.M. 1978. Interaction: The work women do. *Social Problems, 25*, 397-406.

Fulmer, R.M. 1977. *Practical human relations*. Homewood, IL: Richard D. Irwin.

Gilbert, S.J. 1976a. Anxiety, likeability, and avoidance as response to self-disclosing communication. *Small Group Behavior, 7*, 423-432.

Gilbert, S.J. 1976b. Empirical and theoretical extensions of self-disclosure. In G.R. Miller (Ed.), *Explorations in interpersonal communication* (pp. 197-216). Beverly Hills, CA: Sage.

Gilligan, C. 1982. *In a different voice*. Cambridge, MA: Harvard University Press.

Gilligan, C. 1984, October. Invited panelist, *Forum on feminist discourse and the law*. State University of New York at Buffalo Law School.

Goodwin, M.W. 1980. Directive-response speech sequences in girls' and boys' task activities. In S. McConnell-Ginet, R. Borker, and N. Furman (Eds.), *Woman and language in literature and society* (pp. 157-173). New York: Praeger.

Gronn, P.C. 1983. Talk as the work: The accomplishment of school administration. *Administration Science Quarterly, 28*, 1-21.

Hare, A.P. 1972. Four dimensions of interpersonal behavior. *Psychological Reports,* 30(2), 499–512.

Hofstede, G. 1984. Motivation, leadership, and organization: Do American theories apply abroad? In D. Kolb, I. Rubin, and J. McIntyre (Eds.), *Organizational psychology: Readings on human behavior in organizations* (pp. 309–330). Englewood Cliffs, NJ: Prentice-Hall.

Jakubowski-Spector, P. 1974. Facilitating the growth of women through assertive training. *The Counseling Psychologist,* 4(1), 75–86.

Johnson, J.L. 1980. Questions and role responsibility in four professional meetings. *Anthropological Linguistics,* 22, 66–76.

Johnson, P.B., and J.D. Goodchild. 1976. How women get their way. *Psychology Today,* 10(5), 69–70.

Kalcik, S. 1975. ". . . like Ann's gynecologist or the time I was almost raped": Personal narratives in women's rap groups. *Journal of American Folklore, 88,* 3–11.

Kanter, R.M. 1977. *Men and women of the corporation.* New York: Basic Books.

Key, M.R. 1975. *Male/female language.* Metuchen, NJ: Scarecrow Press.

Kramarae, C. 1980. The voices and words of women and men. *Women's Studies International Quarterly,* 3(2–3).

Kramarae, C. 1981. *Women and men speaking.* Rowley, MA: Newbury House.

Kramarae, C. 1982. How she speaks. In E.B. Ryan and H. Giles (Eds.), *Attitudes toward language variation: Social applied contexts* (pp. 84–98). London: Edward Arnold.

Kramer, C. 1975. Women's speech: Separate but unequal? In B. Thorne and N. Henley (Eds.), *Language and sex: Difference and dominance* (pp. 43–56). Rowley, MA: Newbury House.

Kramer, C. Perceptions of female and male speech. *Language and Speech, 20,* 151–161.

Labov, W. 1972. *Sociolinguistic patterns.* Philadelphia, PA: University of Pennsylvania Press.

Lakoff, R. 1973. Language and woman's place. *Language in Society,* 2, 45–79.

Lakoff, R. 1975. *Language and woman's place.* New York: Harper & Row.

Lapadat, J., and M. Seesahai. 1977. Male versus female codes in informal contexts. *Sociolinguistics Newsletter,* 8(3), 7–81.

Levine, V., A. Donnelson, D. Giora, & K.P. Sims, Jr. 1984. Scripts and speech acts in administrative behavior: The interplay of necessity, chance, and free will. *Educational Administration Quarterly,* 19, 93–110.

Maccoby, E.E. 1966. Sex differences in intellectual functioning. In E.E. Maccoby (Ed.), *The development of sex differences* (pp. 25–55). Stanford, CA: Stanford University Press.

Macke, A.S., and L.W. Richardson, with J. Cook. 1980. *Sex-typed teaching styles of university professors and study reactions.* Columbus, OH: The Ohio State University Research Foundation.

McConnell-Ginet, S. 1980. Linguistics and the feminist challenge. In S. McConnell-Ginet, R. Borker, and N. Furman (Eds.), *Women and language in literature and society* (pp. 3–25). New York: Praeger.

McConnell-Ginet, S. 1983. Intonation in a man's world. In B. Thorne, C. Kramarae, and N. Henley (Eds.), *Language, Gender, & Society* (pp. 69–88). Rowley, MA: Newbury House.

McMillan, J.R., A.K. Clifton, D. McGrath, and W.S. Gale. 1977. Women's language: Uncertainty or interpersonal sensitivity and emotionality? *Sex Roles 3*, 545–559.

Miller, M.G. 1983. *Enter the stranger: Unanticipated effects of communication on the success of an organizational newcomer.* Unpublished manuscript, Yale University.

Mintzberg, H. 1973. *The nature of managerial work.* New York: Harper & Row.

Mitchell-Kernan, C. 1972. Signifying and marking: Two Afro-American speech acts. In J. Gumperz and D. Hymes (Eds.), *Directions in sociolinguistics* (pp. 161–179). New York: Holt, Rinehart & Winston.

Naisbitt, J. 1984. *Megatrends.* New York: Warner Books.

Rosener, L., and P. Schwartz. 1980, October. Women, leadership and the 1980's: What kind of leaders do we need? In *The report: Roundtable on new leadership in the public interest* (pp. 25–36). New York: NOW Legal Defense and Education Fund.

Rubin, L.B. 1976. *Worlds of pain: Life in the working-class family.* New York: Basic Books.

Sattel, J.W. 1983. Men, inexpressiveness, and power. In B. Thorne, C. Kramarae, and N. Henley (Eds.), *Language, Gender, & Society* (pp. 119–124). Rowley, MA: Newbury House Publishers.

Schutz, W.C. 1958. *FIRO: A Three-dimensional theory of interpersonal behavior.* New York: Holt & Rinehart.

Shuy, R., W. Wolfram, and W. Riley. 1967. *Linguistic correlates of social stratification in Detroit speech, Final report (Project 16-1347).* Washington, DC: U.S. Office of Education.

Stone, J., and J. Bachner. 1977. *Speaking up: A book for every woman who wants to speak effectively.* New York: McGraw-Hill.

Strodtbeck, F.L., R.M. James, and C. Hawkins. 1957. Social status in jury deliberations. *American Sociological Review, 22,* 713–719.

Swacker, M. 1975. The sex of the speaker as a sociolinguistic variable. In B. Thorne and N. Henley (Eds.), *Language and sex: Difference and dominance* (pp. 76–87). Rowley, MA: Newbury House.

Thorne, B. 1986. Personal correspondence.

Thorne, B. and N. Henley. 1975. Difference and dominance: An overview of language, gender, and society. In B. Thorne and N. Henley (Eds.), *Language and sex: Difference and dominance* (pp. 5–42). Rowley, MA: Newbury House.

Thorne, B., C. Kramarae, and N. Henley. 1983. *Language, Gender, and Society.* Rowley, MA: Newbury House.

Toffler, A. 1980. *The third wave.* New York: Morrow.

Trudgill, P. 1972. Sex, covert prestige, and linguistic change in the urban British English of Norwich. In B. Thorne and N. Henley (Eds.), *Language and sex: Difference and dominance* (pp. 88–104). Rowley, MA: Newbury House.

Zimmerman, D.H., and C. West. 1975. Sex roles, interruptions, and silences in conversation. In B. Thorne and N. Henley (Eds.), *Language and sex: Difference and dominance* (pp. 105–129). Rowley, MA: Newbury House.

4

Attitudes Toward Women and the Experience of Leadership

Robin J. Ely

PREVIEW

The research presented in this chapter is an investigation of how men and women behave in leadership roles and how they are evaluated by their subordinates. I feel it is important that we question the accuracy of sex-role stereotypes as valid descriptions of our own and men's behavior in the workplace and, perhaps more importantly, that we attempt to understand how such stereotypes influence others' perceptions and evaluations of our success. A heightened consciousness about how we enact our roles and how sex-biased expectations may be influencing our interactions with our coworkers might help free us to explore behavioral styles outside the prescriptions of a sexist sex-role ideology.

It is my hope that this chapter will stimulate you to think about your own work experiences as leaders and subordinates and to construct new and helpful ways of understanding those experiences. My interpretations of the results grow from my own knowledge and experience as a professional woman and researcher of organizational behavior. I encourage readers to use their life experiences, as well, to gain deeper insight into the results presented here.

As more and more women enter the work force, questions concerning hierarchical relations between and among men and women in organizations become increasingly pressing. This is especially true when considering the entry of women into positions of authority that traditionally have been reserved for men. Women have become deluged with (very often conflicting) expectations about what is "appropriate" behavior for enacting leadership and followership roles in organizations. As women, we ask ourselves—and our male and female peers, subordinates, and superiors wonder—are we behaving differently from our male counterparts at work? Furthermore, if and when men and women engage in similar leadership processes, are they perceived as equally successful? The empirical work presented in this chapter addresses these questions.

Research on sex differences in leadership style is both inconsistent and complex. Some studies have shown no differences in leadership style as a function of leader sex (Osborne and Vicars 1976; Renwick 1977). Other studies have found that female leaders exhibit more release of tension, express more agreement and more opinions, and solicit more suggestions from their coworkers (Wexley and Hunt 1974), and that women tend to be more supportive than men, but less concerned with avoiding conflict (Thompson 1981). In still other studies, sex differences have been shown to depend on the context in which leadership is exercised. Relevant contextual factors include subordinate sex (Chapman 1975; Eskilson and Wiley 1976; Lockheed 1975), perceived legitimacy of leader role attainment (Eskilson and Wiley 1976; Lockheed 1975; Schneier and Bartol 1980), demands of task (Lockheed 1975; Maier 1970), organizational position (Day and Stogdill 1972), and clarity of role assignment (Lirtzman and Wahba 1972).

Despite the confusion and unreliability of leader-sex effects reported, there are strong theoretical grounds for the prediction of differences between men's and women's actual leadership behavior, and in the perceived effectiveness of their behavior (Rice, Instone, and Adams 1984). Research documenting the existence of sex-role stereotypes suggests that men and women in leadership roles are expected to perform differently from one another, and that they may be evaluated in accordance with those expectations. Nieva and Gutek (1981) suggest further the notion of "sex-role congruency" as an important criterion in the evaluation of men and women in leadership roles. According to this hypothesis, subordinates' satisfaction with and evaluation of leaders may be a function of the goodness-of-fit between sex-role prescriptions and leadership behavior: Women will receive more positive evaluations when they are passive, emotionally supportive, and gentle in their leadership roles, whereas men should be active, unemotional, and assertive.

A pervasive and persistent sex-role ideology permeates research on organizational behavior. Schein (1973; 1975) has shown that successful middle managers are perceived to possess characteristics, attitudes, and temperaments more commonly associated with males, in general, than with females. Similarly, when asked to rate hypothetical situations depicting the use of various kinds of power strategies, both men and women expected women to rely on personal rather than concrete resources, and on helplessness rather than competence in their influence attempts (Johnson 1976). These results are consistent with other studies showing that women in our society are seen as dependent, passive, and subjective, and lacking in such attributes as competitiveness, ambition, and leadership ability (Broverman, et al. 1972).

Stereotypes regarding the capabilities of women appear to influence evaluations of the quality of their work, as well. Pheterson and Keisler (1971) found that paintings presented as the works of women in an art show were judged less favorably than the same paintings attributed to men. Only when women artists were characterized as previously accomplished in their field (i.e., their paintings were described as prize-winning) did the paintings fail to elicit differential ratings according to the artist's gender. Similarly, Goldberg (1968) showed that young women rated journal articles attributed to women authors less favorably than the same articles attributed to men. In addition, the women participating in this study exhibited a stronger bias against women in traditionally masculine fields than those in female-dominated occupations.

Rice, Bender, and Vitters' (1980) study of West Point cadets provides further support for the notion that sex stereotypes influence subordinates' evaluations of women in nontraditional work roles. When male followers with conservative views about appropriate role behavior for women in our society encountered a woman in a nontraditional role (as leader of an otherwise all male group), they described "group atmosphere" as less favorable than when a man served as group leader. Men followers endorsing more liberal views toward women's roles had generally positive reactions to their group experiences regardless of their leaders' sex. Sex-role stereotypes also appeared to influence subordinates' descriptions of their leader's behavior: Group members with conservative attitudes reported that men leaders initiated substantially more structure than their women counterparts.

The notion that men and women in leadership roles achieve success by acting in ways that are congruent with sex-role stereotypes has received some research support. When women were perceived as possessing "masculine" characteristics, such as assertiveness and independence, or using stereotypically masculine supervisory styles, they were viewed as less effective than men behaving in the same manner (Bartol and Butterfield 1976; Haccoun, Haccoun, and Sallay 1978; Rosen and Jerdee 1973). Likewise, Wiley and Eskilson (1982) found that what is perceived as legitimate and effective power use for a man is evaluated negatively when used by a woman.

More recent research findings have failed to support the sex-role congruency hypothesis, however. Rice, et al. (1984) examined the relationship between leader sex and measures of leader effectiveness and leader behavior. They found that, whereas subordinates do have preconceived expectations regarding the proper conduct of leaders, these expectations appeared to be unrelated to leader sex. This study showed that the relationship between leader behavior and perceptions of leader success was generally quite similar for men and women leaders.

One difficulty with these results is that these researchers relied exclusively on subordinates' reports as measures of leader behavior (Rice, et al. 1984). Therefore, it is unclear whether subordinates' ratings reflect actual leader behavior or the subordinates' own implicit leadership theories. The failure to measure actual behavior precludes an assessment of the kinds of behaviors that lead to perceptions of success. Thus, the link between actual behavior and sex-biased evaluation also remains unclear.

This is a difficulty characteristic of most of the research on the effects of sex in leadership situations, since actual behavior is rarely assessed in any systematic fashion. Instead, results generally are based on leaders' reports of their own on-the-job behavior and/or leader descriptions offered by subordinates or superiors. In addition to the effects of sex-role stereotypes on leader evaluations, research has indicated that subordinates may be influenced in their reports of leader behavior by their sex (Butterfield and Bartol 1978; Butterfield and Powell 1981; Lee and Alvares 1977; Wexley and Pulakos 1983), and their personality (Lord, Phillips, and Rush 1980), and by the nature of their task (Weed, Mitchell, and Moffitt 1976). Further, Rice, et al. (1980) found that leaders' descriptions of their own behaviors do not correlate strongly with those of their followers. Still, many research methodologies, as well as most performance appraisal systems in organizations, rely on others' descriptions of leader behavior as though such descriptions are a valid reflection of the actions of leaders. To the extent that raters' characteristics co-vary with leader sex and are inadequately measured or controlled in research designs, the results of studies on sex differences in leadership may be misleading.

OVERVIEW OF THE PRESENT STUDY

Following a design similar to the Rice, et al. (1980) leadership study, groups espousing either liberal or conservative attitudes toward women's roles in society were assembled and appointed either a man or woman to serve as leader for the group. Data collection was extended in the present study, however, to enable direct observation of leader behavior by video tape recording the groups while they were engaged in a decision-making task. In addition, the female component in the present study was enhanced, as compared to the West Point study, by balancing the groups' gender composition, by conducting the study in a university setting where women were better integrated into the social system, and by virtue of the fact that all of the researchers who directed the data collection activities were women. The results discussed in this chapter address three sets of hypotheses, presented below.

Sex and Attitude Effects on Leader Behavior

According to traditional sex-role stereotypes, women in leadership roles should be more passive and dependent, and more solicitous and supportive of their subordinates than men. If sex-role stereotypes are in any way consistent with actual behavior, men should be more task-oriented, and women should be more relationship-oriented. More specifically, men leaders should participate more in group discussion, contribute more to the direction of the group's decision-making process, and have more influence over the decision eventually adopted by the group than women leaders. Alternatively, women should be more solicitous of the opinions and ideas of other group members, and more supportive of others' contributions to the group discussion than men.

Sex and Attitude Effects on Follower Evaluations of Leader

If followers rely on sex-role stereotypes to inform their evaluations of their leaders, as the literature suggests, then followers should rate groups led by men more positively than groups led by women. Additionally, followers should rate men as more task-oriented than women, and women as more relationship-oriented than men.

Based on traditional relations between the sexes, as well as the content of sex-role stereotypes, one would expect both men and women with conservative views to be more comfortable with male than with female leadership (Rice, et al. 1984). Thus, there was a hypothesis that follower attitudes toward women would affect evaluations of men versus women leaders.

There is no clear theoretical basis for predicting the effects of all combinations of leader-follower attributes on the behavioral and evaluative processes that occur between leaders and followers. It is unclear, for example, how women evaluate other women as leaders. On the one hand, one might expect liberal women to show more support and respect for their women leaders. Kanter's (1977) work, however, would suggest alternatively that women's minority status in the broader organizational context might undermine their ability to support one another, independent of their sex-role attitudes. Therefore, these relationships were investigated on an exploratory basis.

Relationship Between Leadership Process and Evaluations of Group and Leader

The concept of sex-role congruency suggests that stereotypically feminine behavior should be associated with more positive evaluations for women leaders and less positive evaluations for men leaders. Likewise, stereotypically masculine behavior should be associated with more positive evaluations for men leaders and less positive evaluations for women leaders. Again, previous research (Rice, et al. 1980) also suggests that these relationships should be more pronounced for followers espousing conservative attitudes toward women.

METHOD

Participants

One hundred twenty-eight graduate students enrolled in the MBA program at the University of Texas at Austin volunteered to participate in the study. Participants were pretested using Spence and Helmreich's (1972) Attitudes toward Women Scale (AWS), which assesses values about women's and men's vocational, marital, family, and social roles. Men's scores ranged from 17 to 45, with a median score of 34; women's scores ranged from 23 to 45, with a median of 37.5. Scores were divided at the overall median of the sample (36.0) to allow classification of participants as either liberal or conservative in their attitudes toward women.

Participants then were divided into 32 four-person groups. A woman was appointed leader for half of the groups; the other half were led by men. Sex of the three subordinate group members was varied as a function of the leader's sex so that each complete group (including the leader) consisted of two women and two men. The groups were also assembled on the basis of the AWS scores, such that of the 16 female-led groups eight were composed of followers with liberal attitudes toward women's roles in society, and eight with followers who were more conservative in their views about appropriate roles for women. The same was true for the male-led groups. Leaders' attitudes varied randomly across groups, so that a leader's attitudes were not necessarily consistent with those of his or her followers.

Procedure

Groups were instructed to role-play as city council members whose task was to reach a consensus within a half hour about what to do with a piece of property that had been donated to their city. They were presented with seven bids, each consisting of a different proposal for use of the property, and each associated with opposition from some segment of the community. The only criterion for deciding what to do with the property was that it be used to "improve the quality of life of the community." The leader's role was to "facilitate the group's discussion."

At the end of each session, participants completed a questionnaire asking for their reactions to and evaluations of the group and the leader.

The questionnaire consisted of a variety of scales assessing team morale, group success, and leader behavior.

Each session was recorded on video tape. These data then were coded using an act-by-act coding scheme modeled after Bales' (1959) Interaction Process Analysis and Hoffman's (1979) valence coding schemes. Codable acts used in the analyses presented in this chapter included verbal utterances regarding (1) direction of the group's process, including statements suggesting, summarizing, or clarifying the process by which the decision could or should be reached; (2) the encouragement or solicitation of other members' contributions to the discussion; (3) justifications of preference for, or opposition to, one or more of the seven proposals received by the city council; and (4) behaviors indicating support, such as statements of agreement. Where appropriate, an act also was coded according to which one or more of the seven proposals the statement preferred. In this way, it was possible to track as a measure of influence the degree to which each member supported or opposed each proposal, including the proposal which was finally accepted by the group. Nonverbal behaviors were considered to the extent that they clarified the meaning or intent of verbal statements.

Coders were two women and two men, counterbalanced across the four conditions. To assess inter-rater reliability, all four coders viewed and coded randomly selected ten-minute segments of interaction. By matching their work, act-by-act, it was possible to determine where coders were in agreement and where they were in disagreement across all acts coded for the reliability analysis. These analyses yielded acceptable levels of reliability: For example, on average, nearly three out of four coders were in agreement on the categorization of any given codable act.[1]

RESULTS

Sex and Attitude Effects on Leader Behavior

Analyses of leader behavior revealed the degree to which men and women behave differently in leadership roles.[2] Follower attitudes were included in the analysis to assess their effects on leader behavior. Table 4.1 presents the means and standard deviations of men's and women's contributions as leaders of the groups.

The only significant and meaningful leader-sex effect, independent of follower attitudes, showed that men leaders were more involved than women leaders in directing the process by which the group reached its decision ($F(1, 27) = 5.11$, $p < .05$). In addition, a significant interaction between leader-sex and follower attitudes on amount of participation in the group revealed that the liberal groups led by men had lower overall

Figure 4.1
Amount of Participation in Groups

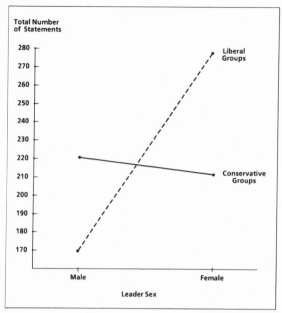

Table 4.1
Mean Percent and Standard Deviations of
Types of Leaders' Verbal Contributions

Type of Statements	Male Leaders		Female Leaders	
	M	SD	M	SD
Proportion of group's statements made by leader	34%	(12%)	36%	(11%)
Decision-making process directive statements:	33	(12)	25	(9)
-Process suggestion	19	(9)	17	(7)
-Summaries of process	6	(5)	4	(3)
-Clarification of process	7	(6)	4	(2)
Solicitations of others' ideas or opinions	15	(6)	13	(8)
Statements in favor of option chosen (influence)	13	(6)	13	(9)
Statements of agreement with others*	5	(3)	7	(4)
Agreements with leader*	18	(11)	22	(13)
Disagreements with leader*	.6	(1)	.6	(1)
Interuptions of leader*	.8	(1)	.4	(1)

Figure 4.2
Leaders' Influence

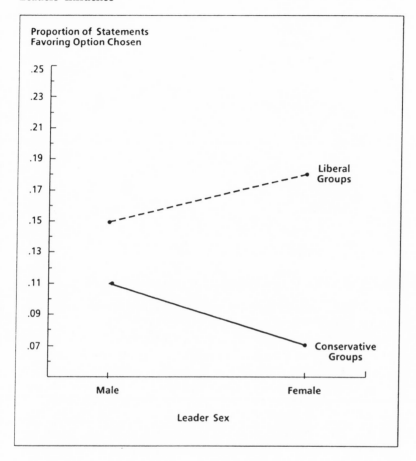

participation than the other groups, whereas participation was highest in liberal groups led by women (F(1,27) = 4.44, p < .05). (See Figure 4.1.)

These analyses also revealed a significant interaction effect between leader-sex and follower attitudes on the amount of influence leaders demonstrated in their groups, as measured by the degree to which leaders had supported the decision eventually adopted by the group (F(1, 27) = 4.3, p < .05). Although men leaders did not seem to have more influence of this sort than women leaders, women leaders of conservative groups were significantly less influential than women leaders of liberal groups, as hypothesized. This effect is shown in Figure 4.2.

Figure 4.3
Followers' Ratings of Group Atmosphere

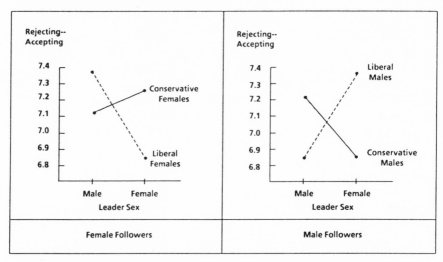

Sex and Attitude Effects on Follower Evaluations of Leader

Leader-sex alone did not explain a significant portion of the variability in followers' evaluations of their groups or their leaders.[3] Instead, the data showed a more complicated relationship between leader-sex and evaluation, one mediated by follower attitudes toward women and follower sex. On the group atmosphere dimension, "accepting-rejecting," there was a three-way interaction effect between leader-sex, follower-sex, and follower attitudes toward women ($F(1, 92) = 5.12$, $p < .05$). As shown in Figure 4.3, this interaction means that members of the same group, with the same leader, evaluated their experiences differently from one another: In conservative groups led by women, women followers reported more positive feelings than did their male group mates; in liberal groups led by women, women followers reported more negative experiences than the men; alternatively, in groups led by men, liberal women reported more positive feelings than did the liberal men; conservative men and women who had men leaders evaluated their experiences equally positively. These results did not support the hypothesis that men receive the most favorable reactions from conservative followers. Instead, it was conservative men and liberal women who rated male-led groups most positively. As predicted, female-led groups were evaluated relatively negatively by conservative men. Somewhat unexpectedly, however, liberal women again were similar to conservative men in their group ratings: Liberal women and conservative men rated their female-led groups equally negatively.

Relationship Between Leadership Process and
Evaluations of Group and Leader

For these analyses, stereotypically feminine behavior was character-ized as: (1) the degree to which leaders solicited group members' ideas, and (2) the degree to which they supported group members' ideas, as measured by the proportion of members' statements with which leaders agreed. Stereotypically masculine behavior included: (1) amount of par-ticipation by the leader, (2) leaders' contributions to the direction of the group's decision-making process, and (3) leaders' influence over the deci-sion adopted by the group, as measured by the proportion of statements the leader made in support of the option chosen by the group. (All behavior measures were proportional to overall individual or group participation.)

Sex-role congruency hypotheses concerning the goodness-of-fit be-tween sex-role prescriptions and leader behavior were assessed through a series of correlation analyses between the leader behavior measures and six eight-point Likert-type questionnaire items (analyzed separately) which served as measures of evaluation. The pattern of correlations sug-gested only a moderate degree of support for these hypotheses. As an-ticipated, women leaders who were more directive of the group's decision-making process tended to receive less favorable reactions from their conservative male and female followers than women leaders who were less directive. Also as hypothesized, these correlations were in the opposite direction for men leaders: Conservatives tended to respond more favorably when men engaged in this stereotypically masculine behavior, and less positively when they did not. The same pattern of results occurred with respect to leaders' participation rates: The more men leaders participated, the more positively conservative followers tended to evaluate them; the more women participated, the more nega-tively their conservative followers evaluated them.

As anticipated, there was less support for the sex-role congruency hypotheses among liberal followers. Sex-role congruent behavior was associated with more favorable evaluations in only two cases: First, the less women leaders participated in their groups, the more positively liberal women evaluated them. Amount of participation by women lead-ers was unrelated to liberal men's evaluations of them, however, and liberal women reacted positively when their women leaders were more heavily involved in the direction of the group's process. The second finding consistent with the sex-role congruency notion was that the more men leaders engaged in directing the group's process, the more positively liberal men evaluated them. This behavior was unrelated to liberal women's evaluations of their men leaders, however. In addition, rather than reacting positively to high participation rates, which is what the notion of sex-role congruency would suggest, these men tended to rate their men leaders lower the more they participated in the group.

Regardless of leader sex, the more influence a leader demonstrated in the group, the more negative were followers' evaluations of the leader. This finding failed to support the hypothesis that only women would be perceived more negatively for demonstrating influence in the group, while men would receive more positive evaluations the more influential they were. In addition, the relationships between leaders' efforts at soliciting other members' ideas and followers' subsequent ratings were the reverse of what had been predicted: The more women engaged in this stereotypically feminine behavior, the more negatively their conservative and liberal followers tended to evaluate them; men, on the other hand, tended to receive more positive evaluations from their followers the more solicitous they were of other members' ideas. Finally, leaders' demonstration of support for other members' contributions, a stereotypically feminine behavior, appeared to be largely unrelated to all leader evaluations.

DISCUSSION

Only a few of the predicted sex differences in leadership behavior were confirmed in the present study. Men engaged more than women in directing the process by which the task would be completed; and women leaders of conservatives demonstrated less influence than women leaders of liberals.

The relationship between followers' attitudes and leaders' behavior suggests that some of the differences observed between men and women by the performance-appraising superior, the trained empiricist, or the casual observer may be at least partly the leaders' attempts to fulfill others' sex-biased expectations. Women conformed to the stereotype of being less influential only in groups that espoused a more conservative sex-role ideology.

That women were less influential in groups espousing conservative attitudes raises the question of how group processes may affect women's ability to perform in nontraditional work roles. This is a difficult question since the processes are not obvious, and thus we may not even be consciously aware of how and when sex-biased expectations are influencing our interactions. Furthermore, when coworkers hold expectations for women that are counter to women's own expectations for themselves, tensions and confusions can create a highly stressful work environment for both parties.

There is some research that has shown that an individual is less likely to conform to another's expectations the more certain she is of her own self-concept. It also appears that if the other's expectations are held with little conviction, they may play a lesser role in the interaction (Swann and Ely 1984). These findings, together with those of the present study, suggest that individuals and organizations must commit to exposing and changing sex-biased expectations if they ever hope to eradicate the effects of sexism on women's and men's work experiences. This could potentially free both men and women to explore behavioral styles outside the prescriptions of a sexist sex-role ideology.

Sexist stereotypes also entered into followers' subsequent evaluations of men and women in leadership roles. The present study suggests that when women do use leadership styles traditionally associated with men, some followers, especially conservatives, may perceive them as less effective than men behaving in the same manner. In addition, conservative men were less comfortable in groups with women leaders than in groups with men leaders, as expected. Conservative women were more comfortable in groups led by women, but, again, appeared to invoke sexist criteria when evaluating both men and women in leadership roles. Of all of the participants in the study, liberal men were most comfortable with women leaders. In addition, masculine and feminine stereotypes appeared to be irrelevant to their evaluations of women leaders.

One of the more surprising results of this study is that liberal women tended to be less comfortable in groups with women leaders than in groups with men leaders. Indeed, these women were as negative in their evaluations of their female-led groups as were the conservative men, and as positive as conservative men in their evaluations of male-led groups. These results suggest the need to take a closer look at women's experiences with each other.

Work relationships between women have not been well researched; in fact, they have largely been ignored in most of the literatures cited above. In the limited (mostly nonempirical) literature that does address women's relationships with one another at work, there is a prevalent finding/belief that women have difficulty sharing power and authority with each other, and often work to undermine one another, one seeking to replace the other. Barry (1979) has suggested that achieving women often are more identified with men's experiences than with the experiences of other women. Nontraditional women may be more comfortable with male leadership since they may be modeling themselves on male roles, and therefore may be more accepting of groups led by men. Unfortunately, this sort of identification with men among achieving women may reduce the possibility of female bonding and mutual support among women, and subsequently, against the empowerment of women as a group. It is also possible that liberal women are more critical of other women in leadership roles because they see themselves as candidates for these positions. Finally, it is possible that men may be participating in these dynamics, perhaps facilitating or otherwise contributing to the negative experiences some women report having when working with other women.

In attempting to understand the liberal woman's relatively negative evaluation of her female-led group, it is important to note that her group was characterized both by female leadership and by a situation where she had no female peers. (In groups with female leaders, there were two male followers, but only one female follower.) Thus, it is difficult to determine whether her experience was a function of female leadership or of the lone status she occupied in her group. Conversely, in male-led groups, liberal women reported more positive experiences, but again, this may have been related to the presence of male leadership, or to the comradeship women could provide for one another.

Previous research advises some caution in the interpretation of the present results since they were generated in a laboratory setting. Adams, Rice, and Instone (1984) found that in field settings attitudes did not introduce a consistent and strong bias in the way men and women were judged as leaders by either their subordinates or their superiors. They reason that the saliency of gender and sex-role stereotypes may wane over time as people are compelled to judge women based on longer-term experience with them. Osborne and Vicars (1976) have drawn similar conclusions from their survey of the research literature on the effects of gender in leadership situations. Just the same, the current results are, at the very least, generalizable to work situations where ad hoc groups of men and women are formed to discuss problems and make decisions.

Finally, it is important to note that these results did not corroborate all of the findings of the West Point (Rice, et al. 1980) study after which this research was modeled. For example, there were several evaluative and descriptive dimensions which did not discriminate men from women leaders in the present study, but which West Point participants used to rate their leaders in reliably sex-typed ways. For example, this study did not support the hypothesis that female leaders are perceived as more relationship-oriented, and male leaders as more task-oriented. In the West Point study, however, followers perceived male leaders as initiating more structure around the task than female leaders.

Differences in the degree and nature of female involvement in these two settings may be partially responsible for this study's failure to replicate those results. These differences stem from at least three factors. First, the proportion of women students is much lower among West Point cadets than among MBA students at the University of Texas. Second, the integration of women into the military academies is much more recent and more controversial than the integration of women into large state universities. Third, women in positions of authority were more salient in the present study since the data collection activities were directed solely by women, while apparently only one of the three researchers involved in the West Point study was a woman. Thus, the environment within which the present study was embedded reinforced the legitimacy of female involvement in nontraditional roles of authority, while the West Point environment perhaps clashed with the idea of female leadership, making salient, especially for the more conservative participants, the notion that women do not belong in leadership roles.

NOTES

This research was supported in part by research funds from the Program in Organizational Behavior, Yale University. I thank Janet Spence, Cristina Banks, Laura Cardinal, and Betty Lou Gaines for their work in the design and data collection phases of this research; Mary Bales, Daniel Hall, and Nasser Aziz for their efforts during the coding phases of this investigation; and Richard Hackman for his comments on this research.

1. A technical note which describes the reliability analyses in greater detail is available from the author.

2. A series of analyses of variance was conducted to examine the main and interaction effects of leader sex and follower attitudes toward women on the behaviors of leaders. Since leaders' attitudes toward women were assessed, but of no theoretical importance to the present hypotheses, their AWS scores were included as a covariate of these ANOVA models.

3. The models used to test these hypotheses included groups as a random effect factor nested within the 2 (leader-sex) × 2 (follower-attitudes) factorial conditions. The mean square associated with the nested "group" factor served as the error term for testing the significance of the "between groups" effects: leader-sex, follower-attitudes, and the leader-sex × follower-attitudes interaction. The mean square error was used to test the significance of the remaining "within groups" effects of interest: follower-sex, the follower-sex × leader-sex interaction, the follower-sex × follower-attitudes interaction, and the follower-sex × leader-sex × follower-attitudes interaction.

REFERENCES

Adams, J., R.W. Rice, and D. Instone. 1984. Follower attitudes toward women and judgments concerning performance by male and female leaders. *Academy of Management Journal*, 27(3), 636–643.

Bales, R.F. 1959. *Interaction process analysis: A method for the study of small groups.* Cambridge, MA: Addison-Wesley.

Barry, K. 1979. *Female sexual slavery.* Englewood Cliffs, NJ: Prentice-Hall.

Bartol, K., and D.A. Butterfield. 1976. Sex effects in evaluating leaders. *Journal of Applied Psychology, 61,* 446–454.

Broverman, I.K., R.S. Vogel, D.M. Broverman, F.E. Clarkson, and P.S. Rosenkrantz. 1972. Sex role stereotypes: A current appraisal. *Journal of Social Issues, 28,* 59–78.

Butterfield, D.A., and K.M. Bartol. 1978. Evaluators of leader behavior: A missing element in leadership theory. In J.G. Hunt and L.L. Larson (Eds.), *Leadership: The cutting edge*. Carbondale, IL: Southern Illinois University Press.

Butterfield, D.A., and G.N. Powell. 1981. Effect of group performance, leader sex, and rater sex on ratings of leader behavior. *Organizational Behavior and Human Performance, 28,* 129–141.

Chapman, J.B. 1975. Comparison of male and female leadership styles. *Academy of Management Journal, 18,* 645–652.

Day, D.R., and R.M. Stogdill. 1972. Leader behavior of male and female supervisors: A comparative study. *Personnel Psychology, 25,* 353–360.

Eskilson, A., and M.G. Wiley. 1976. Sex composition and leadership in small groups. *Sociometry, 39,* 183–194.

Goldberg, P. 1968. Are women prejudiced against women? *Transaction, 5,* 28–30.

Haccoun, D.M., R.R. Haccoun, and G. Salley. 1978. Sex differences in the appropriateness of supervisory styles: A non-management view. *Journal of Applied Psychology, 63,* 124–127.

Hoffman, L.R. 1979. *The group problem solving process: Studies of a valence model.* New York, NY: Praeger.

Johnson, P. 1976. Women and power: Toward a theory of effectiveness. *Journal of Social Issues, 32,* 99–109.

Kanter, R.M. 1977. *Men and women of the corporation.* New York: Basic Books.

Lee, D.M., and K.M. Alvares. Effects of sex on descriptions and evaluations of supervisory behavior in a simulated industrial setting. *Journal of Applied Psychology, 62,* 405–410.

Lirtzman, S.I., and M.A. Wahba. 1972. Determinants of coalitional behavior of men and women—sex-roles or situational requirements? *Journal of Applied Psychology, 56(5),* 406.

Lockheed, M.E. 1975. Female motive to avoid success—psychological barrier or a response to deviancy? *Sex Roles, 1(1),* 41–50.

Lord, R.G., J.S. Phillips, and M.C. Rush. 1980. Effects of sex and personality on perceptions of emergent leadership, influence and social power. *Journal of Applied Psychology, 65,* 176–182.

Maier, N.R.F. 1970. Male versus female discussion leaders. *Personnel Psychology, 23,* 455–461.

Nieva, V.F., and B.A. Gutek. 1981. *Women and work: A psychological perspective.* New York: Praeger.

Osborne, R.N., and W.M. Vicars. 1976. Sex stereotypes: An artifact in leader and subordinate satisfaction analysis. *Academy of Management Journal, 19,* 439–449.

Pheterson, G.I., and S.B. Keisler. 1971. Evaluation of the performance of women as a function of their sex, achievement, and personal history. *Journal of Personality and Social Psychology, 19,* 114–118.

Renwick, P.A. 1977. The effects of sex difference on the perception and management of superior-subordinate conflict: An exploratory study. *Organizational Behavior and Human Performance, 19,* 403–415.

Rice, R.W., L.R. Bender, and A.B. Vitters. 1980. Leader sex, follower attitudes toward women and leadership effectiveness: A laboratory experiment. *Organizational Behavior and Human Performance, 14,* 46–78.

Rice, R.W., D. Instone, and J. Adams. 1984. Leader sex, leader success, and leadership process. Two field studies. *Journal of Applied Psychology, 69*(1), 12–31.

Rosen, B., and T.H. Jerdee. 1973. The influence of sex-role stereotypes on evaluations of male and female supervisory behavior. *Journal of Applied Psychology, 57,* 44–48.

Schein, V.E. 1973. Relationship between sex-role stereotypes and requisite management characteristics. *Journal of Applied Psychology, 57*(2), 95–100.

Schein, V.E. 1975. Relationships between sex-role stereotypes and requisite management characteristics among female managers. *Journal of Applied Psychology, 60,* 3, 340–344.

Schneier, C.E., and K.M. Bartol. 1980. Sex effects in emergent leadership. *Journal of Applied Psychology, 65,* 341–345.

Spence, J.T., and R. Helmreich. 1972. The attitude toward women scale: An objective instrument to measure attitudes towards the rights and roles of women in contemporary society. *Journal Supplement Abstract Service, 2,* 66.

Swann, W.B., and R.J. Ely. 1984. A battle of wills: Self-verification versus behavioral confirmation. *Journal of Personality and Social Psychology, 46,* 6, 1287–1302.

Thompson, M.E. 1981. Sex differences: Differential access to power or sex role socialization? *Sex Roles, 7,* 413–424.

Weed, S.E., T.R. Mitchell, and W. Moffitt. 1976. Leadership style, subordinate personality, and task type as predictors of performance and satisfaction with supervision. *Journal of Applied Psychology, 61,* 58–60.

Wexley, K.N., and P.J. Hunt. 1974. Male and female leaders: Comparison of performance and behavior patterns. *Psychological Reports, 35,* 666–867.

Wexley, K.N., and E.D. Pulakos. 1983. The effects of perceptual congruence and sex on subordinates' performance appraisals of their managers. *Academy of Management Journal, 36,* 666–676.

Wiley, M.G. and A. Eskilson. 1982. The interaction of sex and power base on perceptions of managerial effectiveness. *Academy of Management Journal, 25,* 671–677.

5

Husbands' Job Satisfaction and Wives' Income

Chester C. Cotton
John F. McKenna

PREVIEW

Are you a career woman with an employed husband? Whether your husband has a blue- or white-collar job might make a difference in the extent to which he experiences problems associated with your career achievement. White-collar husbands with achieving wives might be more prone than blue-collar husbands to lower levels of job satisfaction. Results from some studies show that white-collar husbands have difficulties in social and marital adjustment; however, other studies show no effect of wives' achievement at all.

As you read this chapter, check your own situations against the findings of the various research studies that are summarized. To what extent do their results parallel your experiences? A large and growing group—career women with white-collar husbands—may want to remember that while dual-career marriages are unquestionably stressful for wives, they may impose costs on husbands. As wives become more successful, couples may want to address the husbands' adjustments to the changing circumstances in their lives together.

We suppose the possible approaches to managing husband adjustment problems could range from marrying a blue-collar husband who won't be threatened by your success, to taking steps to keep the career progress of both spouses about equal, to hiring a housekeeper and errand runner, to not marrying at all. We believe the future will bring new trends, new arrangements in the ancient social phenomenon that is marriage.

An earlier version of this chapter was presented at the national Academy of Management meeting in Boston, MA, August 1984.

INTRODUCTION

As increasing proportions of women engage in essentially continuous employment throughout the normal working years of ages 20-60, the management literature has begun to address the social and work adjustment processes which members of two-income households will surely confront. Most studies have looked at the implications of this social change for organizations; the few which have focused on the impact on the couple have appeared largely in journals reporting research on marriage and the family. In only three instances did we find such studies reported in the management and organizational behavior literature (Hardesty and Betz 1981; Pfeffer and Ross 1982; Staines, Pottick, and Fudge 1986).

Two approaches to the study of husbands in dual-career marriages characterize contemporary research. One approach compares husbands whose wives work with husbands whose wives do not work on a variety of measures of psychological adjustment. Another approach focuses only on husbands with working wives, comparing those whose wives earn considerably less than the husbands with those whose wives earn as much or more than the husbands.

Impact of the Working Wife

In the most influential study of the correlates of having a working wife, Burke and Weir (1976a) reported that husbands of working wives were less satisfied and performed less effectively than husbands of nonworking wives. This study was conducted with a sample of 189 husband-wife pairs and all of the husbands were either accountants or engineers. These men reported having poorer physical and mental health, doing more worrying, being less happy with their marriages, and being less content with work and life. Burke and Weir conclude that "There is little to suggest that men perceive the roles they fill in dual-career families as contributing to their personal growth and fulfillment" (p. 285). In a subsequent article utilizing the sample described above, Burke and Weir (1976b) reported that members of two-career families had significantly lower needs for social interaction. The husbands reported less need for gratification through relationships with others. They were also less assertive than husbands in single-career families.

Booth (1977) took issue with the methodology and findings of Burke and Weir. He reported a study in which he claimed to have improved upon the sampling and analysis used by Burke and Weir. A key difference in Booth's approach was that he used a probability sample—he included individuals in his sample in the same proportions that such individuals are represented in the overall population. The proportions of professionals, white collar, blue collar, black, white, young, old, and so on individuals in his sample would closely resemble that in the U.S. population. Booth did not report examining differences among groups; for the total sample he found that "wife's employment does not contribute to the marital discord or stress experienced by the husband" (p. 649).

Locksley (1980), using national probability sample data from the Institute for Social Research, found that husbands in dual-career families did not differ from husbands in single-career families in their marital adjustment. She further reported that the variable of wife's degree of interest in her career had no impact on marital compatibility.

In a review of the literature on dual-career family stress and coping, Skinner (1980, p. 476) concluded that "Life for the dual-career male is not without its periods of stress, although the impact of various strains does not appear to be as significant as that reported for women." She also reported that high levels of involvement with career by either partner tend to be associated with lower levels of marital satisfaction.

Pfeffer and Ross (1982) reported on the analysis of a national random sample of 5000 men which they split into "blue-collar," "professional," and "managerial" subgroups. The question they addressed dealt with the impact of a working wife on the wage attainment of men in the three categories. They reported that the negative impact on husband's salary of having a working wife was "larger for managers and professionals than for blue-collar employees" (p. 76). It should be noted that Pfeffer and Ross reported on an analysis of data collected in 1966 and the relationships they observed may have changed.

In the last of the studies dealing with the comparison of single- versus dual-career families' impact on husbands, Staines, Pottick, and Fudge (1986) used a national probability sample to compare certain outcomes of husbands whose wives do not work with husbands whose wives work 20 or more hours per week. They found that wives' employment was negatively associated with husbands' job and life satisfaction. They conclude "the most plausible explanation of the lower job and life satisfaction of husbands of employed wives appears to lie in their feelings of being less adequate as breadwinners for their families" (p. 126).

Note that in most studies conducted with "population samples," (which contain substantial numbers of blue-collar men) no impact on husbands was found for wife's employment. On the other hand, in those studies which either utilized white-collar subjects or categorized subjects by occupational level, emotional (or economic) impacts on white-collar/professional husbands were found to result from participation in dual-career families.

Level of Wife's Employment

When the focus of the research changes to the impact of various levels of wife's economic contributions and/or career achievements on husbands in dual-career families, once again there are conflicting findings. In an examination of wife's occupational superiority and marital troubles, Richardson (1979) utilized a national probability sample and concluded that there was no support for his hypothesis that marital troubles would arise in dual-career families in which the occupational prestige of the wife was equal to or higher than that of her husband.

On the other hand, Keith and Schafer (1980) found, with a probability sample, that men in two-job families tended to be depressed to the extent that they experienced work-family role strain. They concluded that "the work as well as mental health of the husband may suffer when both spouses seek to juggle employment outside the home and family obligations" (p. 487). They also noted that men whose wives spent more time at work were somewhat more involved themselves in "feminine" (sic) household activities and were more likely to be depressed, although they did not report more work-family role strain.

Hardesty and Betz (1980) examined a group of 42 dual-career families in which the woman was a professional. Some 70 to 80 percent of the subjects were college graduates. They found that a wife's income was positively related to degree of individual marital stress for both the husband and the wife. On the other hand, Hardesty and Betz found a positive relationship between wife's career "salience" (commitment) and marital adjustment.

Keith, Goudy, and Powers (1981) interviewed 213 older (60+ years) men from a range of occupational groupings. They reported that men whose wives worked in high status occupations spent more time doing "feminine" (sic) household tasks. However, they found that the intensity of the wives' involvement in the labor force was unrelated to the well-being of these older men.

Kessler and McRae (1982) studied a large national probability sample of white dual-career families in an attempt to determine the influence of wives' employment on the mental health of married men and women. They found that wives' employment is associated with higher levels of depression and lower levels of self-esteem for husbands. On the other hand, they also found no evidence "that increased wife's earnings damages the well-being of husbands" (p. 223).

Rubenstein (1982) reported two findings from different sources which have a bearing on this discussion. First, she reported interim findings from an unpublished major long-term study of the health of 1038 men by social epidemiologist Carlton Hornung and his colleagues at the University of South Carolina. Hornung, et al., found that the men who had lower occupational status than their wives were likely to be subject to psychological abuse (insults, swearing, sulking, threats or actual hitting or throwing of things) by their wives. They were 11 times more likely to suffer from ischemic heart disease—a stress-induced illness—than men in general.

Table 5.1
Analysis of Research Findings by Occupational Level of Sample

Type of Sample	Found No Problems*	Found Problems
Professional		
Burke & Weir (1976a)		x
Preffer & Ross (1982)	Prof/Mar}	x
Hardesty & Betz (1980)		x
Rubenstein (1982)-Psych. Today survey		x
-Hornung study		x
Philliber & Hiller (1983)		x
Professional & Blue Collar		
Booth (1977)	x	
Locksley (1980)	x	
Richardson (1979)	x	
Keith & Shafer (1980)		x
Keith, Goudy, & Powers (1981)	x	
Kessler & McRae		x
Pfeffer & Ross (1982)	x {Blue Col.	
Staines, Pottick, & Fudge (1986)		x

*"Problems" include stress, marital difficulties, physical maladies, lower salary, depression, lower job and life satisfaction and/or lower self-esteem, depending on the study.

Note: Pfeffer & Ross (1982) is listed twice inasmuch as it looks separately at blue collar, white collar, and professional men.

Rubenstein (1982) also reports a reanalysis of data from a *Psychology Today* reader survey which found that in families in which wife's income was higher, husbands reported less happiness with their marriages, less satisfaction with friends and own salary, less involvement with friends, and lower self-esteem. It should be noted that most readers of *Psychology Today* tend to be educated and in white-collar or professional occupations.

Most recently, Philliber and Hiller (1983) looked at relative occupational attainments of husbands and wives and the subsequent changes in their marriages and in wives' work experiences. They learned that "women employed in nontraditional [sex-typed male] managerial/professional positions and married to men of similar status . . . were more likely than expected to leave the labor force, shift to a traditional position, or move to a lower status occupation" (p. 168). They go on to observe that many such marriages end in divorce.

In conclusion, there is some evidence that a wife's occupational attainment is negatively related to husband's mental health, marital adjustment, and satisfaction with work and life when the research focused on the white-collar, managerial, and professional classes. When a broader sample was utilized, including substantial numbers of blue-collar workers, the results in most studies tend to show "no relationship." The studies summarized above are exhibited in Table 5.1.

It appears that level of occupational attainment or, perhaps, social class moderates the impact of dual-career family status on the work and life of husbands. However, social class as a variable affecting husbands' social adjustment at work has not been investigated directly.

In the present study the impact of spouse income level on the adjustment to work of husbands in both white-collar and blue-collar groups is examined. The following research hypotheses were proposed:

H1: For white-collar and professional husbands, the relationship between spousal income and social adjustment to work will be inverse.

H2: For blue-collar husbands, there will be no relationship between spousal income and social adjustment to work.

RESEARCH METHODS

Subjects and Setting

The subjects in this research were recruited from the full-time faculty and staff members of a medium-sized (13,000 students) state university on the West Coast. These subjects were grouped by the researchers into "Professional" (faculty and academic support) and "Sub-professional" (clerical and buildings and grounds) categories. All job groupings were either smaller than 100 (skilled trades, academic support, maintenance) or larger than 300 (faculty, clerical) employees; all members of the smaller units were surveyed while a randomly selected 50 percent of the larger units were polled. All employees selected to participate were sent a survey instrument via the internal mail system of the university. Subjects were asked to respond anonymously and 337 did so, for a return rate of about 45 percent. Of these 337, 188 were in the professional category and 149 were in the sub-professional grouping.

Measures

Subjects were asked biographical questions concerning their gender, marital status, and spouse employment. Subjects were also asked to estimate the percentage of total family income contributed by their working spouse. Each employee's occupational level (faculty, academic support, skilled crafts, clerical, or buildings and grounds) was coded directly and openly on the questionnaire by the researchers prior to distribution.

Job satisfaction data were collected with the *Job Descriptive Index* (JDI) of Smith, Kendall, and Hulin (1969). This instrument gathers job satisfaction data in five areas: pay, promotion, supervision, coworkers, and the work itself. The JDI presents the subject with five lists of mixed positive and negative adjectives. Subjects are to indicate whether an adjective does or does not describe that aspect of their job, a "don't know" option is also provided. Scores for the nine (pay, promotion) or 18 (work itself, supervision, coworkers) adjectives describing each area are summed, to produce a score for satisfaction with that area. It is common to sum the five scale scores into a JDI Total score which is viewed as a measure of overall job satisfaction.

RESULTS

Respondent Sample Characteristics

Of the 337 who responded, only the married men with working spouses (N = 76) were relevant to this particular analysis. Of these, 44 were in the "Professional" group and 32 were in the "Sub-professional" category.

Correlation Results

The group of married male respondents with working wives (n = 76) was divided into white-collar ("Professional") and blue-collar ("Sub-professional") subgroups. For each subgroup, five separate Pearson Product Moment Correlations were computed relating spousal income (as a percentage of household total) to each of the job satisfaction subscales from the JDI. The Pearson Product Moment Correlation procedure summarizes the degree of association between two variables, the degree to which variation in one variable is related to variation in another (Blalock 1972). For this study a significance level of .05 was selected. That is, we were willing to accept a one-in-20 chance of apparently meaningful results occurring by chance alone.

Table 5.2 presents the results of these ten correlation analyses with the correlation coefficient and significance level (if < .05) associated with each. Correlations for particular job satisfaction subscales for white- and blue-collar groups are arrayed side-by-side for each comparison. It will be noted that there is a strong inverse relationship ($r = -.44$, $p < .01$) between the way white-collar males felt about their coworkers and the percentage of household income contributed by their wives. This indicates that white-collar men whose wives contributed larger shares of household income were less satisfied with their coworkers. The inverse relationship was even stronger between spouse income and satisfaction with supervision ($r = .45$, $p < .01$).

Table 5.2
Correlations Between Wives' Income and Five Job Satisfaction Subscales
for Blue- and White-collar Husbands with Employed Wives

Job Satisfaction Subscales	Occupational Level White Collar ($\underline{N}$ = 44)		Blue Collar ($\underline{N}$ = 32)	
	$\underline{r}$	$\underline{p}$	$\underline{r}$	$\underline{p}$
Co-Workers	-.44	.01	.22	n.s.
Supervision	-.46	.01	.06	n.s.
Pay	-.15	n.s.	.07	n.s.
Promotion	-.17	n.s.	-.03	n.s.
Work Itself	-.12	n.s.	-.07	n.s.

Squaring the correlation coefficient gives the coefficient of determination which indicates the percentage of variance in one variable which is explained by variance in the other. Because the direction of causality cannot be determined from correlational findings, one of the following two explanations may be appropriate. The percentage of household income earned by his wife explains roughly 20 percent of a white-collar husband's satisfaction with supervisor and coworkers. Alternatively, a white-collar husband's satisfaction with supervisor and coworkers explains roughly 20 percent of the percentage of household income earned by his wife. An examination of the other three correlations indicates that spousal income was not related to husbands' satisfaction with pay, promotion, or work itself.

None of the correlation coefficients relating blue-collar husbands' job satisfaction subscale scores to their wives' incomes reached significance. While caution should always be exercised in the interpretation of null findings, it appears that percentage of household income earned by spouse may not be related to job satisfaction for blue-collar husbands in this sample.

DISCUSSION

These findings indicate that whether a husband is blue-collar or white-collar/professional makes a difference in whether his job satisfaction is related to his wife's income. The pattern of findings for husbands at different occupational levels reported by previous research is not coincidental. Occupational level differences are supported by the empirical findings.

Some caution should be expressed about the generalizability of these findings. The data are self-reports and the subjects are to some extent self-selected (55 percent didn't respond). All data were collected in one organization, which may neither be typical of other institutions of its type nor be typical of organizations in general. On the other hand, the selection of a widely used, well validated job satisfaction measure, the relatively high questionnaire return rate, and the congruence of the findings with prior research tend to lend credence to these results. Nevertheless, this research should be replicated using alternate measures in different organizational settings with other categories of workers in order to determine how general these findings may be.

Previous research sometimes indicates that a wife's employment or high-status wife's employment is related to lower social motivation (Burke and Weir 1976b), less satisfaction with social relations (Rubenstein, 1982), lower self-esteem (Kessler and McRae 1982; Rubenstein 1982), depression (Burke and Weir 1976b; Keith and Schafer 1980; Kessler and MacRae 1982), and increased marital discord and divorce (Burke and Weir 1976a; Hardesty and Betz 1980; Rubenstein 1982; Philliber and Hiller 1983). Individuals experiencing any of the above may be less satisfied with their coworkers and bosses.

On the other hand, the findings reported here are in disagreement to some extent with those reported earlier. Kessler and McRae (1982) found no evidence that increased spouse earnings would have negative affects on husbands, although they did find negative outcomes from wives' employment. However, their study used a national probability sample— organizational level was not reported used as a moderator. Pfeffer and Ross's (1982) finding that a working wife hurts one's income if one is a professional or managerial male and Rubenstein's (1982) finding that men with highly paid wives were less satisfied with their own earnings are not echoed in these findings. For the sample examined here, there was no relationship between percentage of household income earned by wife and husband's satisfaction with pay and promotion.

Finally, results reported here may appear to conflict with those of the researchers who found "no relationship" between spouse employment level and husband's well-being. However, every study reviewed here that reported finding "no problems" utilized a probability sample that undoubtedly contained, if properly drawn, many blue-collar workers. The results may have been different if professional and blue-collar groups had been examined separately.

The importance of our findings lies primarily in the further questions that they raise. Causality cannot be inferred from correlational research. Thus, our findings could represent one of several possible scenarios: white-collar wives with high earnings cause husbands to be dissatisfied with coworkers and supervision, wives of white-collar men who are dissatisfied with coworkers and supervision are caused to seek and achieve higher incomes, and, lastly, some factor(s) unexamined in this study may cause both outcomes. Do husbands with achieving wives have lower social needs and less satisfaction with coworkers because their spouses are also their favorite *colleagues* and they therefore meet fewer social needs at work? Or do they have lower social needs and less satisfaction with coworkers because their self-esteem suffers by comparison to an achieving wife? Or are they less accepted by bosses and coworkers who could not themselves live with a high-achieving spouse?

Another question is the extent to which individual variables other than collar color influence husbands' adjustment to dual-career marriage. Variables such as self-esteem, central life interest and locus of control might have some bearing on the relationship demonstrated here.

Perhaps the most interesting question is why the observed relationship is true for the educated, middle- to upper-middle-class husband but not for his less educated, less achieving working-class counterpart. The authors experience this finding to be counterintuitive, one not suggested by "common sense." There is a tendency to think of "Joe Sixpack" being more threatened than "Paul Preppy" by a wife with a relatively high income. On the other hand, it can be argued that urban blue-collar women have held jobs in substantial numbers for many decades. Blue-collar men may have grown up with the notion of working mothers, aunts, and neighbor women while white-collar men may have been more more likely to have stay-at-home mothers. Therefore the differences observed here may be transitory, the results of differing childhood experiences on the parts of blue- and white-collar respondents.

Pfeffer and Ross (1982) speculate that white-collar/professional husbands' careers are facilitated by hostess/social secretary wives, needs that may be less common in blue-collar careers. Perhaps a wife's heavy involvement in a "career" or job means that both husband's and wife's weekends, evenings, and vacations are taken up with the routine maintenance that keeps a family establishment operating. If so, little time would be left to socialize with coworkers and bosses (or anyone else).

Regardless of the direction of causality, it does appear that for the current "crop" of white-collar husbands, there is a negative relationship between wives' employment and income levels and at least two dimensions of husbands' social adjustment and psychological health. The practical implications of these findings for white-collar men and women in dual-career households are relatively clear. Awareness that the situation can be problematic is the first step in making adjustments necessary to minimize strain on both members.

REFERENCES

Blalock, H.M., Jr. 1972. *Social statistics.* (2nd ed.) New York: McGraw-Hill.

Booth, A. 1977. Wife's employment and husband's stress: A replication and refutation. *Journal of Marriage and the Family, 39,* 645–650.

Burke, R.J., and T. Weir. 1976a. Relationship of wives' employment status to husband, wife and pair satisfaction and performance. *Journal of Marriage and the Family, 38,* 279–287.

Burke, R.J., and T. Weir. 1976b. Some personality differences between members of one-career and two-career families. *Journal of Marriage and the Family, 38,* 453–459.

Hardesty, S.A., and N.E. Betz. 1980. The relationships of career salience, attitudes toward women, and demographic and family characteristics to marital adjustment in dual-career couples. *Journal of Vocational Behavior, 17,* 242–250.

Keith, P.M., W.J. Goudy, and E.A. Powers. 1981. Employment characteristics and psychological well-being in two-job families. *Psychological Reports, 49,* 975–978.

Keith, P.M., and R.B. Schafer. 1980. Role strain and depression in two-job families. *Family Relations, 29,* 483–488.

Kessler, R.C., and J.A. McRae, Jr. 1982. Effect of wives' employment on the mental health of married men and women. *American Sociological Journal, 47,* 216–227.

Locksley, A. 1980. On the effects of wives' employment on marital adjustment and companionship. *Journal of Marriage and the Family, 42,* 337–346.

Pfeffer, J., and J. Ross. 1982. The effects of marriage and a working wife on occupational and wage attainment. *Administrative Science Quarterly, 27,* 66–80.

Philliber, W.W., and D.V. Hiller. 1983. Relative occupational attainments of spouses and later changes in marriage and wife's work experience. *Journal of Marriage and the Family, 45,* 161–170.

Richardson, J.G. 1979. Wife occupational superiority and marital troubles: An examination of the hypothesis. *Journal of Marriage and the Family, 41,* 63–72.

Rubenstein, C. 1982. Real men don't earn less than their wives. *Psychology Today, 16,* 11, 36–41.

Skinner, D.A. 1980. Dual-career family stress and coping: A literature review. *Family Relations, 29,* 473–481.

Smith, P.C., L.M. Kendall, and C.L. Hulin. 1969. *The measurement of satisfaction in work and retirement.* Chicago: Rand McNally.

Staines, G.L., K.J. Pottick, and D.A. Fudge. 1986. Wives' employment and husbands' attitudes toward work and life. *Journal of Applied Psychology, 71,* 118–128.

6

Have Women's Career and Family Values Changed?

Marsha Katz

PREVIEW

I did this research to document the changing norms that women bring both to the family and the workplace. Many people have stated to me that most women are not interested in their careers. From my own personal and professional experience, I found this to be false. However it seemed impossible to convince my opponents. This chapter provides information demonstrating that women are able and want to have opportunities for advancement. Women are willing to change some traditional practices within the family to achieve this goal.

I hope you will recognize that we must work to achieve an equitable balance between success in work and gratification in personal life for both men and women. I also hope this research will stimulate you to think further about issues of work and family, and ways to combine effectively these two important parts of our lives.

A major change has occurred in the labor force over the last few decades: The number of women in the workplace has doubled since 1950. The participation rate of married women with school-aged children is over 65 percent compared to 39 percent in 1960. Furthermore the participation rate of married women with children under six years old is over 50 percent compared to under 20 percent in 1960 (U.S. Bureau of Labor Statistics 1986).

Married women with paid employment outside the home tend to add the employment workload to their household work. Thus, while women have expanded their influence and responsibilities in the work sphere, they have not necessarily lost their domestic obligations. Research indicates that wives working outside the home do not obtain much more help in household work from their husbands than nonworking wives, nor do working wives and husbands share most of the household activities (Bryson et al. 1978; Nieva 1984, 1985; Pleck 1978, 1986).

Since women bear the primary responsibility for the household and the family's children and have expanded their responsibilities in the work sphere, they are subject to a potential role conflict between family and career (Beutell and Greenhaus 1982, 1983, 1985; Gilbert and Holahan 1982; Hall 1972; Herman and Gyllstrom 1977; Keith and Schafer 1980; Kelly and Voydanoff 1985). Both the job and the family require a large commitment of time and energy, and must at times interfere with each other.

While much of the past research was quite unequivocal about role conflict, some current research reviews suggest that women do not necessarily have role conflicts (Blau and Ferber 1985; Yogev 1982a). Yogev (1982b) suggests that this difference is due to changes in researchers' views of the ability of women to combine work and family. In the 1950s and 1960s, women's participation in the labor force was viewed as threatening to marriage and family. The male was to be head of the household and provider, the female the homemaker and child caretaker. Women working outside the home were believed to cause an increase in conflict and a decrease in marital satisfaction. On the other hand, in the contemporary view, the average family consists of two income earners. Women who have both a family and a career are seen as less negative, and conflict is seen as a normal part of family life, not as causing less marital happiness (Blumstein and Schwartz 1983; Campbell, Converse, and Rogers 1976; Yogev 1982b).

Changes in researchers' perspectives mirror those occurring in society. Younger women, perhaps influenced by social science research or by magazines, television, and the feminist movement, have new attitudes toward work and family. Women are now beginning to plan a career in the same way men traditionally have (Blumstein and Schwartz 1983). These new norms and expectations may have lowered the conflicts experienced by women. Younger females have role models of other women coping with career and family. They should be able to reduce their role conflict by either emulating the pioneers, learning from the pioneers' mistakes, or taking advantage of new work/family patterns that make it easier to combine career and family. Younger women now are free to choose to postpone child bearing until it fits their work schedules (Bistline 1985; Hennig and Jardim 1977; Rapoport and Rapoport 1971) or to work part-time while the children are young (Beutell and Greenhaus 1986; Hayghe 1986; Kaplan and Smith-Avioli 1987; Nardone 1986). Other women choose not to marry at all (Epstein 1971; Herman and Gyllstrom 1977), to marry but not have children (Beckman 1978; Rebecca 1978), or to have fewer children (Valdez and Gutek 1987). Another option is to take jobs that have more flexibility, such as university teaching positions

(Klenke-Hamel 1982) or to work for companies that have flextime or childcare programs (Beutell and Greenhaus 1986). Still others choose to become supermoms, trying to do and to have it all (Hall 1972; Katz 1985).

Younger women may perceive multiple roles as not only creating new conflicts, but also as creating new satisfactions (Nieva 1984). This may not have reduced their workload significantly, but they perceive "doing it all" as a positive trait. Even though they may be working more, they are enjoying their chosen life-style. Young women see family and career as belonging together. Therefore, they should have less role conflict than older women.

Older women may not have incorporated these new values as fully. Those who are working full-time and perform all the domestic chores may perceive it as a conflict situation. They also do not have some of the new options open to them if they are already married and/or have children and cannot delay either to establish their career. The obligations of raising young children and/or the difficulties associated with rearing adolescents is a very demanding job.

This study made three predictions concerning the perceptions and desires of college-educated women between 31 and 60 years old of their ability to combine work and family as well as their beliefs about the desirability of combining work and family. The first hypothesis was that younger women would have less traditional values than older women about pursuing careers and would view women pursuing a career more positively than older women (hypothesis 1). I also anticipated related behavioral differences: Younger women were expected to be more career and achievement oriented than older women (hypothesis 2). Lastly, I predicted that younger women would be less likely to experience role conflict between family and career since their values are more congruent with contemporary society (hypothesis 3).

In general, the study was designed to explore the changing values and attitudes that women are bringing both to the family and the workplace. Although based on a cross-sectional survey, this study documents that women's values towards the combination of family and career have undergone some changes over the last few generations and assesses some of the possible implications due to these changes. It is important that we be aware of changing values in order to meet the needs that these new norms entail.

METHOD

Subjects

One hundred ninety-seven women alumni of the college of arts and sciences and the business school of a midwestern private university completed a mail questionnaire regarding life patterns of college-educated

women. They were selected through a stratified sample by year of graduation from the university alumni list for the years 1945 through 1975. The
return rate was approximately 35 percent.

The women's ages ranged from 31 to over 60. Fifty-four percent were
employed full-time, 19 percent were employed part-time, and 27 percent
were not employed. Income ranged from under $10,000 to over $70,000
per year. Those women employed full-time earned an average of $35,000
a year. Spouses' average income was $45,000 per year.

The women were categorized into four groups: ages 31–35 (N = 47),
36–40 (N = 54), 41–54 (N= 54), 51 and older (N = 41). These age ranges were
selected in order to allow an adequate sample size from each age group.

Questionnaire

This study is a subset of a larger study that covered many aspects of
values between career and marriage. The questionnaires included several
demographic factors: age, income, employment, occupation, and number
of children.

Measurement Scales:

Traditional Sex Role Scale was measured by a seven-point Likert scale.
Respondents were asked to agree or disagree with several statements
pertaining to women pursuing a career. A representative item from the
scale is "Women should actively consider pursuing a profession regardless of their marital and family status" (Holahan and Gilbert 1979). The
alpha score on this scale was .66.

Role Conflict Scales measured the role conflict between pairs of the four
major life roles of worker, spouse, parent, and self as a self-actualizing
person. Six subscales were derived with three or four questions each:
worker versus parent, worker versus spouse, worker versus self, parent
versus spouse, parent versus self, and spouse versus self. Subjects were
asked to respond to the items using a five-point Likert scale that ranged
from "causes no internal conflict" (1) through "causes high internal conflict" (5). A representative item from the scale of professional versus
parent is: "spending most evenings on work-related activities versus
spending most evenings with your family." Satisfactory reliability has
been previously reported for the six scales (Holahan and Gilbert 1979).
The Cronbach alpha scores in this sample averaged .84.

Hypothetical situations were developed by Powell and Posner (1982).
There were five hypothetical questions relating to career/family problems. The five questions were first given with the instructions to
"imagine that you had finished school, and were working full-time and
were not married. What would you do in these situations?" Then each
set of five situations was repeated with different instructions that changed

the family life stage. The second time they were told to imagine that they had "finished school, were working full-time and were married with no children." The third time they were to imagine that they had "finished school, were working full-time and have preschool children," and in the last set of instructions they were told to imagine that they had "finished school, were working full-time and had school-aged children." Each person was given each set of the five questions with the four separate sets of instructions. A representative question is "If you had an important function at home and an important job related function scheduled at the same time, which would you choose?"

Attitudes toward careers versus family consisted of four questions that revealed values toward combining career and family. A representative question is "If you could have only a career or only marriage, which would you choose?"

RESULTS

Employment characteristics varied by age. Young women were more likely to work part-time while older women were more likely to work full-time (Kandall Tau = -.11, $p < .05$). In general, the labor participation rates are similar to findings of other studies of college-educated women (Blau and Ferber 1985).

However, there were no significant differences between the four categories of age on educational level, plans to work in the next year, or the number of hours spent on domestic chores. Sixty-four percent of the women had college degrees, 33 percent had completed their masters degrees and 3 percent had completed the Ph.D. Of the women who were currently working, 98 percent said that they planned to keep working for at least a year. The average amount of time spent on domestic chores was between 11 and 30 hours per week.

The first hypothesis predicting that younger women would have less traditional values than older women was confirmed. On the Traditional Sex-Role Scale, the younger women surveyed were less traditional in their views about women pursuing careers than older women. Despite the fact that younger women are less likely than older women to work full-time, they indicated that they supported the contemporary, nontraditional view regarding sex roles and women's ability to pursue a career. The younger women were more likely to answer the questions in a nontraditional manner indicating that they agreed that women should pursue a career (Kendall Tau = -.20, $p < .001$).

Young women also had significantly different answers on a variety of questions about attitudes toward combining career and family than the older women, particularly when children were involved. Younger women were more likely to say that they did not want children if they

Table 6.1
Attitudes Towards Combining Career and Family by Age

Variable	N[a]	Age	M
If you could have only a career or marriage, which would you choose?[b]	191	31-35	3.5
		36-40	3.4
		41-50	3.7
Kendall Tau = .03 (n.s.)		51+	3.3
If you could choose to have a career and marriage, would you also want children?[c]	166	31-36	2.0
		36-40	2.1
		41-50	1.5
Kendall Tau = -.17**		51+	1.6
When would you go back to work after a child was born[d]	196	31-36	4.7
		36-40	5.3
		41-50	5.3
		51+	6.4

  *p < .05
 **p < .01
***p < .001

[a] N changes because of missing data
[b] 1 = definitely career choice; 5 = definitely marriage
[c] 1 = definitely yes; 5 = definitely not
[d] 1 = immediately after birth; 2 = 3 months-year; 3 = 1-3 years; 4 = 2-5 years; 5 = youngest in nursery school; 6 = youngest in elementary school; 7 = youngest in junior high school; 8 = youngest in high school; 9 = all out of our home

combined career and marriage (Kendall Tau = -.16, $p < .01$) than older women. For those who were employed full-time, the strength of the relationship was even stronger (Kendall Tau = .29, $p < .001$). Younger women also indicated that they would return to work sooner after a child was born than older women (Kendall Tau = .26, $p < .001$). The question was worded so that they would not answer based on what they did in the past, but rather what they think they would do now. However, there was no difference between the age groups about whether or not they would choose a career versus marriage if they had to decide between the two (Kendall Tau = .03, $p < .05$). Table 6.1 shows the means for the questions relating to attitudes toward combining career and family by age.

These differences extended to certain actual behavioral differences in child-rearing patterns. Younger women returned to work earlier than older women had (Kendall Tau = .34, $p < .0001$). Older women also were more likely to have their first child at a younger age than the younger women (Kendall Tau = -.19, $p < .0001$).

Results regarding the second prediction that younger women are more career- and achievement-oriented than older ones was contradictory. There were a number of age differences toward commitment of career. For the level of aspiration, there was a significant difference by age when modified by level of employment (full, part-time or no employment) ($F(5,165) = 6.756$, p $<$ .001). For those who were employed part-time, younger women have higher career aspirations than the older women (Kendall Tau = .34, p $<$ .01). For those women who were employed full-time, there was no significant difference with regard to age.

A similar pattern was found for the need to be successful. The overall analysis was significant ($F(5,165) = 3.8$, p $<$ .01) with the main effect of type of employment being significant ($F(2,165) = 8.8$, p $<$ .001). For those women working full-time, there was no difference by age. For those women working part-time, the need to be successful was more important to the younger women.

In summary, hypothesis two was only partially confirmed. The age of the women makes a difference in attitude only for those who are employed part-time. The women who choose to work full-time are equally committed to their careers regardless of age. However choosing to work part-time may mean something different to the younger woman than the older woman. Younger women who choose to work part-time are more likely to have children ($F(5,199) = 12.02$, p $<$ .001). They may use part-time work as a method to reduce the amount of role overload. In this manner, women can keep their options in their career open for the future. They can be part of the work force without sacrificing their family too severely. It is for many an acceptable compromise.

For older women, the meaning of part-time work may be different. With part-time work, the commitment to their family is less likely to conflict with their jobs. Since it is likely that their children are older, the women may feel that they have more flexibility in their time schedules. The children are likely to be in school, involved with their own activities. These women may choose to work because they need the money, the interaction with other people, the satisfaction of being able to have a career, and so on. But it is not, unlike the younger women, because of an consuming desire to have a career in the future.

Despite the belief that younger women have less role conflict than older women because they incorporate the new beliefs, hypothesis 3 was not confirmed. In fact, the results were in the opposite direction. The younger women said in general that they experience more conflict than the older women (Kendall Tau = -.11, p $<$ .05). Younger women were more likely to experience conflict, especially between the roles of being a spouse and a parent (r = .20, p $<$ .05), and between the roles parents and self (r = .23, p $<$ .005).

DISCUSSION

With the changing environment, there has been much controversy about women's role conflicts. As the feminist movement encouraged women to engage in full participation in the power structure including the labor force, it also denied some of the problems dealing with the family. Betty Friedan (1981) suggested that the new problem confronting the women's movement is how to achieve a more equitable balance between success in work and gratification in personal life.

This study documents some of the changes that have taken place over the last few decades. While many more women of all ages are working, there are considerable differences between the way younger women are combining family and career. The study revealed that younger college-educated women have different values and behavior from older women who have graduated from the same college previously. These younger women have a different view of women's ability to combine marriage and family. Whether this is a lasting change or one that is created by a harsh economic climate is yet to be seen. But there is, very clearly, a difference in attitude towards women's roles.

The young women in this sample indicate that they want to achieve and succeed in the paid employment arena, and that they are willing to make changes in traditional family life-styles. They are considering having children later in life and are willing to go back to work earlier than previous generations. However young women in the study experience more role conflict than older women.

The present study does not explain why the younger women experience more conflict. However, of the six subscales of role conflict, significant results were only found for conflicts including parenting. This suggests that much of the conflict stems from being a parent rather than a paid worker. The parent role has been viewed in the literature as the role causing role conflict or stress. Paid employment is most often viewed as the added-on role, and thus is treated as the variable to analyze in terms of causing role conflict. However, evidence is accumulating that being a mother may be the most important source of stress in women's lives (Barnett and Baruch 1985; Baruch 1984; Veroff et al. 1981). While the values of the younger women indicate that children and career can be combined, they may not have anticipated the role conflict they were experiencing. Unlike the older women, they may feel they have to accomplish everything. Of course, it may be that younger women feel more conflict at this level merely because they are at an age at which they need to learn to deal with these multiple roles, while older women have already done so.

More research is needed on the adaptations that women and men have made in these changing times. Longitudinal research is needed to clarify whether differences found here are generational and not a function of age. In addition, research on other socioeconomic groups might identify different patterns of role conflict. Last, as Betty Friedan states, "in the second stage of this struggle [women's liberation] that is changing everyone's life, men's and women's needs converge. . . . men are now seeking new life patterns as much as women are." More knowledge of how both men and women choose to handle the dynamics of the family and work is necessary to understand the problem of role conflict and the pressures involved in today's changing society.

REFERENCES

Barnett, R.C., and G.K. Baruch. 1985. Women's involvement in multiple roles and psychological distress. *Journal of Personality and Social Psychology, 49,* 135–145.

Baruch, G. 1984. The psychological well-being of women in the middle years. In G. Baruch and J. Brooks-Gunn (Eds.), *Between youth and old age: Women in the middle years.* New York: Plenum.

Beckman, L. 1978. The relative rewards and costs of parenthood and employment for employed women. *Psychology of Women Quarterly, 2,* 215–234.

Beutell, N.J., and Greenhaus, J.H. 1982. Interrole conflict among married women: The influence of husband and wife characteristics of conflict and coping behavior. *Journal of Vocational Behavior, 21,* 99–110.

Beutell, N.J., and J.H. Greenhaus. 1983. Integration of home and non-home roles: Women's conflicts and coping behavior. *Journal of Applied Psychology, 68,* 43–48.

Beutell, N.J., and J.H. Greenhaus. 1985. Sources of Conflict between work and family roles. *Academy of Management Review, 10,* 76–88.

Beutell, N.J., and J.H. Greenhaus. 1986. Balancing acts: Work-family conflict and the dual-career couple. In L.L. Moore (Ed.), *Not as far as you think* (pp. 149–162). Mass.: Lexington.

Bistline, S.M. 1985. Make room for baby. *Association Management, 37,* 96–100.

Blau, F.D., and M.A. Ferber. 1985. Women in the labor market: The last twenty years. In L. Larwood, A.H. Stromberg, and B.A. Gutek (Eds.), *Women and work: An annual review* (Vol. 1, pp. 19–49). Beverly Hills: Sage.

Blumstein, P.B., and P. Schwartz. 1983. *American couples.* New York: William Morrow.

Bryson, R., J.B. Bryson, and M.F. Johnson. 1978. Family size, satisfaction and productivity in dual-career couples. *Psychology of Women Quarterly, 3,* 67–77.

Campbell, A., P.E. Converse, and W.L. Rogers. 1976. *The quality of American life: Perceptions, evaluations and satisfactions.* New York: Russell Sage.

Epstein, C.F. 1971. *Women's place.* Los Angeles: University of California Press.

Friedan, B. 1981. *The second stage.* New York: Summit Books, Simon and Schuster.

Gilbert, L.A., and C.K. Holahan. 1982. Conflicts between student/professional, parental and self-development roles: A comparison of high and low effective copers. *Human Relations, 35,* 635–648.

Hall, D.T. 1972. A model of coping with role conflict: The role behavior of college educated women. *Administrative Science Quarterly, 17,* 471–486.

Hayghe, K. 1986. Rise in mothers' labor force activity includes those with infants. *Monthly Labor Review. 109*, 43–45.

Hennig, M. and A. Jardim. 1977. *The managerial woman.* New York: Doubleday.

Herman, J.B., and K.K. Gyllstrom. 1971. Working men and women: Inter- and intra role conflict. *Psychology of Women Quarterly, 1*, 319–333.

Holahan, C.K., and L.A. Gilbert. 1979. Conflict between major life roles: Women and men in dual career couples. *Human Relations, 32*, 451–467.

Kaplan, E. and P. Smith-Avioli. 1987, August. Changing work patterns among women in dual-earner families: A longitudinal approach. Paper presented at the meeting of the Annual Academy of Management, New Orleans, Louisiana.

Katz, M. 1985. Resolution of role conflict for women with infants. *Birth Psychology Bulletin, 6*, 10–20.

Keith, P.M., and R.B. Schafer. 1980. Role Strain and Depression in Two Job Families. *Family Relations, 29*, 483–488.

Kelly, R.F., and P. Voydanoff. 1985. Work/family role strain among employed parents. *Family Relations, 34*, 367–374.

Klenke-Hamel, K. 1982. Causal determinants of job satisfaction in dual career couples. In J.H. Bernardin (Ed.), *Women in the work force* (pp. 183–204). New York: Praeger.

Nardone, T.J. 1986. Part-time workers: Who are they? *Monthly Labor Review, 109*, 13–18.

Nieva, V.F. 1984. Work and family roles. In M.D. Lee and R. Kanungo (Eds.), *Management of work and personal life* (pp. 15–40). New York: Praeger.

Nieva, V.F. 1985. Work and family linkages. In L. Larwood, A.H. Stromberg, and B.A. Gutek (Eds.), *Women and work: An annual review* (Vol. 1, pp. 162–190). Beverly Hills: Sage.

Pleck, J.H. 1978. The work-family role system. *Social Problems, 24*, 417–427.

Pleck, J.H. 1986. Work schedule flexibility and family life. *Journal of Occupational Behavior, 7*, 149–153.

Powell, G.N., and B.Z. Posner. 1982, August. Sex effects on managerial value systems. Paper presented at the meeting of the Annual Academy of Management, New York.

Rapoport, R., and R.N. Rapoport. 1971. Early and later experiences as determinants of adult behavior: Married women's family and career patterns. *British Journal of Sociology, 22*, 16–30.

Rebecca, M. 1978, March. Voluntary childlessness as a conflict reducing mechanism. Paper presented at the meeting of the Association of Women in Psychology, Pittsburgh, PA.

U.S. Bureau of Labor Statistics. 1986. Special Labor Force Reports, Bulletin 2163.

Valdez, R.L., and B.A. Gutek. 1987. Family roles: A help or a hindrance for working women? In B.A. Gutek and L. Larwood (Eds.), *Women's career development* (pp. 157–169). Beverly Hills, CA: Sage.

Veroff, J., E. Douvan, and R. Kulka. 1981. *The inner American: A self-portrait from 1957 to 1976.* New York: Basic Books.

Yogev, S. 1982a. Are professional women overworked? Objective versus subjective perception of role loads. *Journal of Occupational Psychology, 55*, 165–169.

Yogev, S. 1982b. Happiness in dual career couples: Changing research, changing values. *Sex Roles, 8*, 593–605.

7

A Career Planning Model for Women

Georgia T. Chao
S. D. Malik

PREVIEW

We hope our readers will gain a good understanding of the issues that affect a woman's career choice and subsequent career plans. Our career-planning model illustrates how individual, organizational, and societal factors affect a woman's career. While these factors influence men as well, women are generally more constrained by family plans, organizational expectations of female employees, and sex-role stereotypes of working women. By utilizing the model outlined in this chapter, women should be able to take a positive action toward developing their own careers. The model presents general career-planning strategies and raises several questions for the readers, such as: What are my career strengths and weaknesses? What are my career goals? How can I combine my career ambitions with my nonwork roles of wife and mother? What types of career help can I get from my current organization? Answers to these questions will help to identify career goals and what needs to be accomplished in order to meet them. While implementation of career plans will not guarantee a particular job or career advancement, it will maximize eligibility for the kind of career that a woman values most.

The increase of women in the workforce has been a continuing phenomenon since the 1940s. Currently, women represent over 49 percent of the U.S. workforce (U.S. Bureau of Census 1985), yet little is known about the career planning and development of these women. As more women seek employment and satisfying careers, special attention should be paid to those issues that make a profound impact on their career plans and career development. Issues such as the home/career conflict, dual careers, and societal expectations of working women are generally more salient concerns for women than for men. Furthermore, these issues are adjunct factors that must be resolved within a general career planning model that addresses basic issues of self-assessment, goal setting, and plan implementation.

Hall defines career planning as, "a deliberate process of 1) becoming aware of self, opportunities, constraints, choices, and consequences, 2) identifying career-related goals, and 3) programming work, education, and related developmental experiences to provide the direction, timing, and sequence of steps to attain a specific career goal" (Hall 1986, p. 3). Since career planning can be an ongoing process for all employed people, it represents a proactive course in shaping and developing a rewarding career. The relationship between career planning and career success is supported by Gould's (1979) research that found people who had engaged in career-planning activities rated their careers as more effective than people with less extensive career plans. Thus, career planning is an important function for individuals who have, or would like to have, a vision of their career future.

In addition to the benefits of career planning, the need for self-assessment, career goal setting, and plan implementation will become more important as changes in organizations and their human resource needs evolve in the future. Recent technological innovations, such as industrial robots and office automation have dramatically shifted the locus of American workers away from manufacturing organizations and toward service organizations (Heskett 1987). These changes have created a great deal of uncertainty and ambiguity in the types of career paths that would be available to people in the years to come. Thus, the need for career planning will become more salient to people who cannot rely on traditional career plans that may become obsolete in the near future.

This chapter reviews general issues that affect career planning and integrates them in a model of career planning for women. Our approach toward career planning and working women will be based on a definition of a career as a sequence of work roles over an individual's lifetime (Hall 1986). In addition, we will define work as compensated employment and nonwork as all activities and roles outside the individual's role as a compensated employee. Thus, for our discussion purposes, wives, mothers, and homemakers will be treated as nonwork roles and career planning and development will exclude homemaking as a career. The chapter will discuss career-planning issues from three perspectives: an individual level, an organizational level, and a societal level. A description of each level's relationship to career planning and how it influences a woman's career plans in particular, are presented below.

Individual Issues

Many individual factors, such as a person's need for achievement, career motivation, and support system for his/her career will influence that person's need and ability to plan for a rewarding career. For example, upscale life-styles of a baby boomer generation often necessitate two incomes to support an increased consumer interest in leisure activities and high quality products. A recent survey reported 47 percent of all couples are involved in dual careers (U.S. Bureau of Census 1985). When both husband and wife are working, one spouse's career plans are often dependent upon the other's. Although there are exceptions, typically a woman's career plans are secondary to her husband's. In these cases, a woman's career plans may be constrained by a man's career plans.

Hall (1972) defines an individual's identity as a composite of sub-identities or roles. For example, a person's identity may be an integrated picture of his/her roles as a parent, spouse, citizen, neighbor, vacationer, and employee. Although the number of roles may differ from one individual to another, Hall posits that there are major differences between male and female roles. Male roles are generally sequential—a man is an employee at the office, a father when he is home with the children, and a husband when he is with his wife. Female roles are generally simultaneous—a woman often bears primary responsibilities for the family and household; thus, she does not forget her homemaker and mother roles when she is at work. If the demands of various roles are simultaneously made on a woman, her perceived role conflict between the home and career may be greater than a man's. Attempts to reduce this conflict may require a behavioral role redefinition (e.g., changes in career aspirations/plans to provide adequate time for other roles), behavioral pattern changes (e.g., increase in attempts to work harder to satisfy all role demands), or attitudinal changes on perceived roles and their demands. Possible consequences for each type of coping strategy may include reduced commitment to a career (and, thereby, reducing the potential for future career rewards), or an unrealistic demand for greater efforts (e.g., the Superwoman syndrome). These consequences are more likely when women attempt to match their role orientations with cultural expectations. Thus, if our society disapproves of a woman who forsakes her family in order to build her career, then the options of nonwork role redefinitions are not feasible. The "choice" of becoming less career involved, therefore, becomes a forced decision heavily influenced by sex-role stereotypes rather than an internal decision made by a woman as an individual.

In addition to the different sex-roles, there may be some personality characteristics that differentially affect the career choices and plans of men and women. One of these characteristics was identified by Horner

(1972) who found that many women are motivated to avoid success. According to Horner, women tend to avoid success because they fear that social rejection and isolation will accompany it. Women who possess this success-avoidance motivation are more likely to avoid competitive situations and may not have achievement-oriented goals. Karpicke (1980) studied women college students and found these women also had a greater tendency to exhibit success-avoidance behaviors than did their male counterparts. Heilman and Kram (1983) controlled the type of performance feedback college students received on an in-basket exercise. They found women were more likely to assume blame for poor performance on the exercise and less likely to take credit for successful performance, as compared to men. These differences may have had a profound effect on the occupational choices, aspirations, and subsequent plans for women.

Organizational Issues

Organizational personnel policies and career management programs often play a direct role in the career development of employees. Thus, these policies become an important factor in the career plans of individuals. Women often face barriers to employment or career advancement that are unique to their sex. The number of court cases charging discrimination on the basis of sex, or on sexual harassment have been increasing (Stringer and Duncan 1985; Walshok 1981). In addition, the number of organizations with restrictive benefit policies concerning maternity leave may influence a woman's career goals and subsequent plans.

Other types of problems women may experience on the job are less obvious. Studies examining gender differences in leadership positions may be particularly important to the career planning process of women in management. If male and female leaders are viewed differently, the opportunities for one group (e.g., women) may be less than those for the other group (e.g., men). These views may be based on personality traits (an individual-level issue) but if they affect management decisions like promotions, these views also become organizational issues as well. Schein (1973, 1975) conducted two studies asking male and female managers to describe characteristics of (1) men in general, (2) women in general, and (3) a successful manager. For both gender groups, the characteristics, attitudes, and temperaments identified for a successful manager were more similar to those used to describe men, as opposed to women. Schein suggested that the perceived similarity between managerial and masculine characteristics may increase the likelihood of men to be promoted in management. These findings are supported by a meta-analysis of personality traits and leadership perceptions (Lord, DeVader, and Alliger 1986). Lord et al. reviewed articles identified by Mann (1959), as well as more recent research, and found three traits—intelligence, masculinity-femininity, and dominance—to be significantly related to leadership perceptions. Mann's masculinity-femininity trait generally corresponded to the implicit leadership theory traits of aggressiveness, decisiveness, and unemotionality—traits generally associated with masculinity.

Landy and Farr (1983) reviewed the performance appraisal literature examining gender differences for employees who were rated by their superiors. Their findings indicated females were generally rated lower than males in male-stereotyped jobs, and that males were generally rated lower than females in female-stereotyped jobs. Fewer gender differences were observed in sex-neutral jobs. Landy and Farr concluded that gender differences in the performance evaluations of ratees were integrally related to the type of occupation and that this relationship was more complex than originally believed.

Results from the above studies suggest that a woman's career plans and career development may be affected by the organizational climate (e.g., women in predominantly male occupations or in discriminating/harassing environments may find fewer career opportunities). In addition, the kinds of organizational policies that concern pregnancy, childcare, and personal leaves may also influence a woman's career plans as she integrates her career with her home/family life. These issues can impose constraints on the kinds of career goals a woman sets as well as the success of her career plans. Awareness of these potential barriers, and organizational actions to reduce them may allow women to form better career plans that are more likely to be realized.

Societal Issues

In 1986, women represented 33 percent of all goods-producing workers and 51 percent of all service-producing workers. In addition, the percentage of professional women has increased markedly. Women now represent 20 percent of all lawyers, 18 percent of doctors, and 37 percent of college and university faculty (Bloom 1986). The rising numbers of women in the labor force have been attributed to many factors, including social and political changes initiated by the women's movement and the civil rights movement.

However, the increase of women in the workforce has not affected a total acceptance of women as careerists in our society. A recent book about women and work notes that many people still describe a working woman as an oddity or deviation from a male standard (Douglass 1983). Traditional sex-role stereotypes generally view women as nurturing mothers who stay at home to care for their husbands and children whereas men are described as the careerists, providing financial support for their families (Pepitone-Rockwell 1980). These stereotypes identify two major nonwork roles for women—homemaker and mother—which are often seen as attractive alternatives that pull women away from rewarding careers. Despite the growing number of men and women who deviate from these stereotypes, the sex-role socializations often pose different career questions for men and women to ask themselves initially. Thus, the first career question that women often ask themselves is "Do I want a career?", whereas men are generally socialized to assume they will have a career and their first career question is "Why kind of career do I want?" The difference in the kinds of questions men and women ask can later affect the extent to which the individual will identify with his/her career and be concerned with his/her career plans and future.

Career plans are generally built upon the specific career choice an individual makes. Assuming that a woman has, at least temporarily, decided to begin a career, the choice and subsequent plans are often influenced by the sex-role socializations of the woman and of other people who are in a position to influence her. Psathas (1968) reviewed the theoretical processes of occupational choice and described three factors which significantly affect the decisions of women, but not of men. These factors were: (1) Sex role—the type of sex role a woman wants to fulfill could affect her career choice and ambitions. Women who want to be very feminine, mothers, or primarily housewives will not choose or pursue careers that demand a great deal of time, training, or responsibilities. (2) Family finances—the financial situations of a woman's family or of her husband could significantly affect the resources a woman could access when preparing herself for a career. Often, a family may concentrate most of its limited resources in the career development of sons as opposed to daughters. This differential treatment would be congruent with the traditional sex-role stereotypes. (3) Social class—the social values of a woman's parents, husband, and peers can also affect her occupational choice and career commitment. People in a lower social class are often confined to low-skill career opportunities that require little time for preparation, but would generate income quickly, albeit a modest one for the individual. Middle-class women may be socialized to adopt the traditional sex-roles of their mothers or may be encouraged to seek rewarding careers that will help ensure financial independence and support for themselves. Finally, upper-class women are not under severe economic pressures to begin a career. For these women, the attractiveness of nonwork roles, such as socialite or woman of leisure, may be very high and their career choices and plans may reflect a lower career motivation and commitment (Sonnenfeld and Kotter 1982). Psathas (1968) concluded that, in order to understand how women choose their occupations, it is essential that certain factors, unique to women be understood. Despite the age of the Psathas review, significant differences in career choice are still being observed. Knight, Sedlack, and Backhuber (1983) found that male college graduates were more likely to enter professional, technical, and managerial occupations and that female college graduates were more likely to enter clerical or sales positions.

Summary

Figure 7.1 illustrates how the individual, organizational, and societal levels are interrelated, with elements in each level influencing and reacting to elements in another level. For example, a woman's decision to begin a career occurs at the individual level. However, it is shaped not only by what she perceives her goals to be (individual), but also by what she can achieve in a specific work environment (organizational), and by how she may be influenced by others (societal). In addition, her career goals are generally set within a larger framework of nonwork roles. How work and family responsibilities are integrated may be affected by societal

Figure 7.1
An Example of How Individual, Organizational, and Societal Levels Affect Career Planning for Women

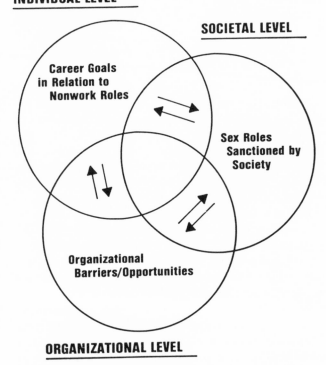

sanctions of these roles for women as well as organizational support for both roles. When many women enter the workforce, their individual needs may change the kinds of organizational policies that affect their careers and the kinds of opinions or expectations society has about career women. Finally, these organizational and societal changes may alter career opportunities or needs for current careerists as well as for the next generation of men and women.

A model describing theoretically based components of the career-planning process for women is presented within a framework of the above three levels of analysis. Following the model, a discussion of its implications for women and a guide for future research is presented.

A CAREER PLANNING MODEL FOR WOMEN

The concept of career planning builds upon an individual's career choice. Only after an initial choice has been made can a person set career goals and identify appropriate paths and preparations toward goal attainment. However, factors that may influence an individual's career choices may also affect his/her subsequent plans; hence, our model on career planning will include important factors that are central to career choice as well as career planning.

The model integrates societal, organizational, and individual factors that influence a woman's career planning (see Figure 7.2). A discussion of each component of the model and propositions describing how the components affect career planning, is presented below.

Individual Level Factors

Role Models

Bandura's (1977) work on social learning theory and Katz and Kahn's (1978) work on role theory demonstrate the importance of role models and their effect on people. Role models often represent a standard of excellence that an individual values and imitates. The selection of a particular role model is typically based on a person's perceptions of his/her similarity to the role model and his/her desirability to assume characteristics (e.g., knowledge, skills, abilities, and attitudes) of the role model (Decker and Nathan 1985). For most children, daughters choose their mothers as appropriate role models while sons see their fathers as the models to follow. Given the fact that earlier generations of women were not as career-oriented as the current generation (the percentage of women in the workforce generally decreases as one goes back in time [U.S. Bureau of Census 1985]), many housewives cannot serve as actual models of career women for their daughters. In addition, many women

Figure 7.2
A Career Planning Model for Women

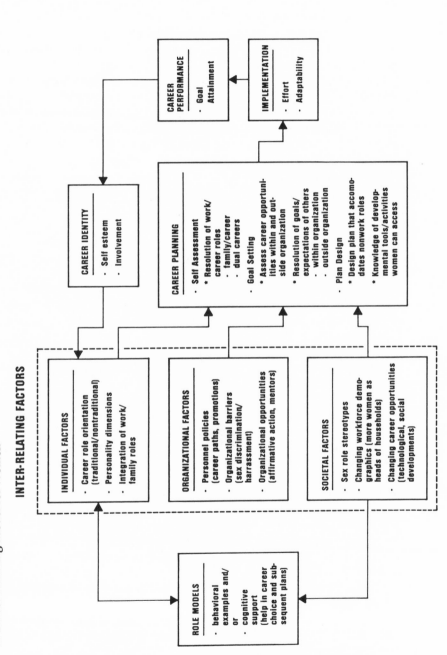

promote their nonwork roles of homemaker and mother as attractive roles for their daughters. Thus, most girls have a variety of work and nonwork roles they can model, whereas most boys have one model of a working father. For women who select nonwork roles, the issue of career planning becomes irrelevant. However, nonworking women validate social stereotypes of appropriate roles for women and these stereotypes may pose problems for women who decide to have careers.

Research examining the modeling process provides support for the effects of role models on career choice and role orientations (Boles and Garbin 1971). Early research examining social determinants of career choice showed significant relationships between a parent's occupation and a child's subsequent occupational choice (Sonnenfeld and Kotter 1982). Role models often encourage young people to follow in their career paths. Boles and Garbin's (1971) interviews of 51 striptease artists revealed that most of the women who worked as feature strippers were recruited into their profession by a family member. In addition, most of their subjects had role models in the profession. The significant relationship between a parent's occupation and a child's subsequent occupational choice may also be due to the clear previews these role models provide of their careers. Card and Farrell (1983) surveyed 461 Army Reserve Officer Training Corps (ROTC) college cadets and 470 non-ROTC college students on the types of role models they had and the extent to which they had realistic understandings of a military career. A comparison of male and female subgroups showed the male subjects had more role models in the military than did the female subjects. Furthermore, the men had more realistic ideas about their military careers than women did.

Not only do role models provide behavioral examples, they may also provide cognitive support for an individual. Haber (1980) studied the career aspirations of lower- and middle-class women and found that an important influence of career choice and commitment was the mother's own cognitive support of her daughter's career choice, and that the mother's own career orientation was a less important factor. Thus, it was more important for a mother mentally to support her daughter's career choice than actually to set a behavioral example. Lunneborg (1982) posited that a woman's career choice was congruent with her immediate family environment. She found a significant effect for both behavioral and cognitive support from a woman's parents and a woman's decision to pursue a nontraditional career.

London (1983) defines career identity as the extent to which a person defines his/her life by the type of work he/she performs. The importance of a woman's career to her overall life can dramatically influence her career involvement and future career planning. Psathas (1968) noted that nonwork factors, such as marriage, children, and a spouse's attitudes, are major considerations in a woman's career involvement and that these factors typically do not receive comparable attention by men in their career development. Shann (1983) provides evidence to support Psathas because the men in her study did not accommodate family issues in their career plans for the years when they could expect to be raising a family. However, Farmer (1985) did find that men who were more secure in their career goals were more likely to consider these factors in their career plans.

The results from these studies leads us to the first proposition of our model: a woman's role models will have an important impact on her decision to begin a career (as opposed to a nonwork role), on her exposure to different career opportunities either through behavioral example or cognitive support (career choice), and on the extent to which she will make career plans and develop a strong career identity. Role models will serve as initial vocational guidance counselors and may act as primary information sources for career choice and early career planning.

Although the selection of a role model is an individual level factor, it may be heavily influenced by societal definitions of appropriate roles for boys and girls. Most children select the same gender parent as an appropriate role model; however, this identification may be modified to the extent to which both parents support stereotypes of gender-appropriate roles. If parents adopt stereotypic sex-roles for themselves and present these roles as the appropriate ones for their children to model, then the societal definitions of gender-appropriate roles may exert a stronger influence on the modeling process. Thus, the selection and identification with a particular role model may be affected by societal definitions of gender-appropriate roles as well as individual level factors related to a person's value system.

Personality Traits

Individual factors, such as need for achievement, locus of control, and self-esteem, are influenced by a person's role orientations, but represent general personality traits. These factors will help determine the extent to which career plans will be developed. Proposition 2 states that certain personality traits will predispose an individual to career planning. Specifically, people with a high need for achievement, an internal locus of control, and high self-esteem will be more likely to engage in career-planning activities than those without these characteristics.

Research on need for achievement and women has generally compared working women with nonworking women, or compared women in traditional and nontraditional careers (Moore and Rickel 1980). Baruch (1967) found women in professional careers to have higher need for achievement scores than housewives. Sorrentino (1973) found need for achievement scores to be positively related to managerial level and nontraditional work roles for women managers. In addition, Moore and Rickel (1980) described characteristics of women in traditional and non-traditional managerial roles and found significant differences between these groups. Women in nontraditional managerial roles were higher in need for achievement, job involvement, and production orientation than women in traditional managerial roles (e.g., nursing supervisors). In addition, nontraditional women managers described themselves more often as having managerial and "male" characteristics than did traditional women managers. This difference may affect the extent to which they will plan for their future career development. However, it is worth noting that several studies (Mandelbaum 1981; Shann 1983; Walker, Tausky, and Oliver 1982) found more occupation-related differences in work values than gender-related differences. This finding indicates that many of the gender-related differences may be focused in the career choice area; but once the choice is made, there are few differences in the work values of men and women within an occupation. Since men and women generally value their work equally, traditional arguments that a man's career is more important than a woman's, or that a woman's career should be subordinate to her roles as wife and mother, are unfounded. Thus, career planning is as important to women as it is to men. Although these studies indicate that women with high need for achievement are career-oriented and are likely to be promoted, few studies have examined the relationship between need for achievement and career planning. Proposition 2a states that women with high need for achievement would be more likely to engage in career-planning activities than women with low need for achievement.

There is evidence that locus of control may also be a personality factor important in career development issues. Burlin (1976) found significant differences in locus of control and ideal career aspirations for women. Basically, her findings support a relationship between internal locus of control and ideal career choices of nontraditional careers. However, the relationship between locus of control and realistic (vs. ideal) occupational aspirations was not significant. Gould (1979) found marginal support for a relationship between locus of control and career planning. A signficiant correlation between these variables indicated that internal locus of control people were more involved in career planning than externals; however, a nonsignificant beta weight was found for locus of control when this variable was regressed against a career-planning criterion. Perhaps one explanation for Gould's findings may be the low reliability of his measure for locus of control (coefficient alpha = .68) or the nature of his sample (subjects were municipal employees with an average tenure of ten years). From the general literature on this personality trait, proposition 2b states that people with an internal locus of control are more likely to exert direct control over their lives and hence, engage in more career-planning activities than people with an external locus of control.

Hall (1976) identifies self-esteem as another important personality trait that helps define an individual's identity. People who have high self-esteem seek successes in life that would reinforce their positive self-images. For example, an individual with high self-esteem may set specific career goals that help define activities for the person to strive for and gain success. If the individual is successful, his/her self-esteem is enhanced and leads to a more competent self-identity. Furthermore, the likelihood of future goal setting and motivation toward success is increased in order to maintain the positive identity. The available research in this area supports a positive relationship between self-esteem and some career issues. Betz (1983) reported higher self-esteem ratings for working women than for homemakers. Gould (1979) found a positive correlation between self-esteem and career planning. In addition, self-esteem was marginally supported as a predictor of career planning when this variable was entered in a stepwise multiple regression analysis ($B = .11$, $p < .06$). From this research, proposition 2c states that people with high self-esteem will be more likely to engage in career-planning activities than people with low self-esteem.

Summary of Individual Factors

All of the individual factors that we have discussed are relevant factors influencing career choice and career planning for men and women. However, several of these factors differentially affect women. Explanations for the differences may be attributed to societal influences of appropriate roles for women and/or individual differences in personality traits. Role models often present attractive nonwork roles for many women. In addition, gender differences in some measures of personality may explain differences in the career development of men and women. For example, Lenney's (1977) review of the literature on women's attitudes in achievement-oriented situations found women generally showed lower self-confidence than men did across a variety of achievement-oriented situations. Although the differences may be due to contextual features of the achievement-oriented situations and not totally due to actual gender differences, the lower self-confidence may lead women to set lower career goals and less ambitious plans. If these relationships are true for a significant number of women, at least two implications regarding career planning can be made. First, a stereotype of women setting low career goals/plans may have negative consequences for those women who do not accept the stereotype. Second, self-awareness and development programs designed to increase a woman's self-confidence in achievement-oriented situations, may reduce this barrier to more effective career planning. It should be noted that the factors presented here do not define the domain of all individual level variables that impact on career planning. They are presented here only as examples of factors that have theoretical arguments supporting a relationship with career planning efforts.

If a woman does perceive a need for career planning, the actual goals and plans that are developed are not only based on these individual level factors but must also consider the opportunities and barriers found within the organization and within the woman's general career field.

Organizational Level Factors

Personnel Policies

Personnel policies may be clearly stated in an employee handbook, or may be readily obtained from managers or personnel specialists. These policies represent the organization's formal position on a variety of issues regarding human resources management. An organization's personnel policies can have a direct influence on a woman's career-planning efforts. The design of several major personnel functions, such as staffing systems, training and development programs, and performance appraisal systems help shape a woman's perceptions of her career opportunities within the organization. In addition, the compensation system and types of benefits an organization offers to its employees can have a direct impact on a woman's career plans. Relatively low salaries that are associated with traditionally female-stereotyped occupations may motivate many women to plan for nontraditional careers. Fringe benefit policies regarding pregnancy leave and/or childcare may also affect career plans. A recent Supreme Court decision (*California Federal Savings & Loan Association* v. *Guerra* 1987) ruled in favor of a California state statute allowing women to take up to 18 weeks of unpaid maternity leave from their employers and guaranteeing their jobs (or comparable jobs) back when they return to work. This type of policy reduces the amount of uncertainty many pregnant women face by explicitly stating the organization's responsibility in accommodating a woman's nonwork role of being a mother.

When women do return to work, their roles as mothers and employees may be further accommodated by company-sponsored childcare facilities. These day-care centers typically offer two advantages for mothers: the costs of day-care are often subsidized by the organization, thus offering an economical advantage. Furthermore, the convenience of a day-care center that is located near or within the organization offers mothers the opportunity to visit their children during work breaks or lunch. Advantages to the organization are also two-fold: employers may be able to retain valuable employees by offering them an alternative to expensive childcare or career abandonment for full-time motherhood. Second, the convenience of an on-site day-care center minimizes the number of work hours that are lost from travel, visits, and/or telephone calls that are made by employees who need to attend to their children.

Other kinds of personnel policies can also facilitate the integration of work and nonwork roles. Flextime offers employees more discretion on when they may start or stop their workday. This benefit allows women more flexibility in taking care of family matters without suffering negative consequences associated with tardiness or absenteeism (Cascio, 1986). In addition to flextime benefits, many organizations have offered job-sharing or part-time work as methods of hiring or retaining valuable employees who are unable to devote themselves to full-time careers (Gordon, 1986). These practices help accommodate nonwork roles while still retaining many women in the work force.

In addition to the above policies, several organizations have instituted career management programs that help encourage women to plan rewarding careers that also benefit the organization. Campbell and Moses (1986) describe such a program at AT&T that has as one objective the promotion of women into management positions. The program utilizes an assessment center to identify those women who have good management potential. These women then participate in a career-planning program that involves goal-setting, performance feedback, and career support/follow-up by the woman's superior as well as the program coordinator. Results from this program indicate that the promotion rates for women into management are comparable to the promotion rates of men.

An organization's personnel policies may set barriers or define opportunities for a woman's career development. How these policies affect a woman's attempt to integrate her work and nonwork roles, and how they define the kinds of career opportunities available to a woman can have a direct influence on her career goals and plans.

Organizational Climate

Although personnel policies represent the organization's formal position on human resources management, oftentimes the organizational climate will determine how these policies are actually implemented. If organizational climate describes the employee's perceptions of the organization's "personality," it includes perceptions about how the organization treats its work force and shows concern for its employees' career development.

A general review of the number and kinds of employment litigation involving sex discrimination would suggest that many organizations do not have a climate that would support the career development of women. A sample of court cases illustrate the difficulties women have experienced in gaining equal pay for equal work (*Corning Glass Works* v. *Brennan* 1974), equal pension benefits that are not based on sex (*Retired Public Employees Association of California* v. *State of California* 1982), and freedom from sexual harassment (*Bundy* v. *Jackson*

1981). Clearly, many women have suffered negative career consequences from discriminatory management policies.

On the positive side, many organizations have established a climate that would support a woman's career development. AT&T's concern about the managerial development of its women was manifested in its career-planning program (Campbell and Moses 1986). Many personnel policies may be a reflection of an organizational climate that supports women. Voluntary affirmative action plans, special training programs for women, and career-planning/career-management policies can serve as concrete examples of a positive climate. Recently, the Supreme Court has supported affirmative action plans that help women move into nontraditional jobs (*Johnson* v. *Transportation Agency* 1987).

On an informal level, many managers have served as mentors for women and this relationship has proved to be a powerful career development technique (Kram 1985). Mentors generally serve as organizational role models who teach the protégé the knowledge, skills, and abilities that are needed to fast-track the protégé's career. Mentors provide a protégé with challenging job assignments, organizational visibility, and often exercise power to advance the protégé's career. Mentorship is generally viewed as the most intense work relationship in organizations and the relationship extends beyond organizational boundaries by evolving into a solid, personal friendship (Hunt and Michael 1983). However, since most senior managers are men, their mentoring relationships with women are riskier than more traditional mentoring with other men. The literature about cross-gender mentoring identifies several risks when men mentor women (Clawson and Kram 1984; Fitt and Newton 1981). Cross-gender mentorships are more difficult than same-gender relationships because the male mentor may lack an understanding of a female protégé's perspective about her work and career future (and vice versa). Thus it is harder to develop a protégé who does not share the mentor's interests, attitudes, or background. Furthermore, the rarity of these relationships make them subject to public scrutiny and the possibility of a sexual relationship (whether it is actual or only organizational gossip) could harm the career developments of both parties.

Summary of Organizational Factors

A woman's perceptions about the organization's concern for her career development, as well as the kinds of personnel policies that may affect her work and nonwork roles, represent a critical source of information for career planning. Policies related to pregnancy leave, childcare, flextime, and job sharing may facilitate a woman's efforts to blend work and nonwork roles. The extent to which the organizational climate supports a woman's career development and the extent to which policies support all of the work and nonwork roles will determine the kinds of career goals a woman will set for herself. Proposition 3 states that a woman's knowledge and understanding of the organizational climate and personnel policies will influence her ability to set realistic career goals and appropriate plans for attaining those goals.

Societal Level Factors

The influx of women into the work force has been a consequence of several important social factors. Changes in our society show more women are delaying marriage or are not marrying at all. In addition, the high divorce rate has left many women as the sole income source for their families. These developments have caused more women to seek work in order to support themselves. As these women begin their careers, many can take advantage of the medical advances related to birth control and pregnancy, as well as the societal advances in child day-care and preschool programs. These developments have given women more control over their family planning; thus, women are now in a better position to accommodate their family lives with their work lives.

In addition to the medical advances that allow women to plan for a better integration of their work and family lives, many new products and services are currently available that allow women to be time-efficient with their household responsibilities. A partial list of these products and services would include: microwave ovens, frostless freezers, self-cleaning ovens, programmable appliances (e.g., coffee pots and ovens may be programmed to begin food preparation by themselves), no-wax floors, shopping by mail order and television, convenience foods (frozen entrees, easy-to-prepare meals, etc.), and affordable cleaning/maid services. These innovations are labor-saving devices that ease the burden of household maintenance chores.

In addition to these changes, technological innovations in organizations have dramatically shaped the number and kinds of career opportunities that are currently available or will be available in the future. The applications of industrial robots and computer technology in manufacturing organizations are often aimed at minimizing human labor costs by replacing many jobs with machines. With these applications, the factory of the future may be visualized as an organization staffed by a small number of technicians (Hunt and Hunt 1983). In contrast, the increasing demand for services has identified this type of organization as the area of employment growth. Thus, general shifts of available jobs will be seen as more manufacturing jobs are lost to automation and more service jobs are created to meet a heightened consumer need.

Finally, the kinds of sex-roles that are sanctioned by society may affect how certain career choices and plans are valued by the individual. The effects of sex-role stereotypes are mitigated by the individual's personality and by the particular encouragement or discouragement of these stereotypes by those people who are most influential with the individual (i.e., the role models). The impact of the societal factors leads us to our fourth proposition: Changes in our society will affect the number of women who are motivated to seek careers, the general support for these working women, and the kinds of career opportunities available to them. The extent to which these changes are perceived as important to a woman would influence the extent to which they will affect her career plans. Currently, we are seeing more women who need to support themselves. They are taking advantage of the kinds of products and services that facilitate work and nonwork roles, as well as searching for the kinds of career paths and opportunities that would be available in the future.

Career Planning and Results

Efforts actively to develop career plans have been found to enhance positively an individual's career development (Gould 1979; London and Stumpf 1982). These efforts may range from career planning booklets and workshops that are conducted within organizations to more personal planning efforts with the guidance of career counselors. Career plans are based on a self-assessment of career-related strengths and weaknesses as well as an understanding of how the career fits into one's overall life. For many women, the work-nonwork resolution may involve work/family conflicts and/or dual careers with working husbands. Once the assessment has been completed, the plans help define career goals and identify appropriate paths toward those goals. For many women, the types of goals that are set may be influenced by the kinds of opportunities that are available or blocked by the organization, or by other organizations that may be potential employers. In addition, the goals may be influenced by the sanctions imposed by a woman's support group (her spouse, children, parents, role models, and general society). Once goals have been formulated, they may be implemented to guide one's job/career performance. Although career progress is affected by factors other than an individual's performance (e.g., promotion opportunities; competition, etc.), a person's job performance is a critical factor that the individual can exert some control over. Therefore, it can help shape the person's career role or identity which, in turn, helps shape the individual's overall identity and general personality.

Summary

The career-planning model presented here draws its foundation from the literature and research examining general career planning as well as issues specific to the careers of women. The model is developmental as well as dynamic. It incorporates those factors that affect a woman's developmental process of career choice as well as factors that affect career development once the choice has been made. Thus, the model provides a bridge between the research examining career choice issues of young women who have not yet entered the workforce, and research examining the development of women who are employed in their chosen careers. The model is also dynamic, for many factors that affect career plans are typically related to the individual's current life stage. As one progresses through the life stages, both work and nonwork factors may change in their relevance and importance to future career plans. For example, the home/career conflict is usually most salient to women who have young children and this conflict becomes less evident as the children mature and become less dependent on their mother.

DISCUSSION

An individual engaged in career planning is rarely able to accurately predict when appropriate career opportunities will become available to him/her. Instead, career planning takes place within environmental uncertainty, and the goal of career planning is to be prepared for a maximum number of opportunities that can or cannot be anticipated. Thus, the individual must be aware of his/her capabilities and potential as well as the external environmental factors that can set parameters on his/her career options and range of planning activities.

One way of conceptualizing the process involved in career planning is to apply the literature from the business strategy area which suggests that people in top management positions who are responsible for directing organizations' use of environmental scanning as a technique to reduce environmental uncertainty (Fahey and King 1977; Thompson and Strickland 1984). Environmental scanning requires these people to monitor and interpret social, political, economic, and technological events in order to maximize opportunities and minimize risks (Fahey, King, and Narayanan 1981). Data collected during scanning are used by top management to set goals or to modify existing goals in order to take advantage of opportunities and to avoid threats.

The processes involved in environmental scanning can be applied to individual career planning. Astin (1985) proposes that environmental factors are important influences on career development activities because they define the structure of opportunities available to the individual. Super and Hall (1978) specify that an individual engaged in career planning must gather information in order to design a particular career plan. Along the same lines, London and Stumpf (1982) identify sources of information that can help a person understand the kinds of opportunities that may be a part of his/her career plans. These information sources can be informal (e.g., family and friends) or formal (e.g., career libraries, professional societies, Chamber of Commerce, etc.). Furthermore, they may involve sources specific to a chosen career (e.g., trade associations, corporate annual reports, etc.) or they may be more general (e.g., church groups, political parties). In summary, the sources of information that can help a person plan a career may be located in a variety of environments—social, political, religious, and organizational environments can all be potential references for career-planning information. These environments may represent factors that affect the individual, the organization, or society as a whole.

If the model presented in this chapter captures the major processes that describe most women as they plan their careers, several implications for women can be made at the individual, organizational, and societal levels. At the individual level, the model proposes that planning can help a woman integrate her work and nonwork roles to enhance her identity as a careerist and as a woman. Planning activities can help a woman articulate her career goals and shape her work behaviors toward goal attainment. The career performance may then promote her career identity which, in turn, can positively affect general personality dimensions such as need for achievement and self-esteem. A career can be a primary arena for a woman to satisfy many psychological as well as economic needs. Indeed, a review of the literature (Baruch, Biener, and Barnett 1987) on women and their reported work and family stress suggests that work holds several advantages for women. The data indicate that working women suffer less stress than nonworking women. Furthermore, when women view their work as a career rather than just a job, they reported greater work satisfaction and less role conflict with nonwork roles. These findings suggest the rewards from career planning activities may be quite substantial for women.

At the organizational level, employers could maximize the utilization of a significant portion of the work force by the effective career management of its working women. The professional development of women in organizations via thoughtful career planning will elevate the bottom-line effect of many affirmative action plans beyond one of the ineffective tokenism. This help can take the form of progressive personnel policies to support work/nonwork roles of women. In addition, an organizational climate that supports the career development of women is imperative for their career growth. Changes in managerial attitudes toward women have occurred in recent years. An attitude survey was administered to executives in 1965 and to a second group of executives in 1985 (Sutton and Moore 1985). A comparison of these two groups showed significant changes in managerial beliefs about women. In 1965, a majority of the respondents believed women rarely wanted or expected top-level positions. In contrast, only 10 percent of the 1985 executives held that belief. These results indicate a changing organizational climate that supports more women advancing their careers. However, the support for women

Irons, E.D. and G.W. Moore. 1985. *Black managers: The case of the banking industry.* New York: Praeger Publishers.

Kanter, R.M. 1980. *A tale of "O": On being different in an organization.* New York: Harper & Row.

King, M.C. 1975. Oppression and power: The unique status of the black woman in the American political system. *Social Science Quarterly, 56,* 121–128.

Kraiger, K. and J.K. Ford. 1985. A meta-analysis of ratee race effects in performance ratings. *Journal of Applied Psychology, 70:* 56–65.

Ladner, J. 1971. *Tomorrow's tomorrow: The black woman.* New York: Doubleday.

Larwood, L. and M.M. Wood. 1977. *Women in management.* Lexington, MA: D.C. Heath.

Leggon, C.B. 1980. Black female professionals: Dilemmas and contradictions of status. In La Frances Rodgers-Rose (Ed.), *The black woman.* Beverly Hills: Sage Publications.

Linville, P.W., and E.E. Jones. 1980. Polarized appraisals of out-group members. *Journal of Personality and Social Psychology, 38,* 689–703.

Lykes, B.M. 1983. Discrimination and coping in the lives of black women: Analyses of oral history data. *Journal of Social Issues, 39,* 79–100.

Malveaux, J. 1985. The economic interests of black and white women: Are they similar? *The Review of Black Political Economy, 14,* 5–27.

Merton, R.K. 1957. *Social theory and social structure.* Glencoe, IL: Free Press.

Morse, R. 1983. *The Black female professional,* (Occasional Paper No. 21). Howard University–Washington, DC. Mental Health Research and Development Center, Institute for Urban Affairs and Research.

Nieva, V.F. and B.A. Gutek. 1982. *Women and work: A psychological perspective.* New York: Praeger.

Puryear, G.R. and M.S. Mednick. 1974. Black militancy, affective attachment, and the fear of success in black college women. *Journal of Consulting and Clinical Psychology, 42,* 263–266.

Roche, G.R. 1979. Much ado about mentors. *Harvard Business Review, 57,* 14–28.

Sherman, M.F., N.C. Sherman, and R.J. Smith. 1983. Racial and gender differences in perception of fairness: When race is involved in a job promotion. *Perceptual and Motor Skills, 57,* 719–728.

Simpson, J.C. 1981, January. Black female managers are making the right moves to fight racism and sexism in their pursuit of corporate power. *Black Enterprise,* pp. 20–25.

Smith, A. and A. Stewart. 1983. Approaches to studying racism and sexism in black women's lives. *Journal of Social Issues, 39,* 1–15.

Steptoe, S. 1986, March 24. Strangers in a strange land. *The Wall Street Journal* (A special report—The corporate woman), pp. 22–23.

Struggle for the executive suite: Blacks vs. white women. 1980, September. *Black Enterprise,* pp. 25–27.

Szafran, R.F. 1984. Female and minority employment patterns in banks. *Work and Occupations, 22*(1), 55–76.

Terborg, J.R. 1977. Women in management: A research review. *Journal of Applied Psychology, 62,* 647–664.

U.S. Bureau of the Census. 1984. Women's share of managerial occupations increased sharply between 1970 and 1980: Census data show. (United States Department of Commerce News, CB).

U.S. Department of Labor, Office of the Secretary, Women's Bureau. 1983. Time of change: 1983 handbook on women workers, (Bulletin 298).

Wallace, P. 1980. *Black women in the labor force*. Cambridge, MA: MIT Press.

Weathers, D. 1981. Black executives: Winning under the double whammy. *Savvy*, 2, 34–40.

Wiley, M.G. and A. Eskelson. 1982. The interaction of sex and power base on perceptions of managerial effectiveness. *Academy of Management Journal*, 25, 671–677.

Wortman, M.S. 1982. An overview of the research on women in management: A typology and prospectus. In H. John Bernardin (Ed.), *Women in the workforce*. New York: Praeger.

Yarkin, K.L., J.P. Town, and B.S. Wallston. 1982. Blacks and women must try harder: Stimulus person's race and sex attributions of causality. *Personality and Social Psychology Bulletin, 8*, 21–24.

9

Tokenism and Academic Culture: Women in Canadian Business Schools

Linda Dyer
Irene Devine

PREVIEW

Our research considers the underrepresentation and concomitant difficulties experienced by full-time tenure-track women in business schools. Discrimination faced by lone women in a traditional man's world has become more subtle and less conscious but has not yet disappeared. Academic women still are under the spotlight and are limited by the stereotypes others have of them. The professional implications of token status may include little opportunity for academic collaboration, few political alliances, reduced social support and barriers to advancement. Women students, too, can be adversely affected by witnessing men professors' treatment of women faculty. Faculty who objectify and devalue women can create long-lasting impediments to academic, professional and personal growth to both women faculty and students.

Our results will be of interest to women and men in educational and business settings where there is only token representation. We believe that if women and men become more aware of and confront the actions and attitudes associated with tokenism, they will then be halfway to instituting behavioral and attitudinal changes. Renewed support for affirmative action also would increase the proportion of women. Alternatively, the reader may think of other methods of reducing gender-related salience in her own workplace. Meaningful social change will allow women access to the same institutional opportunities as men, and only then will organizations benefit from the full participation of women and men.

We, as female professors teaching in a Canadian business school, have been reading about and researching the difficulties faced by managerial women in male-dominated, profit-making companies. We were interested in the lot of women who, like us, work in educational institutions.

Some researchers have observed that women academics tend to be somewhat less satisfied than men with their colleagues, and with promotion and merit pay procedures (Fedler et al. 1983). Legal records also document numerous academic employment discrimination grievances filed by individual women scholars in the United States (Farley 1982). These women often noted that their difficulties emanated from the fact that they were female. It is reasonable to assume that many of these problems may spring from being a woman in a male-oriented organization. If this is so, and business schools can understand and address these issues, the need for legal action may decrease.

Traditionally, most profit-making companies are established by men, managed by men, and peopled with men. In the past decades, though, increasing numbers of women have been hired into these companies. Their path is not an easy one; many researchers have noted that women have difficulty fitting into male-centered organizations (Bartol 1978; Marshall 1984). First, advancement in hierarchical organizations is fundamentally a political process (Harragan 1977). Women are rejected for promotion to upper-level positions because they do not fit the normative model of the ideal (male) executive (Offe 1976; Martin, Harrison and Dinitto 1983). Women are less likely to be viewed as qualified or as the best choice for the job (Epstein 1975), particularly for positions that entail extensive authority over others (Wolfe and Fligsteen 1979) or the right to make decisions affecting substantial resources or capital (Silver 1981). Yet to the extent that an individual has access to and control of resources, and is central to organizational interactions, she or he becomes more important to ensuring organizational effectiveness (Smith and Grenier 1982). Thus the formal system in organizations puts women at an overall disadvantage (Bartol 1978).

A second reason for the difficulties women face when they advance to upper-level positions is that they are disproportionately few in number—they are tokens (Kanter 1977). Because they are few, they get more attention than their male peers, and this increased visibility creates performance pressures. Being noticeable is a two-edged sword: successful deeds may get more recognition, but mistakes are also more public. Token women get used as showpieces to demonstrate that the specific organization has women in its upper-level ranks and their acts may be viewed as symbols of how women-as-a-group perform.

Kanter also found that token women are typecast into stereotyped roles, and women find this very stressful. For instance, women in professional positions report being mistaken for secretaries or treated like dates during their professional encounters. They also frequently are asked to do tasks that are traditionally female, such as counseling or being on Equal Employment committees.

Third, Kanter reported that male managers tend to exaggerate the differences between their own and the female managers' cultures, which results in female exclusion from informal groups. For example, the normal flow of events gets interrupted by reminders of the women's difference by men's apologies for swearing in their presence. Sexual innuendos and traditional "men's" topics (like sports) tend to increase when token women are present.

Thus, tokenism exacerbates the problems women experience in male-dominated organizations. The women may work there, but feel socially isolated—they do not belong (Devine 1985; Marshall 1984; Richbell 1976). In order to understand the implications of this, we must appreciate the impact of the informal system of relationships on an individual's success. Informal social contacts are essential for information and guidance, especially for new organizational members (Schein 1979). In fact, informal processes may even undermine or contradict the formal system. For example, decisions may be informally made during a golf game, or information necessary to a task may be passed along in a washroom when women are not present. Further, the informal system is more powerful the closer one is to the top, where evaluations and rewards more commonly are determined by subjective criteria. Exclusion from this informal system not only leads to feelings of estrangement, but to a lower probability of good performance and career success (Devine 1985; Marshall 1984).

Most of the information we have about the obstacles and barriers that women in upper-level positions in organizations face comes from research done in the private sector; it is not clear whether these conclusions are generalizable to other organizational contexts. Thus it appeared useful to explore logical and empirical extensions of these structural and process arguments in the university context.

In 1983-1984, women faculty represented just 15 percent of full-time faculty in Canadian universities. Furthermore, the female professors tend to be ghettoized in traditional female disciplines (Inch 1985), such as teaching, nursing, and library science. Thus, in business schools, the expected ratio is even more skewed. The percentage of women in the higher academic and administrative ranks is even smaller. We would predict that the processes that occur when tokens are present in male-dominated organizations would also apply in this context.

The present research was an attempt to test the theoretical and empirical generality of these issues in an academic setting. More specifically, do female faculty members in Canadian business schools face difficulties that are similar to those reported by women in upper-level positions in the business community? Kanter's categorization of the outcomes of tokenism (namely increased visibility, role stereotyping, and social exclusion) was used as a springboard for this exploratory investigation. The research questions follow:

Are women in business schools likely to report higher visibility and more attention than is accorded their male colleagues?

To what extent do women feel that they are typecast into stereotyped roles?

To what extent do women feel they are excluded from the informal system?

METHOD

The Participants

The names of 38 female and 38 male full-time faculty members were drawn from the membership list of the 1984 Administrative Sciences Association of Canada, as well as from lists of other professional organizations. All recognizably female names were included in the sample, and each was matched with the (male) name appearing immediately before it on the list. A questionnaire was mailed to each person; two questionnaires were returned for individuals who had left their university with no forwarding address. For the remaining questionnaires, there was a 41 percent response rate. The final sample was comprised of 30 business school professors (15 female and 15 male).

Demographic information was collected about length of employment, rank, age, and estimation of the percent of women faculty in the business school. Average length of employment at the university was 7.7 years; the women had been in their departments for a briefer time (6.2 years) than had the men (9.2 years). The respondents ranged in rank from instructor (five female, no male), through assistant professor (six female, two male) and associate professor (three female, five male), to full professor (one female, seven male). Fifty-seven percent of the respondents were in the 40–50 year age group; the others were mainly in their thirties. Estimates of the percent of women faculty ranged from 1 percent to 40 percent, with an average of 13.6 percent women.

The Instrument

The questionnaire contained a short story which described scenarios about events that might happen in a university context. These scenarios were intended to elicit recall of the day-to-day activities that participants may have experienced. None of the scenarios focused specifically on the academic tasks of teaching or doing research; we did not want people to generate comments about their *skills* as academics, rather, we were interested mainly in *interactions* among department members.

The scenarios were divided into four segments, and each segment was followed by a series of open-ended questions about issues raised in the text. For example, one scenario read:

8:30 A.M. You are about to leave your house. You are thinking about a proposal you will be making at the University Graduate Studies' committee meeting this morning. The support of this committee is important if your department is to get its graduate diploma program approved.

You mentally rehearse the major points you wish to cover. You also consider your appearance. It is important that you look professional during this presentation, because you sense that the success of the proposal depends to a great extent on the image you create. You will be the only representative of the Business School at the meeting.

10:40 A.M. The meeting is over. Actually it went quite well. There were a few changes to the proposal, but it was accepted. You are pleased. As you are collecting your papers to return to your office, a friend from the History Department who was also at the meeting calls out to you.

"All through your presentation I was wondering what was different about you," your friend says. "Did you get a haircut recently? It makes your face look quite different." You stop to chat briefly, but soon you excuse yourself, remembering all the work that is piled up on your desk.

Questions. Is there a dress code in your department? How do people usually dress? Under what conditions (if any) is it important for you to pay attention to your appearance? Would your colleagues be likely to comment on haircuts or other changes in your appearance? How does this make you feel? Have you ever found that people pay more attention to how you look or speak, rather than to what you say?

The events and questions were presented in a neutral tone and no mention was made of the gender of the protagonist. In fact, respondents were told in a cover letter that we were trying to describe the academic culture of Canadian business schools. No mention was made of gender differences. Space was left for the subjects' answers to the open-ended questions.

Protocol Analysis

The written answers were content-analyzed by two scorers to determine the subjects' experiences of visibility, role stereotyping, or exclusion (as described below).

Perceived visibility. This dimension was made up of factors characterized by responses such as: (1) Colleagues pay attention to my mistakes; (2) colleagues pay attention to my successes; (3) colleagues see me as representing women as a group; (4) colleagues draw attention to my discrepant (nonjob-related) characteristics; and (5) colleagues are envious of my achievements.

Perceived role stereotyping. This dimension was made up of factors characterized by responses such as: (1) I am mistaken for a student or secretary; (2) I am asked to do jobs that "only a woman could do"; and (3) colleagues sometimes treat me—(a) as if I were their mother, (b) as if I were their date, (c) patronizingly, (d) as if I am so "tough" that I'd never need help.

Perceived exclusion. This dimension was made up of factors characterized by responses such as: (1) Colleagues exaggerate their "maleness" in their conversations with me; (2) colleagues apologize when they think I feel excluded from the group; (3) I am left out of the informal social groups; and (4) colleagues test my loyalty to the department.

The scorers rated each protocol along each dimension (visibility, role stereotyping, and exclusion), using seven-point bipolar rating scales (1 = respondent did not mention anything relevant to this category or mentioned a relevant issue but described it in positive affective terms; 7 = respondent mentioned issue in negative affective terms). Scorers were given examples of anchors related to each of the dimensions in question, for instance, one of the scales used to rate exclusion read:

1 (Low anchor): "I feel I know all the grapevine talk. I spend a lot of time socializing with my colleagues."

7 (High anchor): "I don't care to socialize too much with the people here. What is important is that I do my work and go home. There's too much gossip anyway."

Inter-rater reliability for the factors was acceptable, but somewhat low. Some comments were so ambiguously stated that raters did not agree on how to rate them. Reliabilities for the factors described above ranged from .66 to .72. Those with lower reliabilities were dropped from further analysis. On other categories, there was no variability because no subject ever mentioned the issue—for example, colleagues' apologies for exclusion from the group.

We conducted another content analysis of the protocols, which categorized the affective tone of the comments. Again, the gender of the subjects was unknown during the analysis. The unit of analysis was the idea, and each idea was coded as a positive, a negative, or a neutral comment on the department norms of interaction between individuals. Examples of positive comments were: "This questionnaire has made me realize how much I enjoy working in this faculty," and "I love it! Wouldn't work anywhere else." Neutral commented included: "Dress varies from suits and ties to casual jeans and sport shirts." Negative comments were: "This faculty is far less cohesive as a group than the one I used to belong to at another institution"; and "Boring, narrow, superficial, culture-less life, not befitting a true university academic."

RESULTS

We found evidence of gender differences in two sources of organizational difficulties for female faculty members—increased visibility and role stereotyping—but not for perceived exclusion.

Women significantly more often reported visibility in terms of attention to their discrepant characteristics than did the men in our sample. The mean score for women was 4.20 (on a seven-point scale) and the mean score for men was 2.64 ($t(28)$ = 2.35; p < .025, one-tailed). For instance, women made comments like, "There was a part-time faculty member who commented on my appearance every time I saw him, and I felt insulted by his attention as though we had nothing else to discuss. I came to dislike him intensely." Another said: "I make every effort to wear clothing that even the most conservative, religious zealot would not find to be in the least provocative, however, given that I am not ashamed of being a woman, this is at times difficult, and an imposition not requiring effort on the part of the male members of the faculty." Typical male comments were: "My weight fluctuations attract notice, but these are 20 pounds or so," and "No, my colleagues are not likely to comment on my haircuts, etc."

Women also reported being the focus of informal stereotyping significantly more so than men. The mean score for women was 3.60 and for men, 2.50 ($t(28)$ = 2.18; p < .025). These informal stereotypes included such comments as, "I downplay my young child. One does not want to be seen at work as a mother," and "Too much attention [to sex-role etiquette like opening doors], too obviously. It is almost always commented on as it is done. These 'little gestures' are detrimental to my work climate."

There was, however, no difference between male and female responses to the issue of exclusion from the informal group. The women in the sample scored 4.44 and the men scored 4.41. There are two possible explanations: one is that neither women nor men experience problems of exclusion in the business school setting. The other possibility is that both men and women report equally high levels of feelings of exclusion and isolation from their peers. These possibilities will be pursued presently.

In order to determine whether the sex ratio of the work environment was related to participants' responses, we correlated the perceived female/male ratio with the three major dependent variables. Interestingly, there was a negative correlation of –.49 between the amount of role stereotyping and the perceived female/male ratio (p < .01). In other words, the fewer the women at the workplace, the more informal role stereotyping was reported. This lends support to Kanter's (1977) proposition that a more balanced number of males and females reduces or eliminates the organizational problems that women must face. The perceived ratio was not related to visibility or exclusion, however. None of the other subject variables, such as age, length of employment at the university, or state of tenure, had an impact on the major dependent variables.

The results of our evaluation of protocols as positive, neutral, or negative concerning departmental atmosphere indicated that only a slim majority of the comments were positive (51 percent). These comments usually referred to the politeness and friendliness of department members. The remaining 49 percent of the affective comments were negative; most of these pertained to isolation experienced by the professors. Four subjects said nothing positive about their departments.

DISCUSSION

Women academics were found to differ from men in two ways: first, they more often reported that (primarily) men colleagues paid attention to discrepant characteristics like their physical attributes; and second, women were more likely than men to report that they accepted, or were asked to accept, stereotyped informal roles. Our findings were similar to those reported by female tokens in private corporations.

Discriminatory behavior towards women is not necessarily deliberate, yet the effects may be destructive. Token female faculty members are likely to experience greater performance pressures because of their increased visibility. Their teaching and research activities may be more closely monitored by colleagues than the activities of their male peers. So, for instance, the research topics selected by female professors may be labeled nonmainstream for the field, whereas their male peers' similarly nonmainstream research may pass unnoticed and uncriticized. Some women may respond by becoming workaholic in attempting to satisfy performance demands or by withdrawing completely from public scrutiny. Either of these outcomes may be stress producing.

Second, women are expected to conform to stereotypes that are inappropriate to the professional context. For example, when senior male faculty members treat junior female faculty members as if they were their secretaries or their wives, and not as competent colleagues, females may hesitate to defend themselves. They may experience anxiety that they are jeopardizing their chances for promotion. These inappropriate stereotypes, thus, are likely to cause higher levels of stress among female than among male professors.

Contrary to what we expected, women and men reported equivalent amounts of exclusion from the informal system. We were quite surprised by the relatively high frequency of negative comments that arose when professors discussed their academic lifestyle. Some faculty described an individualistic, lonely, competitive environment where colleagues keep to themselves and miss meaningful social interaction. This is counter to the stereotype of academics as an easygoing, collegial, contented group.

Several external factors could explain these findings. First, the questionnaires were mailed at the end of a term (December, 1985), just before the Christmas break. At that time many professors were spending long hours grading examinations, a task which might have created a temporary negative attitude toward the workplace. Second, the questions asked may have predisposed respondents to make negative comments. We tried to make the text as neutral as possible, but certain questions, such as: "Have you ever felt left out of an informal group?" may have triggered recall of difficulties rather than rewarding experiences. The third explanation is that our inferences are accurate, and the social climate of business schools is relatively impoverished and stressful for both male and female academics. We believe that there are two salient features of the university system that differentiate it from typical business organizations, and accentuate professors' dissatisfaction with their interpersonal relationships.

First, professors have a relatively high level of task autonomy as compared to managers in the private sector; teaching and research are usually conducted independently of peers, with a major portion of performance feedback coming from external reviewers and students. Compared with many other types of organizations, the business school has low requirements for interdependence. This may serve to reduce the frequency of day-to-day working interactions with others, and academic men as well as the women may feel more isolated than may employees of business organizations.

Second, there is greater latitude for individual variability in universities. Eccentricities are tolerated, even expected, while in upper level positions in private organizations, "similarity" is a criterion for promotion and acceptance (Kanter 1977). Further, Canadian business schools are marked by great diversity in the cultural background of the professors. There are few Ph.D. business programs in Canada; a majority of academic positions are filled by graduates of foreign universities. Although such wide cultural variability has its advantages, it heightens feelings of difference and isolation from one's peers. Groups as a whole are less cohesive and many feel the effects of social isolation and not belonging. Women, then, become only one of the minority subcultures and we find other minority members describing problems of feeling left out of the dominant culture. Women and others who perceive themselves as isolated in their professional environments need to plan strategies to develop social relationships, seek closer collegial ties, and establish professional networks as one way of increasing their relative satisfaction.

Even though both male and female faculty members in Canadian business schools describe feelings of exclusion and social isolation, the minority group of women also describe feeling more visible than their male colleagues did and more typecast according to sex-role stereotypes. So it would seem that token women in educational institutions face barriers to successful career development and advancement that are similar to top level women managers. Regardless of the type of organization in which they work, there is still much to be done before women take their place equally alongside their men peers.

CONCLUSION

In conclusion, we have seen that in many ways, women academics in business schools face the same difficulties of visibility and role stereotyping as do their counterparts in the private sector. These outcomes of tokenism are likely to result in performance pressures and stress. We also have seen that women (as well as men) in the business schools we surveyed feel that they do not fit in. By raising awareness of the dynamics and results of tokenism, and by developing our networking strategies, we may find a way to alleviate the problems experienced by women faculty members, and to develop the blueprint for more satisfying work lives.

REFERENCES

Bartol, K. 1978. The sex structuring of organizations: A search for possible causes. *Academy of Management Review, 3,* 805–815.

Devine, I. 1985, November. The social isolation of professional women in organizations. Paper presented at Canadian Research Institute for the Advancement of Women, Annual conference, Saskatchewan.

Epstein, C. 1975. Institutional barriers: What keeps women out of the executive suite? In F.E. Gordon and M.H. Strober (Eds.), *Bringing women into management* (pp. 7–21). New York: McGraw-Hill.

Farley, J. 1982. *Academic women and employment discrimination.* Ithaca, NY: Cornell University Press.

Fedler, F., T. Counts, and R. Smith. 1983, August. A survey of job satisfaction of women professors in mass communication. Paper presented to the Mass Communication and Society Division, Annual Convention of Association for Education in Journalism and Mass Communication, Oregon State University.

Harragan, B.L. 1977. *Games mother never taught you: Corporate gamesmanship for women.* New York: Warner Books.

Inch, J. 1985, November. Affirmative action needed to boost women academics. *Canadian Association of University Teachers Bulletin,* p. 13.

Kanter, R.M. 1977. *Men and women of the corporation.* New York: Basic Books.

Marshall, J. 1984. *Women managers: Travellers in a male world.* New York: Wiley.

Martin, P.Y., D., Harrison and D. Dinitto. 1983. Advancement for women in hierarchical organizations. *Journal of Applied Behavioral Science, 19,* 19–33.

Offe, C. 1976. *Industry and inequality.* London: Edward Arnold.

Richbell, S. 1976. De facto discrimination and how to kick the habit. *Personnel Management, 8,* 30–33.

Schein, E.H. 1979. Organizational socialization and the profession of management. In D.A. Kolb, I.M. Rubin, and J.M. McIntyre (Eds.), *Organizational psychology* (pp. 87–103). Englewood Cliffs, NJ: Prentice-Hall.

Silver, C. 1981. Public bureaucracy and private enterprise in the USA and France: Contexts for the attainment of executive positions by women. In C.F. Epstein and R.L. Coser (Eds.), *Access to power: Cross-national studies of women and elites* (pp. 219-236). London: George Allyn and Unwin.

Smith, H.L., and M. Grenier. 1982. Sources of organizational power for women: Overcoming structural obstacles. *Sex Roles, 8,* 733-746.

Wolf, W., and Fligstein, N. 1979. Sex and authority in the workplace. *American Sociological Review, 44,* 235-252.

10

Occupational Sex Segregation in Canada and the United States: Does Affirmative Action Make a Difference?

Dallas Cullen
Alice Nakamura
Masao Nakamura

PREVIEW

Twenty years ago, casual observation of any office would have shown men and women working at different jobs. What about today? Has there really been a change in the pattern of the types of jobs that men and women do? It would seem that there have been changes since, for example, women are an increasing proportion of managers compared to a few years ago. Many would argue that this change has been due to the implementation of affirmative action and equal employment opportunity programs. But, at the same time, we can see that men have not become secretaries in the same proportions. What does this say about these programs?

One perspective on such programs is afforded by comparing the United States, which has had federally mandated and enforced affirmative action and equal opportunity programs, and Canada, which has had no comparable federal programs. This chapter makes this comparison and provides insights into occupational segregation in the two countries, as well as the changes that have occurred between 1950 and 1981.

As can be easily observed, men and women usually work at different jobs. Men are managers, women are secretaries. Men are doctors, women are nurses. Men are university professors, women are grade school teachers. Men are engineers, women are home economists. Patterns of male jobs and female jobs, referred to as occupational segregation, have been repeatedly demonstrated for the United States (e.g., Gross 1968; Oppenheimer 1970; Blau and Hendricks 1979; Beller 1982; Bergmann 1986) and for Canada (e.g., Gunderson 1976; Armstrong and Armstrong

1978; Nakamura, et al. 1979b; Merrilees 1982; Robb 1984). One reason why public attention and research effort has been focused on the phenomenon of occupational segregation by gender is because women's jobs tend to pay less than men's jobs (e.g., Treiman and Hartman 1981; Bergmann 1986). On average, working women in the United States and Canada earn about 60 percent of what working men earn (e.g., O'Neill 1985, for the U.S.; Gunderson 1979, for Canada), and a large portion of this earnings differential seems to be attributable to the segregation of working women in low-paying jobs.

Many in both the United States and Canada believe that discrimination by gender on the part of (largely male) employers is one important factor contributing to the occupational segregation of women. Many have also hoped that this discrimination could be lessened by the adoption of laws and other measures making it illegal and costly for employers to discriminate on the basis of gender. The reasoning has been that once discriminatory barriers were lowered, more women would enter better-paying, previously male-dominated occupations. As a result of this, the occupational distribution of working women and men would become more similar, and the earnings gap between working women and men would shrink.

In the 1960s and 1970s, a number of equal employment opportunity measures were introduced in the United States. The most significant of these measures were at the federal level: the Equal Pay Act of 1963, Title VII of the Civil Rights Act of 1964, Executive Order 11246 issued in 1965 (which mandated affirmative action by federal contractors and grantees), and the 1972 amendments to Title VII, which gave the Equal Employment Opportunity Commission (originally created by Lyndon Johnson) the authority to bring discrimination suits. Equal employment policies were also instituted in Canada during the 1960s and 1970s (e.g., Gunderson 1985). However, these policies were mostly provincial rather than federal. They were also less vigorous than the U.S. measures in several important respects. For instance, in Canada discrimination suits must be initiated through the action of the affected individual. There is no Canadian counterpart of the U.S. Equal Employment Opportunity Commission. Also, although there are some affirmative action programs in Canada, they cover a limited number of organizations and individuals, and compliance with them is largely a voluntary matter.

What we would like to know is whether the more far-reaching (and much more costly) U.S. affirmative action and equal opportunity measures were more effective in reducing occupational segregation than the Canadian measures. Evidence that this is so would bolster the case for tougher Canadian measures. Moreover, it would also constitute new evidence that occupational segregation can, in fact, be reduced by measures attacking gender-related employment discrimination. In studies based solely on U.S. data, the effects of equal opportunity and affirmative action programs are inextricably mixed with the effects of changes over time in other factors such as family structure, technology in the home and workplace, and the industrial mix of the economy that could also have resulted in changes in the extent and nature of occupational segregation by gender.

Starting with published U.S. and Canadian census data for hundreds of detailed occupational categories, we have compiled occupational data for 22 major categories that are comparable over the periods of 1950 to 1980 for the United States and 1951 to 1981 for Canada (for more information on this recoding, see Nakamura, et al. 1979a). Using this unique data set, we first establish that the patterns of occupational segregation by gender were very similar and have exhibited little change in both Canada and the United States over the periods of 1950/51 and 1970/71. We then look for signs of greater reductions in occupational segregation in the United States compared to Canada over the periods of 1970/71 to 1980/81. This latter period is when we might expect to see some divergence in the U.S. and Canadian patterns of occupational segregation, since it was in the early 1970s that the U.S. measures outlawing employment discrimination on the basis of gender began to be vigorously enforced.

OCCUPATIONAL SEGREGATION
OF U.S. AND CANADIAN WOMEN

As Canadians do know, and U.S. citizens may know, the commonalities between the two countries are numerous. Geographically, Canada is slightly larger, but its population is approximately one-tenth that of the United States. Similarities between the two countries ensure a common culture that is basically a U.S. culture. U.S. multinational corporations control a significant part of Canada's economy. Canadians watch U.S. television stations, they attend U.S. movies, they read U.S. books and magazines, they listen to U.S. music, and they observe U.S. political events. Few U.S. citizens do the reverse.

However, Canada and the United States are not identical. The observed work behavior of U.S. and Canadian women, and a number of factors that are thought to affect this work behavior, are really quite different. For instance, female employment rates have been and still are substantially lower for Canadian than for U.S. women. On average, Canadian women do not stay in school for as many years as their U.S. counterparts. Also, employed wives in Canada must file separate tax returns, rather than file jointly with their husbands as most U.S. wives must do (Nakamura and Nakamura 1981). Thus, even though it has long been known that working women are occupationally segregated in both countries, it cannot simply be assumed that the patterns of occupational

Table 10.1
Proportion of Workers Who Are Women, by Occupation for the United States and Canada, 1950/51–1980/81

Occupation	1950/51 U.S.	1950/51 CAN.	1960/61 U.S.	1960/61 CAN.	1970/71 U.S.	1970/71 CAN.	1980/81 U.S.	1980/81 CAN.
Teaching	68.4	67.2	64.4	64.4	65.2	60.4	66.9	59.7
Clerical	62.3	56.1	68.1	61.0	74.8	68.4	77.7	77.8
Medicine and health	61.4	68.5	67.2	72.1	73.1	74.3	76.2	77.8
Service	53.4	45.1	57.9	46.7	55.1	46.2	54.0	52.7
Social sciences	34.3	27.8	32.8	29.4	39.7	37.4	45.4	52.5
Materials handling	34.3	27.2	36.2	19.4	24.1	19.7	24.6	22.6
Artistic, literary	34.1	30.7	35.0	31.2	32.2	27.2	41.1	39.4
Sales	26.6	33.3	28.5	32.0	29.6	30.4	38.9	42.3
Fabricating, repairing	26.6	22.6	27.6	22.8	31.8	23.7	27.7	24.6
Processing	20.8	14.8	19.8	13.7	24.3	17.8	34.0	22.3
Religion	17.1	39.7	15.5	28.9	10.1	15.7	13.4	29.9
Managerial, administrative	12.8	8.7	14.6	10.4	17.5	15.7	30.7	25.1
Not elsewhere classified	9.7	13.4	9.3	9.2	18.3	13.0	21.1	16.4

Other crafts	9.6	8.4	10.0	9.1	15.8	12.4	21.5	21.2
Machining	9.2	4.8	9.7	4.3	14.1	5.7	12.4	6.8
Farming	8.4	3.9	9.1	11.7	9.3	20.9	14.6	21.6
Natural sciences, engineering	6.3	6.9	5.2	4.8	8.0	7.3	16.3	13.9
Fishing, hunting, trapping	1.5	0.0	1.3	0.1	4.1	1.6	6.4	5.5
Transport	1.3	0.5	1.7	0.6	5.1	2.4	9.1	6.5
Forestry	1.2	0.0	1.1	0.4	2.8	1.9	5.4	6.1
Construction	1.1	1.0	0.9	0.8	2.0	0.9	3.0	1.9
Mining	0.8	0.0	0.4	0.0	3.9	0.5	2.5	2.1
All occupations	27.7	22.0	32.5	27.3	37.9	33.5	42.6	40.4

Source: Calculated from 1951 Census of Canada Vol, IV, Table 4; 1961 Census of Canada, Vol III - Part I, Table 6; 1971 Census of Canada Vol III - Part 2, Table 8; 1981 Census of Canada, Cat. No. 92-917, Table 1; 1960 U.S. Census, Vol. I, Part 1, Table 201; 1970 U.S. Census, Special Report PC(2) 7A, Table 1; 1980 U.S. Census, Special Report PC 80-2-7C, Table 4.

Table 10.2
U.S. and Canadian Occupational Distributions for the Female Labor Force, 1950/51–1980/81

Occupation	1950/51 U.S.	CAN.	1960/61 U.S.	CAN.	1970/71 U.S.	CAN.	1980/81 U.S.	CAN.
Teaching	5.5(5-6)	6.8(5)	6.0	7.4	7.8	8.0	7.2	6.2
Clerical	27.1(1)	30.4(1)	30.5	31.4	34.3	35.6	33.9	36.3
Medicine and health	5.5(5-6)	6.6(6)	6.6	8.8	7.8	9.2	9.3	8.7
Service	22.1(2)	19.7(2)	22.1	20.0	17.6	16.9	14.6	15.7
Social sciences	0.8(13-14)	0.5(15)	0.9	0.7	1.3	1.1	1.9	2.1
Materials handling	1.4(10-11)	1.7(10)	1.4	1.7	2.2	1.5	1.5	1.2
Artistic, literary	1.4(10-11)	1.0(12)	1.5	1.1	1.0	0.8	1.3	1.4
Sales	11.4(3)	8.9(4)	10.4	8.6	8.8	9.4	8.4	9.4
Fabricating, repairing	10.2(4)	9.6(3)	9.6	6.9	8.3	5.7	5.2	4.9
Processing	5.1(7)	5.0(7)	3.5	2.8	2.7	2.3	3.8	2.3
Religion	0.2(18-19)	1.1(11)	0.2	0.6	0.1	0.1	0.1	0.2
Managerial, administrative	1.8(9)	3.4(8)	2.3	3.4	3.0	2.2	6.9	5.4
Not elsewhere classified	0.8(13-14)	0.4(16-17)	0.6	0.6	0.6	0.8	0.8	0.5

Other crafts	0.6(15)	0.6(14)	0.5	0.5	0.6	0.5	0.6	0.6
Machining	1.3(12)	0.7(13)	1.1	0.5	1.5	0.5	1.1	0.4
Farming	3.7(8)	2.8(9)	1.9	4.4	0.9	4.1	0.9	2.3
Natural sciences, engineering	0.4(16)	0.4(16-17)	0.4	0.4	0.8	0.6	1.4	1.2
Fishing, hunting, trapping	0.0(20-22)	0.0(20-22)	0.0	0.0	0.0	0.0	0.0	0.0
Transport	0.2(18-19)	0.1(19)	0.2	0.1	0.4	0.3	0.7	0.6
Forestry	0.0(20-22)	0.0(20-22)	0.0	0.0	0.0	0.0	0.0	0.1
Construction	0.3(17)	0.3(18)	0.2	0.2	0.3	0.2	0.4	0.3
Mining	0.0(20-22)	0.0(20-22)	0.0	0.0	0.0	0.0	0.0	0.0
All occupations	100.0	100.0	100.0	100.0	100.0	100.0	100.0	100.0

[1]Number in parentheses are the occupations' country-specfic ranks for proportion of workers in the occupation who are female.

Source: Calculated from 1951 Census of Canada Vol. IV, Table 4; 1961 Census of Canada, Vol III - Part 1, Table 6; 1971 Census of Canada Vol III - Part 2, Table 8; 1981 Census of Canada, Cat. No. 92-917, Table 1; 1960 U.S. Census, Vol. I, Part 1, Table 201; 1970 U.S. Census, Special Report PC(2) 7A, Table 1; 1980 U.S. Census, Special Report PC 80-2-7C, Table 4.

segregation are similar. The extent of similarities in these patterns has not been investigated by other researchers since the definitions of the occupational categories for which data are published are not the same from country to country, or over time in either country. The reclassification we have undertaken is not completely accurate, and the resulting occupational groupings are quite highly aggregated (though not nearly as aggregated as the white-collar and blue-collar sorts of classifications used in some studies). Nevertheless, these reclassified data are probably adequate to reveal major trends or changes in the overall patterns of occupational segregation in the United States and Canada (for further evidence on this point, see Nakamura, et al. 1979b).

The U.S. and Canadian proportions of workers who are women for the 22 occupations, and for all occupations combined, for the years 1950/51, 1960/61, 1970/71 and 1980/81 are shown in Table 10.1 The occupations are listed in all our tables, including Table 10.1, according to the 1950 U.S. proportions of workers in each occupation who are women. For example, teaching, where 68.4 percent of the 1950 U.S. work force was female, comes first because it has the highest degree of female concentration according to this measure. The numbers in Table 10.2 show the U.S. and Canadian proportions, respectively, of all employed women in the labor force in each country in each of the occupations, and the numbers in parentheses in the first two columns show the country-specific rankings of these proportions from largest to smallest. Thus, we see that in 1950 in the United States, 5.5 percent of all women in the labor force were employed in the teaching profession, and we also see that the teaching profession tied with medicine and health as the fifth largest female occupational group. Table 10.1 shows the extent to which various occupations are female-dominated or male-dominated, while Table 10.2 allows us to see the importance of each occupation in terms of female employment. For instance, we see that the clerical profession is both female-dominated and a major employer of women. On the other hand, whereas the ratios of women to all workers are higher in each census year in the social sciences than in the work force as a whole, it can be seen from Table 10.2 that the social sciences is not a major employer of women.

As can be seen from the first three pairs of columns in these tables, the patterns of occupational segregation are very similar for 1950/51 through 1970/71. In both countries, a significant proportion of women were employed in clerical occupations, followed by service, sales, and fabricating and machining (a manufacturing classification). Similarly, very few women in either country worked in the natural resource occupations of fishing, forestry, and mining. Moreover, from 1950/51 to 1970/71, there was little change in the extent of occupational segregation in both countries, in the sense that the proportion of women in the traditionally female occupations remained almost the same. If the affirmative action

Table 10.3
Summary Statistics on Occupational Segregation of Women

	U.S.	CANADA
Percentage of all women workers in Clerical, Service and Sales occupations:		
1950/51	60.7	59.0
1960/61	63.0	60.0
1970/71	60.7	61.9
1980/81	56.9	61.4
Percentage of all women workers in fabricating, repairing; Teaching; and medicine and health occupations:		
1950/51	21.2	23.0
1960/61	22.2	23.1
1970/71	23.9	22.9
1980/81	21.7	19.8
Percentage of all women workers in teaching, clerical, and medicine and health occupations:		
1950/51	38.2	43.8
1960/61	43.1	47.6
1970/71	49.9	52.8
1980/81	50.4	51.2
Percentage of all women workers in service, Social sciences, and materials handling occupations:		
1950/51	24.3	21.9
1960/61	24.4	22.4
1970/71	21.1	19.5
1980/81	18.0	19.0

Source: Calculated from Tables 10.1 and 10.2.

and equal employment measures enacted in the United States were effective, we might expect to find that working women in the United States were less occupationally segregated than their Canadian counterparts in 1980/81. Looking at these figures in the fourth pair of columns of Tables 10.1 and 10.2, however, it is not at all obvious that this is the case.

Summary information in Table 10.3 provides a sharper picture of these U.S. and Canadian similarities in the occupation-specific concentrations of women and the distribution of women over occupations in 1950/51, 1960/61 and 1970/71 versus 1980/81. From Table 10.2 we find that the top three occupational groups of women in the United States in 1950 were clerical, service, and sales. From the top segment of Table 10.3, we find that over the census years 1950/51 through 1970/71 these three occupations accounted for roughly 60 percent of female employment in both the United States and Canada. Nor is there any sign of change in this pattern in Canada between 1971 and 1981. On the other hand, the 56.9 percentage for the United States in 1980 does represent a low over the 1950–1980 period. This might be interpreted as a sign of lessening occupational segregation in the United States.

The next three largest occupational groups of women in the United States in 1950 were fabricating and repairing, teaching, and medicine and health. These three occupations accounted for approximately 22 percent of all female employment in the first three census periods. There is a slight dip in the proportion of all women working in these occupations in 1980/81 versus 1970/71 in both the United States and Canada.

Looking now at Table 10.1, we find that the highest occupation-specific concentrations of women are in teaching, clerical, and medicine and health professions. From the third segment of Table 10.3, we see that from 1950/51 through 1970/71 roughly 40 to 50 percent of all women workers in the United States and Canada were employed in these three most female-intensive occupations, with the proportion growing slightly between 1970 and 1980 for the United States and falling slightly between 1971 and 1981 for Canada. From section four of Table 10.3 we see that about 20 percent of women workers were employed in the next three most female-intensive occupations—service, social sciences (includes, among others, lawyers, librarians, and social workers) and materials handling (includes stevedores and packagers) over the period of 1950/51 through 1970/71, with this percentage falling slightly for Canada and somewhat more for the United States from 1970/71 to 1980/81. Thus the evidence from section four of Table 10.3, like the evidence from section one of this table, might possibly be viewed as an indication of greater reductions in occupational segregation by gender in the United States than in Canada over the period 1970/71 through 1980/81. The observed changes are relatively small, however, compared to the observed fluctuations in the percentages of interest over the 1950/51 through 1970/71 period.

It might be argued that the broad occupational groupings used in our analysis mask or cover shifts in specific occupations. For example, the occupational group of medicine and health includes both doctors and nurses. Shifts may have occurred between these two occupations, with the overall percentage of women in the larger occupational group remaining the same. While this is true, the shifts in the United States and Canada have been fairly similar. For example, in Canada in 1971, women were 10.1 percent of all physicians; they were 17.1 percent of all physicians in 1981. In the United States comparable figures are 9.0 and 13.3 percent, for 1970 and 1980. A similar pattern is observed for lawyers. Women were 4.8 percent of this occupation in Canada in 1971, and 15.1 percent in 1981. The 1970 and 1980 figures for the United States are 4.8 and 13.6, respectively.

From the information presented so far, we would argue that women are occupationally segregated in both the United States and Canada. This is true whether we look at the employment of women in the most female-intensive occupations, or if we simply look at the employment of women in the occupations in which the largest number of women are employed. Second, we would argue that, in the time period of 1950/51 to 1970/71, there are clear U.S.–Canadian similarities in the patterns of female occupational segregation. Finally, we do not find any major erosion in these historical similarities in 1980/81.

OCCUPATIONAL SEGREGATION AND EARNINGS

Of course, equal opportunity and affirmative action measures in the United States could have played an important role in moving women from lower- to higher-paying occupations without necessarily altering any of the specific aspects of occupational segregation focused on in the previous section. Thus, in this section, we look for evidence of specific effects on the concentrations of women in occupations that traditionally have been higher versus lower paying.

We have defined occupations as traditionally higher or lower paying based on the average wage and salary incomes of both all wage earners and all women wage earners in Canada in 1951 (see Nakamura et al. 1979a, for this data). Using criterion, the three highest paying occupations are managerial and administration, natural sciences and engineering, and social sciences. Table 10.4 shows that the proportion of all women workers in these three occupations has risen from 1950/51 to 1980/81 from 3.0 to 10.2 percent for the United States and from 4.3 to 8.7 percent for Canada. The 1970/71 to 1980/81 changes of 5.1 percentage points for the United States and 4.8 percentage points for Canada account for most of the rise for both countries over the 1950/51 to 1980/81 period. Moreover, from Table 10.2 we see that the largest shares in observed U.S. and Canadian increases in the proportions of women working in the three highest income occupations are due to the increases in the proportions of women working in the managerial and administrative category. The increases in the proportions of women working in higher income occupations have tended to be slightly larger for the United States than for Canada.

Table 10.4
Further Summary Statistics on
Occupational Segregation of Women

	U.S.	CANADA
Percentage of all women workers in managerial, administrative; natural sciences, engineering; and social sciences:		
1950/51	3.0	4.3
1960/61	3.6	4.5
1970/71	5.1	3.9
1980/81	10.2	8.7
Percentage of all women workers in service, religion and farming:		
1950/51	26.0	23.6
1960/61	24.2	25.0
1970/71	18.6	21.1
1980/81	15.6	18.2

Source: Calculated from Tables 10.1 and 10.2.

Again using our criterion, the three lowest income occupations are service, religion, and farming. From the bottom portion of Table 10.4, we see that the proportion of total female employment in these three occupations has been falling over the period of 1950/51 through 1980/81 in both the United States and Canada, with the decline being somewhat greater in the United States. It is also true that the female concentrations (that is, the ratios of female to all workers) have risen steadily since 1950/51 in both the United States and Canada in farming, and have fluctuated without showing any downward trend for the service and religion occupations. But this just means that men have been moving out of (or failing to enter) these occupations at a rate at least as high as the female rate of exit (or nonentry).

In summary then, the proportions of women employed in the three highest-paying occupations have been rising, and the proportions employed in the three lowest-paying occupations have been falling, in both the United States and Canada. The patterns of change are basically similar in the two countries, although the rate of change in the United States seems to be a little greater.

CONCLUSIONS AND IMPLICATIONS

We have found that women workers are occupationally segregated in the United States and Canada, and that the pattern of this occupational segregation has changed somewhat over the period of 1950/51 to 1980/81. The nature of this occupational segregation and the observed changes in it are found to be quite similar, however, for both the United States and Canada. This is true even in 1980/81, despite the introduction of more vigorous and far-reaching equal opportunity and affirmative action programs in the United States than in Canada.

Could it be that the value of affirmative action and equal opportunity programs lies more in the social climate they help to create than in their specific provisions, including enforcement? As was mentioned before, Canada is both aware of, and familiar with, affirmative action programs, but any that have been implemented have been voluntary. Our data suggest the possibility that enforcement provisions of the sort adopted in the United States have, at best, only a modest effect in the short run. Perhaps the efects of these programs are due more to the social climates they create. Effects of this sort would have been observed in both the United States and Canada, because of the extent to which Canadians are exposed to U.S. news, magazines, and television programs.

These possibilities have clear implications for both organizations and individuals in the years ahead. How much commitment to affirmative action and equal opportunity should there be? In the United States, the government has been backing away from such programs, while in Canada (paradoxically) the government is slowly moving towards them. What should be the response of these moves? Perhaps these programs have accomplished all that can be done at this point: a recognition of the necessity for expanding employment opportunities. It may be that the changes brought about by this initial consciousness-raising will continue even in the absence of difficult-to-enforce, mandated programs.

Our data also suggest that any changes in response to such programs will be slow. It seems that the reality for most women in Canada and the United States is that they will continue to work in the low-paying, pink-collar jobs. Given this, a concerted focus on equal pay for work of equal value (comparable worth) might benefit larger numbers of women than would a focus on affirmative action and equal opportunity. Equal pay for work of equal value can provide immediate economic benefit for women by raising the wage levels in the occupations where women are clustered, while affirmative action and equal opportunity programs seek to move women into the traditionally higher-paying male occupations. While the two issues clearly go together, the effects of equal opportunity and affirmative action programs may be more indirect and long-term than those of equal pay for work of equal value.

Individuals choose occupations for many reasons, one being interest in the work itself and another being the wages paid for that work. Women who seek higher wages must enter traditionally male occupations; affirmative action and equal opportunity programs may help them to do so. But what of those women (and men) who find the traditionally female occupations intrinsically appealing or satisfying? Must they forego higher wages to do a type of work they enjoy? Equal pay for work of equal value holds out the hope of higher earnings in the future in some of the traditionally female occupations.

It may also be time to focus more of our attention on conditions in which large numbers of women are employed, regardless of the degree of female concentration in those occupations. How will these occupations be affected by free trade, or by trade restrictions and barriers? How are they affected by general economic measures used to stimulate the economy, control inflation, or reduce a government's budget deficit?

If occupational segregation is to be the reality for women for the foreseeable future, perhaps more attention needs to be devoted to both those general economic conditions and organization-specific policies that effect those occupations in which large numbers of women work. Does an organization truly have an equal opportunity program if, while it is slowly moving small numbers of women into managerial and professional positions, it is also, through the adoption of technology, eliminating or downgrading a large number of its clerical positions? What do we mean by equal employment opportunities?

REFERENCES

Armstrong, P., and H. Armstrong. 1978. *The double ghetto: Canadian women and their segregated work.* Toronto, Canada: McClelland & Stewart.

Beller, A.H. 1982. Occupational segregation by sex: Determinants and changes. *Journal of Human Resources, 17,* 371–392.

Bergmann, B.R. 1986. *The economic emergence of women.* New York: Basic Books.

Blau, F., and W.E. Hendricks. 1979. Occupational segregation by sex: Trends and prospects. *Journal of Human Resources, 14,* 197–210.

Gross, E. 1968. Plus ça change . . . ? The sexual structure of occupations over time. *Social Problems, 16,* 198–208.

Gunderson, M. 1976. Work patterns. In G.C.A. Cook (Ed.), *Opportunity for choice.* (pp. 93–142). Ottawa, Canada: Statistics Canada.

Gunderson, M. 1979. Decomposition of male-female earnings differential: Canada 1970. *Canadian Journal of Economics, 12,* 479–485.

Gunderson, M. 1985. Discrimination, equal pay, and equal opportunities in the labour market. In W.C. Riddell (Ed.), *Work and pay: The Canadian labour market.* (pp. 219–265). Toronto, Canada: University of Toronto Press.

Merrilees, W.J. 1982. Labour market segmentation in Canada: An econometric approach. *Canadian Journal of Economics, 15,* 458–473.

Nakamura, A., and M. Nakamura. 1981. A comparison of the labor force behavior of married women in the United States and Canada, with special attention to the impact of income taxes. *Econometrica, 49,* 451–489.

Nakamura, A., and M. Nakamura. 1985. A survey of research on the work behaviour of Canadian women. In W.C. Riddell (Ed.), *Work and pay: The Canadian labour market.* (pp. 171–218). Toronto, Canada: University of Toronto Press.

Nakamura, A., M. Nakamura, and D.M. Cullen, in collaboration with D. Grant and H. Orcutt. 1979a. *Employment and earnings of married females.* Ottawa, Canada: Statistics Canada Census Analytical Study. Catalogue 99–760E.

Nakamura, M., A. Nakamura, and D.M. Cullen. 1979b. Job opportunities, the offered wage, and the labor supply of married women. *American Economic Review, 69,* 787–805.

O'Neill, J. 1985. The trend in the male-female wage gap in the United States. *Journal of Labor Economics, 3,* S91–S116.

Oppenheimer, V. 1970. *The female labour force in the United States: Demographic and economic factors governing its growth and changing composition.* Berkeley, CA: University of California Institute of International Studies.

Robb, R. 1984. Occupational segregation and equal pay for work of equal value. *Relations Industrielles/Industrial Relations, 39,* 309–416.

Treiman, D.J., and H.I. Hartmann. 1981. *Women, work, and wages: Equal pay for jobs of equal value.* Washington, DC: National Academy Press.

11

Women Supervisors Experience Sexual Harassment, Too

Lillian Wilson Clarke

PREVIEW

This chapter on sexual harassment of women supervisors was written largely as a research review but it also conveys my personal experiences and observations. Because of this dual outlook, I hope this chapter will imbue women readers with an empathetic attitude toward other women who are struggling for professional survival and contribute to an improved sense of self-worth for readers who are alone in dealing with sexual harassment. This chapter is designed so that readers can determine whether they have received unwanted sexual advances which may be protested under federal legislation and whether reporting such incidents would improve working conditions.

WOMEN SUPERVISORS AND SEXUAL HARASSMENT

Women who work are likely to experience sexual harassment at some time in their working lives. As many as 18,721,000 (42 percent) of all employed women in the United States experienced overt sexual harassment in 1980, based on estimates derived from a random sample of women in all occupations in the federal government (U.S. Merit Systems Protection Board 1980) and labor force data from the U.S. Department of Labor (National Commission on Working Women 1978). The number of women in middle- and top-level administrative positions has more than doubled in the last five years (Wakefield 1984), and evidence indicates that these women are more likely to be sexually harassed than less-educated working women (Gutek 1985; Whitmore 1983). In this chapter, the problem of sexual harassment as it relates to women supervisors and the detrimental effects it has on human dignity and productivity will be explored. Then, individual and organizational solutions will be presented.

The Problem of Sexual Harassment

Sexual harassment in the workplace, as experienced by the victim, includes conduct ranging from explicit demands for sexual favors, to subtle derogatory remarks relating to the sex of an employee, and to retaliatory action when an employee resists harassment (Chapman 1981). The coercive nature of the interaction distinguishes it from sexual attention that is part of a mutually consenting relationship. In 1980, the Equal Employment Opportunity Commission established guidelines on sexual harassment that stipulate:

Unwelcome sexual advances, requests for sexual favors, and other verbal or physical conduct of a sexual nature constitute sexual harassment when (1) submission to such conduct is made either explicitly or implicitly a term or condition of an individual's employment, (2) submission to or rejection of such conduct by an individual is used as the basis for employment decisions affecting such individual, (3) or such conduct has the purpose or effect of unreasonably interfering with an individual's work performance or creating an intimidating, hostile, or offensive work environment. (Mastalli 1981)

In spite of the fact that women are legally entitled to protection from these behaviors, the problem of sexual harassment is believed to be endemic to the workplace due to women's structurally inferior status (MacKinnon 1979). Most women are employed in lower status "women's occupations," such as nursing and secretarial work, which are subordinate to higher status male-dominated professions, such as medicine and management. Women who do enter "men's fields" are usually vertically stratified into lower-ranking positions. In both situations, women are dependent on the approval and good will of male supervisors for hiring, retention, and advancement. Being at the mercy of male supervisors adds direct economic clout to male sexual demands. In addition, women's lower earning power deprives them of the material security and the independence which might increase their ability to resist harassment.

Concern about sexual harassment has increased as women enter the work force in greater numbers. Because women currently comprise 43 percent of the labor force, anything that affects them also affects U.S. companies and public sector organizations. Thus, it is not surprising that sexual harassment also has an impact on the organization's productivity and the job satisfaction of its female workers (Gutek 1985).

The Case of Women Supervisors

Contact between women and men at work increasingly is occurring with women in the role of peer or even as supervisor (Gutek, Morasch, and Cohen 1983). Research indicates that well-educated women are more likely to be sexually harassed than less-educated women (Gutek 1985). Consequently, the woman supervisor or manager is one probable target of sexual harassment.

One explanation for the difference between better-educated and less-educated women is that women with more education may be less tolerant of undesirable working conditions, less willing to put up with sexual harassment as part of the job, and more likely to report it. For example, Gutek (1985) reported several waitresses as saying they expect unwelcome sexual advances in their work. These women might be less inclined to report harassment than a highly educated professional woman who probably doesn't expect to encounter such treatment.

On the other hand, better-educated women may experience more sexual harassment because they are likely to be more occupationally dependent on a specific job than less-educated women, who may have more opportunities for employment within their job class. For instance, a waitress might leave one job and readily find another. However, an ambitious woman in advertising may want a job in a limited number of prestigious firms. The same is true for the aspiring lawyer, researcher, manager, or college professor. The career-minded lawyer is not likely to leave a prestigious law firm unless she has an equally good offer elsewhere. Similarly, an assistant professor at a highly regarded university is not likely to say "I don't have to put up with that: I'll quit." The woman with an advanced degree may be a particularly vulnerable target if her specific job is valuable to her and if she is ambitious. In addition, she may have high expectations for being treated in a professional manner which may make her less inclined to identify sexual overtures as harassment.

Lastly, the sex ratio of the occupation provides another explanation for why women supervisors might experience more harassment. Women *or* men who are in a statistical minority more often report sexual touching and comments by the opposite sex (Gutek 1985).

Most of the research centers around supervisor-subordinate relations. The implications are less clear in the case of supervisor-supervisor harassment, or for a woman supervisor being harassed by a higher up. How will her future advancement be jeopardized? What are the implications involved in reporting the incident? What differentiates the avenues of redress for the woman supervisor from the woman subordinate?

At the supervisory level, it may be especially difficult to prove sexual harassment. Consider the case of Jeanne Toure (pseudonym), an acquaintance of mine who is a supervisor at a large firm:

A new division head was assigned to manage several departments, one of which was Jeane Toure's, and Toure enjoyed working with him. In fact, they coauthored several professional papers. The supervisor, Carlton

Freeman, worked well with all of the employees under his supervision, at first.

Freeman had casually flirted with Toure from the beginning of his employment, but Toure ignored his continued flirtations in view of the fact that he had not been overtly coercive—that is, Freeman had not been overtly coercive until Toure decided to install a new operating procedure in her department.

Toure spent many hours after work devoting time to plans for the new procedure. As Toure worked alone one weekend, Freeman came into Toure's office ostensibly to review her progress. During the interchange, Freeman chased and physically attacked Toure. Although Toure was shocked and dismayed, she was not caught off guard. Her countermoves restricted the damage to a push and a pull match and a few broken fingernails. There were no witnesses. Toure did not know what steps she should take to see that this type of incident did not happen again. She also pondered whether she had a plausible case for the Civil Rights Commission. Toure was angry, but at the same time, she was fearful of retaliatory measures from Freeman if she reported him. The productive working relationship had been broken, and Toure stayed home from work the following day to consider the best possible action.

In the Toure case, there were no records of the sexual propositions, nor was compliance to sexual demands made a condition of employment or of promotion. Thus, it does not technically meet the definition of sexual harassment outlined by the U.S. Civil Rights Commission. This situation posed a dilemma for Jeanne Toure. Should she have reported the incident? Ignored it? Cut off communcation with Freeman? What impact would any action have on her professional image? If it were public knowledge, how would her relationships with coworkers be affected?

Consequences of Harassment

The woman supervisor who has been sexually harassed must anticipate how colleagues will react to her plight in choosing a plan of action. The woman supervisor, then, is in a delicate position. She must be forceful and yet carefully avoid any opportunity her male colleagues may have to label her "strident" in her feminism.

The woman supervisor must become knowledgeable of the answers to questions such as these: What are the statistics on hiring and promotion of women into management in their own organizations? How many women are currently in senior management positions? What is the company's attitude toward women in managerial roles? How do corporate policies support this attitude? How open and honest are their relationships with male co-workers? with other women? In what ways have they been expected to accommodate in order to succeed in management? What have they gained as a result? What have they lost?

Where organizations already have a procedure in place, what can the woman supervisor do to help train the staff about sexual harassment? Women supervisors can write articles for company newspapers, present seminars, and develop visual aids explaining the existing policies and procedures and extolling professional behavior. The attitude represented should not be one that accuses the organization of wrongdoing (a backlash would result from this approach) but rather an attitude promoting the benefits of separating gender and work. Gutek (1985) explained that organizations might try to separate work and sex more generally as a goal of preventive medicine. If the woman supervisor takes this position, it will gain considerably more attention than if it were from a subordinate. Top male managers, as well as other employees, must know that top female managers are not satisfied with less than professional treatment. The upwardly mobile female executive might not be able to count on the camaraderie of men peers. Because she is competing with men for the same job and salary, they could be unsympathetic to her situation. In fact, in order to exclude her from the social network, some of them might make threats or demands, display sexual cartoons or posters, make gender-related jokes or comments, ask personal questions, pressure her for dates, or physically touch her. She may indeed be "lonely at the top."

Woman colleagues and subordinates will not necessarily be supportive, either. They may lose respect for the woman supervisor who is harassed if they learn that she is faced with the same problems they have and that channels of redress are no more viable for her than for them.

The woman supervisor may be left with no place to turn. Her only alternative is to report the incident to a superior, who will very likely be a man. Unless these top managers have demonstrated their disapproval of sexual harassment, this avenue of redress may not be successful. If the person doing the harassing is viewed as more valuable to the organization than the person harassed, reporting it may put the woman supervisor's job at risk.

Further, sympathetic male colleagues who would never themselves behave in an unprofessional manner, will likely fail to see the true dimension and consequences of the problem. Indeed, for them, problems of sexual harassment are likely seen as isolated incidents that must be handled as they arise and not as an endemic problem with far-reaching consequences. The problem is rooted in our culture. And, like all cultural problems, the members who do not suffer tend to be the most myopic.

Company policy means nothing if it is not taken seriously, so the woman supervisor's good example becomes imperative. To bring the issues of corporate masculinism to the surface, women supervisors must be willing to speak with honesty and clarity about the need for change (Loden 1985). More important, they must demonstrate through their actions that a realistic alternative is available.

Personal. Faced with the specter of unemployment, discrimination in the job market, and a good possibility of repeated incidents elsewhere, many women try to endure harassment. But the costs of endurance can be very high, including physical as well as psychological damage. According to Whitmore (1983), women report more personal and psychological difficulties emanating from sexual harassment than from the actual demands of their work. Victims and researchers may have difficulty assessing the true repercussions of harassment, but it is safe to say that the more serious the sexual harassment, the more likely victims suffer significant work and emotional problems. Some examples cited by MacKinnon (1979) demonstrate this phenomena:

The anxiety and strain, the tension and nervous exhaustion that accompany this kind of harassment take a terrific toll on women workers. Nervous tics of all kinds, aches and pains (which can be minor and irritating or can be devastatingly painful) often accompany the onset of sexual harassment. These pains and illnesses are the result of insoluble conflict, the inevitable backlash of the human body in response to intolerable stress which thousands of women endure in order to survive.

Without further investigation, the extent of the disruption of women's work lives and the pervasive impact upon their employment opportunities can only be imagined. One woman, after describing her own experiences with sexual harassment, concluded:

Many women face daily humiliation simply because they have female bodies. The one other female union member at my plant can avoid contact with everyone but a few men in her department because she stays at her work bench all day and eats in a small rest room at one end of her department. (MacKinnon 1979)

For many women, work, a necessity for survival, requires self-quarantine to avoid constant assault on sexual integrity. Many women try to transfer to another department, which may even entail financial sacrifice, to escape the individual man. But once a woman has been sexually harassed, her options are very limited:

If she objects, the chances she will be harassed or get fired outright. If she submits, the chances are he'll get tired of her anyway. If she ignores it, she gets drawn into a cat-and-mouse game from which there is no exit except leaving the job. (MacKinnon 1979)

The consequences of complaining to the perpetrator usually are negative. The refusal is ignored or interpreted as the "no" that means "yes." If the refusal is understood, the harasser may accuse the woman of prudery. "What's the matter, aren't you liberated? I thought nothing bothered you" (MacKinnon 1979). The presumption seems to be that women want sex with men, so a woman who declines sexual contact with this particular man must reject all men. A woman who says "no" to sexual harassment may be criticized for trying to take away one of the few compensations for an otherwise meaningless, drab, and mechanized workplace.

When the harassment is interracial, the harasser may use different rationalizations. If the man is black and the woman white, he may resort to emotional blackmail, arguing "you're not the woman I took you for" (MacKinnon 1979). Similar sexual extortion may exist between white men and black women, and the chances are more readily available since white men are generally in positions of authority over black women.

Women's confidence in their job performance can be shattered by these events. They are left wondering whether praise they received prior to the sexual incident resulted from the man's perception of the sexual potential in the relationship—or whether the later accusations of incompetence are a result of her refusal to acquiesce to his demands.

When the harassment is subtle it may not be illegal, but it can be just as annoying. Consider this account from a 30-year-old female project leader in the finance department of a large company: "Not a day passes without my boss either sharing a particularly lewd joke with me or asking me what I did with my boyfriend the night before—complete with leers and smirks. My requests for him to cease have fallen on deaf ears; he seems to enjoy my discomfort and chides me for being a 'poor sport.' Prior to my divorce, he was totally inoffensive" (Collins and Blodgett 1981).

That such an attitude on the part of male managers is discouraging is evident from many comments. Typical was the remark from a 32-year-old financial officer in a small company: "I was the victim of harassment, and it was a miserable experience. When I voiced complaints to my so-called feminist male boss and colleagues, I was made to feel crazy, dirty—as if I were the troublemaker." Another woman wrote, "Sexual harassment eats away at the core of a woman's being, destroys self-confidence, and can contribute to a lowered feeling of self-worth" (Collins and Blodgett, 1981).

To be sure, most women are not certain that they can deal with an unwanted sexual approach and, in fact, they wonder whether anything they do would make them safe from such behavior in the workplace. A full 78 percent of them disagree with the statement, "If a woman dresses and behaves properly, she will not be the target of unwanted sexual approaches at work" (Collins and Blodgett 1981).

Interpersonal. Besides direct negative personal consequences, a climate of strained interpersonal relations with superiors, peers, and subordinates may result from harassment. Gutek's (1985) survey of sexual harassment in the workplace showed that supervisors can influence the work climate in a way that encourages or discourages sexual overtures and sexual hostility. Several women in the survey said supervisors ignored or laughed about sexual overtures. In one case where a coworker made sexual remarks to a woman, her male supervisor told her she should feel complimented. In another instance, when a woman was pinched by a coworker, the supervisor laughed and told her she had no sense of humor. The mere presence of a male supervisor rather than a female supervisor may reduce male workers' inhibitions about approaching women, even though the supervisor may not approach women himself.

The female supervisor is, of course, in a minority with her peers. What is her role when incidents of sexual harassment are reported to her? She has no authority, nor is it her place to police the workplace. Yet she may feel isolated and helpless in this situation, for as long as this behavior is allowed to continue, her authority within her own department and her ability to negotiate sucessfully with other departments is subtly but seriously undermined. How can she, then, act as a change agent in areas outside her purview, especially where these areas impact detrimentally upon her own efficiency and authority?

These problems lead me to conclude that where the organizational climate discourages sexual harassment, a woman supervisor who takes a forthright stand against it may be encouraged. On the other hand, if top level administrators avoid taking a stand against sexual harassment, the woman supervisor may pay a penalty for speaking out against it, and further, may even herself become a victim of sexual harassment.

If this is the case, subordinates may wonder how the sexually harassed female supervisor can maintain the authority needed to protect and supervise them if she is unable to protect her dignity from her male coworker's advances. Questions may arise regarding whether she sent out confusing signals to her male counterparts. Perhaps this happens because she did not know the rules of the game that is played in male-dominated organizations. Besides, reporting the incident might result in long-term consequences for the female supervisor and retaliation from the attacker.

There are no easy answers to such problems, and it goes to the heart of the dilemma faced by the woman supervisor. Where the woman is merely a token, the political implications may outweigh the satisfaction achieved by reporting the incident. Men with female supervisors apparently feel not only that their female supervisors have little power or influence in the organization, but also that their supervisors have little control over them (Gutek 1985). This may reflect their feeling that it is inappropriate for a woman to supervise a man. Harasssing the female supervisor may be an acting out of these underlying feelings of resentment which may exist in male subordinates and coworkers.

Women do find ways of fighting back short of, and beyond, leaving their jobs. Women have also begun to oppose sexual harassment in more direct, visible, powerful ways. The striking fact that black women have brought a disproportionate number of the sexual harassment lawsuits to date points to some conditions that make resistance seem not only necessary but possible. Protest to the point of court action before a legal claim is known to be available requires a quality of inner resolve that is reckless and serene, a sense of "this I won't take" that is both desparate and principled. It also reflects an absolute lack of any other choice at a point at which others with equally few choices do nothing (MacKinnon 1979).

Black women's least advantaged position in the economy is consistent with their advanced positions on the point of resistance. Of all women, they are the most vulnerable to sexual harassment, both because of the image of black women as the most sexually accessible and because they are the most economically at risk. These conditions promote black women's resistance to sexual harassment and their identification of it for what it is. On the one hand, because they have the least to fall back on economically, black women have the most to lose by protest, which targets them as dissidents, hence undesirable workers. At the same time, since they are so totally insecure in the marketplace, they have the least stake in the system of sexual harassment as it is because they stand to lose everything by it. Since they cannot afford any economic risks, once thay are subjected to even a threat or loss of means, they cannot afford not to risk everything to prevent it.

This view, while certainly true in some respects, is probably simplistic, for it is tied to a greater awareness of the need to struggle and the realization that gains come from action. Compared with having to struggle on welfare, for example, any battle for a wage of one's own with a chance of winning greater than zero looks attractive. In this respect, some black women have been able to grasp earlier and more firmly the essence of the situation, and with it the necessity of opposition, than other more advantaged women.

Other factors may contribute to black women's leadership on this issue. To the extent they are sensitive to the operation of racism on an individual level, they may be less mystified by the sexual attention in the workplace and realize that the attention is not "personal." Their heritage of systematic sexual harassment under slavery may make them less tolerant of this monetized form of the same thing (MacKinnon 1979).

Organizational. On an organizational level, because harassing men relate to women workers as women rather than as workers, they may be wasting valuable work time—both their own and the women's. In addition, if they supervise the woman they harass, they are probably not making effective use of them as employees. The man who is looking for a potential sexual partner when he hires a secretary will probably not get the most effective secretary. And the sales manager who is eager to have sex with a female member of the sales staff may spend lots of time with her, but whether he is helping her be a better salesperson is questionable (Gutek 1985).

Over 20 percent of women have quit a job, been transferred, been fired, or quit applying for a job because of sexual harassment. This represents a fairly substantial loss for organizations, directly through the loss of these employees and indirectly through lowered morale, as well as lowered commitment to the job where they were harassed and possibly future jobs (Gutek 1985).

SOLUTIONS AND ASSESSMENT STRATEGIES

It is unlikely that passing more laws will solve a problem that is exacerbrated by stereotyping, organizational climate, and socially controlled circumstances. An environment that encourages sexual harassment discourages optimum productivity. The challenge to management is to provide an organizational and socio-cultural environment which encourages productivity rather than sexual harassment. Harassment must be confronted fully by the top people in the organization in order to increase production.

Men are not likely to give up their positions of power easily. Women supervisors must be prepared to take advantage of every opportunity to press toward the ultimate goal—equality in the workplace. What can the woman supervisor do? How can she focus attention on the benefits of solving this problem? Of course, the woman supervisor cannot be expected to wrest power from top managers and change attitudes that have existed for many years. Rather she must become fully aware of what the issues are and what policies are in existence and then use that knowledge as a starting point from which to shape future events.

Specific solutions women supervisors may effect are: act as role models, seek other employment, promote professional conduct, provide emotional support to other women, promote women to serve in policy-making positions, establish promotion qualifications, develop media instruments, and report clear-cut cases.

Beyond this, how can the woman supervisor work within established frameworks to improve the organizational and socio-cultural work environment? Listed below is an elaboration of some strategies for action which were developed by the Committee on Civil Rights in 1982 and published in a booklet titled *Sexual Harassment on the Job.*

1. *Establish a procedure for handling complaints of harassment.* Many large organizations already have a sexual harassment policy and may have established a set of procedures. These steps provide a mechanism for uncovering and handling sexual harassment, as well as provide substantial protection against lawsuits, provided the steps are in operation. Where clear cut cases of harassment are reported and are successfully resolved, the result will be that this "hot" issue will be taken seriously.

2. *Determine whether there is a sexual harassment problem.* A confidential investigation to determine the extent of sexual harassment may be conducted through the personnel department. The results of the survey should be reported and employees should be notified of the existing company policy and procedures. Let workers know that they can report complaints and have them investigated discreetly and promptly.

3. *Seek legal counsel.* Because some workers and supervisors may not know exactly how the law defines sexual harassment, they should be able to discuss the topic with someone other than their immediate supervisor. Anyone who believes that workers should go to their immediate supervisor with any complaint or problem is unaware of, or blind to, the effects of organizational structure and the influence of supervisors on people's careers (Gutek 1985). This person should be a member of the legal profession. If the harassment has reached the point where it should be reported, the victim must be convinced that it is a clear cut case which fits the legal definition of sexual harassment.

4. *Prepare and distribute a policy statement on harassment.* The goals of eliminating sexual harassment and separating sex and work is in the best interest of the organization. In the short run, disseminating information about a well-conceived policy and set of procedures and putting them into action are important steps in encouraging professional behavior from all employees. These goals are best achieved in the long run by incorporating them into the ongoing practices of the organization: orientation for new employees, messages in the company's newsletter or newspaper, inclusion in the performance appraisal system, and ample role models of professional behavior from the chief executive officer on down (Gutek 1985).

5. *Train the personnel staff about sexual harassment.* Seminars, films, and other training programs on sexual harassment specifically are useful tools for education. Information on sexual harassment should be included in orientation for new employees. Posters, prominently displayed, should tell employees where to call or visit if they have been sexually harassed. A short memo announcing a new policy and procedures is highly effective. In the corporate world, a memo of this type is often analagous to legislation. In addition, a personal statement from the chief executive officer or an endorsement from top management demonstrates support for the policy.

6. *Prepare executives, middle management, and supervisory personnel.* Any effort at change that lacks the support of top management will be substantially less successful than one with such backing. Furthermore, the rest of the organization must know that top management backs the change. Through management level conferences, codes of behavior should be discussed. At these meetings it should be made clear that sexual harassment of female employees is considered unpro-

fessional and that anyone who practices it or condones its practice within his or her department will be held responsible. Sexual harassment should be considered in all performance reviews. This is rarely the case.

Evaluation of harassment might be more productively and efficiently handled in a category on unprofessional conduct. An organization has a right to expect employees to follow certain standards of conduct, including treating others with respect and dignity. In the case of harassment, the organization's human resources are being squandered. Sexual harassment, like other unprofessional conduct, affects the well-being of employees and the productivity of the organization. The organization serious about eliminating the problem should create sanctions against harassment in the reward system.

7. *Assign responsibility for coordinating the overall effort to prevent harassment.* Someone other than the supervisor should be responsible for coordinating the effort to prevent harassment. The coordinator might come from the company's legal staff, be it an outside consultant, a personnel specialist, or an ombudsperson. A combination of people with these backgrounds might form a team to investigate sexual harassment complaints. The coordinator should thoroughly understand sexual harassment, its psychological and organizational dimensions, as well as its legal definition. The job of coordinator also requires the whole range of skills in handling people. Finally, the organization should act on the recommendations of the coordinator and an investigative team if there be one. Thus, before they begin, managers should be prepared to follow the recommendations of the coordinator.

CONCLUSION

It is likely that some harassment in some work environments will exist as long as men and women work together; however, women supervisors can make a difference. Buoyed by support from the federal government through the EEOC, women now have avenues of redress through the court system that did not formerly exist.

On the other hand, subtle forms of harassment and retaliation against women which do not come under the law, may continue to occur and to cause emotional and physical damage. In spite of this, the work environment can be improved and women can gain respect as human beings, without outlawing mutually agreeable relationships. In conclusion, as more women demand career opportunities equal to men and a nondiscriminatory, harassment-free work environment, the growing general awareness of the problem of sex discrimination will become more acute.

REFERENCES

Chapman, Gordon R. (Ed.). 1981. *Harassment and discrimination of women in employment.* Washington, DC: Center for Women Policy Studies.

Collins, Eliza G.C., and T.B. Blodgett. 1981. Sexual harassment . . . some see it . . . some won't. *Harvard Business Review*, 59(2), 76–95.

Committee on Civil Rights. 1982. *Sexual harassment on the job*. Washington, DC.

Gutek, Barbara A. 1985. *Sex and the workplace*. San Francisco: Jossey-Bass.

Gutek, Barbara A., Bruce Morasch, and A.G. Cohen. 1983. Interpreting social-sexual behavior in a work setting. *Journal of Vocational Behavior, 22*, 30–48.

Loden, Marilyn. 1985. *Feminine leadership or how to succeed in business without being one of the boys*. New York: Times Books/Random House.

MacKinnon, Catharine A. 1979. *Sexual harassment of working women*. New Haven, CT: Yale University Press.

Mastalli, Grace L. 1981. Appendix: The legal context. *Harvard Business Review, 59*(2), 76–94.

U.S. Merit System Protection Board. 1981. *Sexual harassment in the federal workplace: Is it a problem?* Washington, DC: U.S. Government Printing Office.

National Commission on Working Women. 1978. *An overview of women in the workforce*. Washington, DC: Center for Women and Work.

Wakefield, Deborah Gay. 1984, November. Gender and power communication in middle- and top-level administration. Paper presented at the Southwest Region of the American Business Communication Association.

Whitmore, Robin L. 1983. *Sexual harassment at UC Davis*. Davis, CA: University of California, Women's Resources and Research Center.

12

Women Entrepreneurs: Problems and Opportunities

Robert D. Hisrich
Candida G. Brush

PREVIEW

This chapter will give the reader a better understanding of the characteristics, problems and keys to success for the woman entrepreneur. Although we feel the differences between men and women entrepreneurs are primarily demographic, it is demographics such as a lack of education in financial planning and limited occupational experience in business management, that often create the biggest obstacles for women entrepreneurs at start-up. Personal issues for women entrepreneurs, such as risk, confidence, and multiple roles are also discussed along with tips for self-improvement in these areas. Readers should consider how their own background and occupational experiences will impact their choice of venture and ability to overcome obstacles, particularly in the area of finance. We suggest keeping in mind your personal motivations, business skills, work experiences, and education as these relate to the strengths needed to run your particular business. We feel women entrepreneurs should also recognize and trade on their assets, such as organizational skills, and remember that the future is bright as many more women elect to become self-employed.

Susan Hogan is in the process of starting a new business. After studying for a degree in special needs education, Susan worked in the field for five years until reaching a point of frustration with the school system and boredom with her job. Her father, a self-employed contractor, suggested she open a business based on her lifetime hobby—horticulture. Taking his advice, she started a small retail shop selling herb wreaths, seasonings, plants, and other items. Her average annual revenues are $95,000 and she employs one assistant. Susan's biggest problems have been lack of capital, determining where to get marketing information, and developing a promotion plan that works. The growth and success of her store has been hampered by her lack of business experience, particularly in the field of finance.

This scenario is typical of many women entrepreneurs. Susan is one of the approximately 3.5 million women who are self-employed. According to Bureau of Labor Statistics, the number of self-employed women increased by 74 percent between 1974 and 1984, three times the rate of increase for self-employed men in the same time period. While the phenomenon of women-owned businesses is not necessarily new, especially in such fields as beauty care, childcare, and education, the growth in the past several years has also occurred in traditionally male-dominated fields such as construction, manufacturing, and financial consulting. Both the growth in self-employment and the venturing out into new areas has created significant public interest as well as demand on the part of these new entrepreneurs for guidance and information.

This growth in self-employment has occurred in spite of the significant risk and effort involved in creating and building a new enterprise. Certainly the financial and emotional costs can be high, but a woman frequently has to face a number of additional problems: being in a male-dominated arena, having few role models, not having an established network, and lacking confidence in her business skills. These factors indeed increase her risk of failure. In spite of this, the number of self-employed women has virtually sky-rocketed in the last ten years. Who are these women willing to add the stress of entrepreneurship to their life already full with family concerns? What opportunities are driving them? What problems are they facing, and how are they being overcome?

Most of what is known about the demographic characteristics of entrepreneurs, their family, educational and occupational backgrounds, their motives for starting their own companies, and their typical business problems, is based on studies of male entrepreneurs. This is not surprising since men still make up the majority of people who start and run their own business. Wortman (1986) established a research typology for entrepreneurship as a mechanism for an evaluation of the research in the field. Interest in women entrepreneurs as research subjects is a more recent phenomenon. Several studies have investigated characteristics, personalities, motives, and types of businesses of, and problems encountered by, women entrepreneurs over the last few years. Indeed, these studies of women entrepreneurs have investigated many of the same questions addressed in previous research of men entrepreneurs.

Schwartz (1979) investigated 20 female entrepreneurs and reported that the major motivators were: the need to achieve, the desire to be independent, the need for job satisfaction, and economic necessity. Also these female entrepreneurs tended to have an autocratic style of management—closely watching and controlling their business operations. While credit discrimination was the major problem confronted during the capital formation stage, underestimating the costs of operating the business and marketing the product or service were also problems they experienced.

Research by DeCarlo and Lyons (1979) of 122 black, white, Hispanic, and Indian women entrepreneurs found that minority and nonminority women enterpreneurs differed significantly from women in the general population on tests measuring achievement, autonomy, aggression, conformity, independence, benevolence, and leadership. Differences were found between minority and nonminority women, with minority women being somewhat older than their nonminority counterparts. Minority women entrepreneurs reported starting their businesses at a later age than the nonminority women. While nonminority female entrepreneurs had a higher need for achievement and independence; minorities placed greater value on conformity and benevolence.

The demographic characteristics, motivations, and business problems of 21 women entrepreneurs was explored by Hisrich and O'Brien (1981). Women entrepreneurs have particular business problems in the areas of obtaining lines of credit, being in a weak collateral position, and overcoming society's belief that women are not as serious as men about business. These problems were related more to the respondents' types of business than were educational level or background.

Do these women entrepreneurs reflect the type of business they were in? This question (as well as others) was addressed by another study by Hisrich and O'Brien (1982). The results indicated that women entrepreneurs were older and more educated than both the general populace and the respondents of previous studies. They also had very supportive parents and husbands. Female entrepreneurs in nontraditional business areas (finance, insurance, manufacturing, and construction) were different than their counterparts in more traditional business areas (retail and wholesale trade). One particularly significant difference was the apparent lack of external financial sources available to women entrepreneurs in nontraditional business areas.

THE WOMAN ENTREPRENEUR

The preceding studies produced useful insights into the nature of the woman entrepreneur, but none of them were general in scope. To fill this large gap in the body of knowledge, we carried out a major research project in 1982 that surveyed 468 women entrepreneurs from all areas of the country (Hisrich and Brush 1983). This research study, mailed to 1151 women entrepreneurs in 18 states, included a mixture of scaled, dichotomous, multiple answer, open, and ranking questions designed to assess the motivation for starting the business, general demographic characteristics, management skills, social and psychological factors, educational and occupational influences, and overall business data. In addition, 195 of these women participated in a follow-up study done in 1986 to measure the growth and changes in their businesses (Hisrich and Brush 1987).

The mail survey was sent to 344 of the original 468 respondents from 17 states who had indicated their names and addresses on the 1982 survey. This study assessed the characteristics of the venture five years later (size, product lines, ownership, legal form, sales, profits, number of employees, and income derived), aspects of the woman entrepreneur (management skills, networking, resources used, personal and business problems, and selected demographic characteristics), and the nature of any problems involved.

Characteristics

According to our findings, the typical woman entrepreneur is 34–45 years old, the first born child in a middle-class or upper-class family, is well-educated, has a well-educated supportive spouse, and operates a venture in a traditional woman's business area. Education played an important role in the upbringing of the women entrepreneurs. Not only were their parents more highly educated than the general populace (particularly their fathers), the women themselves also tended to be married to more educated men (see Table 12.1). The importance of education is exemplified in the following comment of one woman:

In my family, education was very important. The kind of education was a mix of vocational (useful) versus liberal arts. My mother was a dentist in a day when

Table 12.1
Education Level of Women Entrepreneur, Spouse, and Parents

Education	Woman Entrepreneur (N = 138)	Spouse (N = 86)	Mother (N = 114)	Father (N = 110)
Some high school	2%	4%	13%	19%
High school graduate	4	1	39	25
Some college/Technical school	29	27	22	17
College graduate	31	27	23	20
Graduate degree	34	41	3	19

most women did not even graduate from High School. But it was my father who was the motivator in my instance. I have two daughters—one is a sports journalist and the other a strategic planner with a Fortune 500 company. I was their motivator.

This high education level of the women entrepreneurs and their parents reflects both the social class while growing up and their parent's occupation. Most of the women entrepreneurs (67 percent) indicated that they grew up in a middle- or upper-class environment, which corresponds with their parents' occupations. Almost half of the fathers had managerial or professional jobs, while 32 percent were self-employed. Perhaps more significant is the career pattern of the mothers. While the majority, as might be expected, were homemakers, 28 percent had

Table 12.2
Major Fields of Undergraduate and Graduate Study

| Major Field | Undergraduate | | Graduate |
	First Major (N = 124)	Second Major (N = 38)	(N = 60)
Art	12%[1]	8%[2]	7%[3]
Business	15	24	20
Communications	6	3	10
Education	3	11	17
English, Literature	13	11	7
Health Services	7	3	8
Humanities	10	14	-
Law	-	-	12
Library Science	-	-	3
Math, Science, Engineering	10	5	5
Medicine	-	-	5
Social Sciences	24	22	7

[1]This is the percentage of those who attended college. Nearly 90% of the respondents completed this question.

[2]A second major or area of concentration was reported by 27% of the respondents.

[3]This is the percentage of those who answered the question. Approximately 43% responded, indicating that some started graduate studies but did not complete a degree.

managerial or professional positions and 13 percent were self-employed. Of the women entrepreneurs, 28 percent grew up in a family where both the parents held white-collar jobs or were self-employed.

For the most part, those women who were married at the time of the survey had the advantage of having a well-educated, well-paid spouse. Nearly three-quarters of the husbands had an undergraduate or graduate college degree, and most of them were employed in a managerial, technical, or professional position. While their average annual income was in the $30,000 to $40,000 range, more than 25 percent earned above $50,000. These women, then, were usually in a financially sound environment in which to begin their new business venture.

The woman entrepreneur tends to follow the typical educational path. Table 12.2 indicates the breakdown of college majors and graduate degrees earned. Most of the women had a liberal arts background, with concentrations in the social sciences (psychology, sociology), arts, and humanities. A significant number (15 percent) earned a degree in business administration, accounting, or related fields, but only a few majored in science or engineering. Nearly half of the graduate degrees were earned in business, education, and law.

The vast majority of the respondents had some work experience before launching their venture. Only 12 percent were homemakers or students immediately preceding their entrepreneurial career. The most common areas of past experience were administration (17 percent), secretarial (12 percent), and education (11 percent). Nearly 11 percent were professionals—lawyers, CPAs, or stockbrokers. Very few had upper-level management experience, and those with mid-level positions were likely to be involved in marketing or public relations rather than financial or operations areas.

The Entrepreneurial Venture

What was the nature of the entrepreneurial venture of these women entrepreneurs given this demographic composition and background? For 78 percent of the women entrepreneurs, their present venture was their first entrepreneurial effort. However, the majority (67 percent) had previous experience in the field of their present venture. This is highly correlated with the nature of the present entrepreneurial effort: 90 percent of the participants were engaged in service-related businesses while the remainder were in financial businesses and manufacturing. Thus the women tended to be in areas they knew best when beginning their new venture. Of course, this helps reduce any psychic risk or fear of failure. Also, the type of business ventures were not very innovative; few blazed trails into new markets or started a business based on product or service innovations. Instead, they elected to be new competitors with established or similar products in existing markets. The majority of businesses were retail and wholesale establishments (19 percent); management and business consulting (15 percent); advertising and public relations (11 percent); publishing, printing, and communication (10 percent); and financial, accounting and insurance (10 percent). The professionals were primarily attorneys. Some businesses were considered unique because they were male-dominated business areas (plumbing, petroleum, and construction). The majority of the businesses were young—less than four years old.

Motivations and Rewards

Our participants were queried regarding perceived gains associated with self-employment, including their motivations, the inspiration for their business idea, and the departure point for actually starting the new business. The four most important motivations, in order, were independence (29 percent), achievement (24 percent), opportunity (14 percent), and job satisfaction (13 percent). Over three-fourths of the women picked one of these four as the most important motivation for their entrepreneurial career. Less than 10 percent indicated that the desire for status, power, or money was the greatest motivation.

This emphasis on more personal, psychic driving forces is reflected in both the inspiration and departure point for the venture. More than half of the women got their business idea from personal experience—they saw a need not being filled. About 15 percent saw their personal desire for self-employment as the main idea generator, and 10 percent were encouraged by someone else to open a particular business. The departure point (bringing motivation and inspiration together into a new business) was caused by frustration with a current job coupled with interest in the area of business. While change in the family structure, such as divorce, widowhood, children leaving home, or demands of parenting, was mentioned as the departure point by about one-fourth of the women, 9 percent said they had no other employment opportunities.

In light of these motivations, what kinds of gains have these women entrepreneurs made over time? In the five years that elapsed between the surveys, several changes occurred in the business ventures of the women entrepreneurs in areas of legal form (i.e., sole proprietorship, partnership, incorporation, or S corporation), size in terms of employees and revenues, scope of markets served, and business problems. In our 1981 study 55 percent of the businesses were sole proprietorships, 23 percent were incorporated, and an additional 10 percent operated as S corporations (a corporation form between a limited partnership and a regular corporation). This changed significantly as in the follow-up study 51 percent are now incorporated, 8 percent are S corporations, and 33 percent remain as

Table 12.3
Numbers of Employees 1981–1986

Employees	1981		1986	
	Full-Time	Part-Time	Full-Time	Part-Time
None	31%	29%	23%	29%
1-10	53	62	60	64
11-20	14	7	11	5
21-30	3	4	4	1
51-100	1	0	1	2

sole proprietorships. The change to a more formal legal structure is fairly typical of growing enterprises. In terms of controlling interest in this business structure, only 86 percent of the women entrepreneurs own more than 50 percent of their enterprise.

Over the five years between the two studies, the size of the businesses have increased only slightly in numbers of employees (see Table 12.3). The typical business employed less than ten part- and full-time employees in 1981 and the same is true for current operations. There is a decrease in the percentage of responses in the "none" category from 31 percent to 23 percent, reflecting some growth.

There has been steady growth in gross revenues for the women business owners in the past five years as well (see Table 12.4). In the 1981

Table 12.4
Gross Revenues 1981–1986

	1980	1981	1984	1985	1986
RANGE					
$29,999	23%	17%	17%	14%	11%
$29,999-99,999	25	25	20	14	17
$100,000-499,999	36	40	54	57	46
$500,000-999,999	9	10	6	9	17
$1,000,000-4,999,999	7	8	3	6	9
$5,000,000	0	0	0	0	0
MEAN	$65,000	$72,000	$79,000	$86,000	$100,000

study, 47 percent grossed less than $100,000 while only 16 percent grossed over $500,000. In the follow-up study, 29 percent of the respondents had revenues of under $100,000, 26 percent over $500,000. The mode was in the $100,000–$499,999 bracket and the average has grown from $65,000 to $100,000, reflecting an increase of 54 percent in six years or an average annual growth rate of about 7 percent per year.

Another important measure of growth is changes in the scope of the business and plans for expansion. In 1981, 73 percent of the businesses served only local markets while only 7 percent and 3 percent served national and international markets respectively. Currently, 48 percent operate on a local scope while 17 percent and 15 percent serve national and international markets, a good indication of expansion and growth. In addition, women entrepreneurs also show their interest in moving forward by their willingness to add new products or services and drop older ones. Twenty-five percent indicated they had dropped mature products or services and 72 percent presently have plans to expand by: adding new services/products, moving to larger facilities, increasing volume, or servicing new markets. While nearly 25 percent planned to sell their venture, 17 percent intend to acquire another business and 8 percent hope to sell a division or product.

Business Problems and Solutions

The education and occupational background of the woman entrepreneur suggests that she is not particularly well-prepared for her new role. When asked to appraise their own management skills, these women rated themselves high in idea generation/product innovation and dealing with people; good in marketing/sales, business operation, and planning; and weak in finance. Lack of financial skills were the source of many of the problems identified at start-up. Nearly 87 percent of the women mentioned financial problems, including problems with obtaining lines of credit, having a weak collateral position, and lacking experience in financial planning. Additionally, many identified lack of business training, lack of management experience, and lack of guidance and counsel as problems encountered during start-up (see Table 12.5).

As might be expected, as the business matured, the problems changed. In commenting on current problems, the women generally mentioned fewer areas of concern (21 percent listed three or more as compared to 40 percent at start-up). Financial problems continued to be the leader, but problems with employees, legal problems, and inexperience with planning for growth all increased.

In the follow-up survey of 1986, the biggest obstacles to running a business were identified as time management, selecting and keeping good employees, limited capital, and fluctuating cash flows. Many prob-

Table 12.5
Problems and Risks Encountered

	Start-up	Current
Business and Personal Problems		
Lack of Experience in Financial Planning	29.8%	25.2%
Obtaining Lines of Credit	27.3	13.7
Lack of Business Training	26.6	7.9
Lack of Guidance and Counsel	22.3	13.7
Weak Collateral Position	20.9	12.9
Lack of Management Experience	20.9	9.4
Cash Flow	8.6	5.0
Employee Problems	1.4	7.9
Lack of Experience in Planning Growth	-	7.9
Lack of Respect for Business Women	18.0	10.8
Lack of Involvement with Colleagues	17.3	9.5
Demands of Company Affecting Personal Relationships	17.3	19.4
Greatest Perceived Risk		
Financial	60.2	59.7
Psychic	22.0	16.8
Family	12.1	9.2
Social	3.5	6.7
Other	2.2	7.6

lems were described as pervasive: inadequate time for managerial functions, heavy operating expenses, slow collection of accounts receivable, and inadequate sales. On the other hand, after being in business an average of seven to ten years, these women had little difficulty with decision making, purchasing, facilities, the company's credit position, knowledge of competition, and distribution of their product or service.

The occupational and educational experiences of most women entrepreneurs give them a disadvantage in business and financial skills. They have little decision-making, negotiating, or budgeting responsibilities, have not developed planning and analysis skills, and frequently lack any personal credit history. What can a woman entrepreneur do to compensate for these weaknesses?

First, women need to address the problem of not having a financial track record. Obtaining a personal loan and paying it off is the beginning of establishing a personal credit history. Developing a relationship with a bank by opening a savings account, a checking account, and getting to know the loan officer will help the woman entrepreneur know how to approach the business lending situation. Carol Bonner of Aircraft Technical Publishers offers this advice:

Study with experts, test your understanding and comprehension, then evaluate your results. You have to work at it and not give up.

Second, weak business skills or lack of a business education can be compensated for through seminars, workshops, self-help books, and college courses. The women surveyed reported many different sources used to improve or maintain their business skills.

Seminars, experts, self-help books, and trade association workshops were all popular sources of information. In addition, these women frequently reported seeking business guidance from fellow entrepreneurs, accountants, lawyers, and industry associates.

For women who are contemplating ventures, the best advice is to get management experience in the area of their venture before starting the business. Barring this, many volunteer groups or community service organizations have a need for treasurers or project chairpeople and this experience can be valuable in business management. Some women business owners have said that the process of refinancing their home, subcontracting for home construction services (plumbing, electrical work, or framing) has also been helpful as these require such business skills as budgeting, negotiating, and supervising.

A third possibility for the woman entrepreneur is to find complementary business partners or employees who have expertise in weak areas. Hiring outside experts and seeking mentors are also ways that women entrepreneurs can compensate. Research shows that approximately 32 percent of women business owners have mentors. The owner of a ladies clothing store explains:

My mentor provided not only business guidance, but coaching and knowledge. This combination of moral support and answers to questions helped me to succeed.

Personal Problems and Solutions

Many women indicated that difficulties or deficiencies in areas other than business skills cause ongoing problems in their businesses. Lack of respect for businesswomen, lack of involvement with colleagues, and company demands negatively impacting personal relationships, were all indicated by about 20 percent of the women as problems in start-up. As the company matured, the first two concerns were less frequently mentioned, while problems with personal relationships increased slightly (see Table 12.5).

Risks other than financial were often a concern with these women. While financial risk was deemed the greatest for both start-up and current operations, about 40 percent of the respondents were more concerned about psychic, family, or social risks (see Table 12.5). One woman stated: "The risk is more than financial, it is your friendship too, because you do not have time to accept or return social engagements."

Risk is very personal and threatening to any entrepreneur. For some women, risk taking is particularly difficult, reflecting internalized societal expectations and lack of business experience. The owner of a Scandinavian antique shop explained:

Our socialization creates high psychic risk in us. We fear failure in business because we haven't experienced the financial risks when we were young. That makes us conservative in our financial risk posture and often affects our business.

Lack of confidence is often expressed by a low self-assessment of business talents. The first step in dealing with lack of confidence is recognizing the tendency toward self-criticism. This requires honest self-appraisal and listening. Second, a concerted effort to state business strengths and skills positively without qualification should be made. Networking exercises developed by human resources experts suggest that women should learn how to brag about themselves or explain what they do well without using titles. Through these and other methods, women entrepreneurs should develop their confidence in their business dealings.

Along with the perception of personal risk and the lack of confidence, there were other personal problems mentioned: emotional stress, time management, and balancing the dual roles of family and business. Over 80 percent of the women indicated that one of these was the largest personal problem faced in operating a business. Since women entrepreneurs characteristically are married with families, self-employment creates new demands in this area as well. She must perform the role of a wife, a teacher, a counselor, a daughter, a cook, a maid, a household manager, as well as other roles depending on the situation. Establishing a business means she will also become a teacher, a marketer, an idea developer, a personnel manager, a stockholder, a president, a financier, a negotiator, a secretary, and an administrator as well.

How does a woman entrepreneur manage these roles and decrease the resulting stress? While no one has all the answers, some women entrepreneurs have offered the following advice:

1. Organize your time—Plan as best you can but learn to be flexible with your plans.
2. Delegate—Learn to delegate unimportant household and business activities to competent assistants. Get the less important mind-cluttering issues out of your head and focus on important issues.
3. Learn to say "No"—You don't have to do everything. Focus on your priorities rather than details.
4. Build a support system of family and friends—Emotional and moral support for your efforts is helpful in maintaining your stability.

The Strengths of Women Entrepreneurs

The problems many women have at business start-up are due in part to their education, occupation, and experience. However, the demographic profile described earlier also provides certain advantages that are often underestimated. For example, a liberal arts background provides a good general education allowing the woman entrepreneur to envision the "big picture" rather than be too specialized in her knowledge of the business. Certain occupational backgrounds also may provide strong "people" skills, that can translate into harmonious employee relations. For example, teaching experience can be very helpful to an aspiring woman business owner, as it facilitates training employees and explaining the product or service to suppliers or buyers and provides confidence in making presentations. Likewise, women with backgrounds in health care services can transfer their experience in being sensitive to people's needs to the business world. The owner of an advertising business stated:

I had a terrible confidence problem when I started my business, but I soon realized that my teaching experience, where I had to project, teach and elicit feedback was most valuable in working with clients.

Sometimes unrecognized by women entrepreneurs themselves, but often an asset, are the organizational and planning abilities that most women develop in running households, planning for food and shopping needs, organizing household repairs, interior decorating, and the logistical problems of transporting children or elderly relatives to and from various activities. These tasks require a great deal of planning and organizational ability which is an asset in business management. Women entrepreneurs should recognize and feel more confident given this experience.

Finally, the fact that many women entrepreneurs have professionally employed spouses is a major advantage as they are then not dependent on the profits of the business to support themselves and the family. The business can therefore exist for a greater period of time without the cash drain of a salary, giving it a better chance to succeed. This financial cushion, of course, may not be available for single or divorced women.

THE FUTURE

The future for women entrepreneurs appears very bright. Over the past 25 years there has been significant growth in woman-owned businesses as well as more opportunities in many fields. Today women entrepreneurs are more confident, have better skills, and are willing to take more risks than ever before. However, there may still be some time before a woman entrepreneur has complete acceptance in all fields and industries. This acceptance and the future of women entrepreneurs will be influenced by the roles of business, society, and education.

The role of business in the future is illustrated in the comment of a woman entrepreneur: "It would be nice to have acceptance in the world as a business person without having to overcome stereotypical views of women." The growth of woman-owned businesses has been increasing. This will have a significant impact on the business world, as women entrepreneurs will no longer be a minority in terms of absolute numbers. Financial institutions, governmental organizations and industry will become more familiar and comfortable with female-owned businesses as they lose their status as unique.

Second, since many woman-owned businesses are young—less than five years old—they are likely to grow and expand in the future. The increase in size will aid further in establishing the presence of the woman entrepreneur in the business community. Of course, this maturing and growth will be accompanied by new problems: harvesting products; meeting intense competition; and dealing with declining markets, rising wages, and business reorganization.

Perhaps the slowest and most difficult area to change will be societal values about women entrepreneurs. In the words of one businesswoman, this is likely to change only if, "women could be brought up the way men are: success oriented, goal oriented, and with the understanding it is important to do something with your life." Cultural norms and activities assigning women the responsibility for home and family are changing somewhat. However, even though some men are accepting family partnerships, role reversals, and shared household duties, the sex and role stereotypes still remain. As more women become economically and emotionally independent through careers or self-employment over the next decade, negative attitudes about women entrepreneurs and their dual roles will be less closely held. The women entrepreneurs of the 1960s, 1970s, and 1980s have laid the groundwork for more social acceptance of occupational choices. By 1990, the pressure for women entrepreneurs to "do it all" will be less and adjustments for family responsibilities and household duties will be more routine rather than the exception.

Perhaps even more important in the future is the role of education as is indicated in the following comment by a successful businesswoman: "Schools should create an environment that encourages women to learn finance, focus on careers and expect to be their own source of financial support." While the majority of previous research studies have not focused on women entrepreneurs, there is a major effort underway to learn more about their distinct characteristics and problems. As the number of women entrepreneurs increases and their established businesses continue to grow, the body of literature on women entrepreneurs will have a corresponding increase.

Women entrepreneurs who have successfully established a business can contribute greatly to the educational process by participating in high school or college classes as guest speakers, by hiring women students, or by being a mentor or role model for a potential women entrepreneur. This type of support is invaluable and can create motivation and inspiration for a future woman entrepreneur.

In all, the future for women entrepreneurs is bright and can perhaps best be illustrated by this comment of a woman entrepreneur:

In starting your own business, it's always sink or swim. But in the future, there will be more women succeeding and they will be role models for younger women. It will be okay to be a successful business or professional person and still be a successful woman. I am optimistic, but realistic about the hard work that entrepreneurship requires.

Still, of course, the real decision for a woman is whether or not to become an entrepreneur. One successful woman entrepreneur gave this advice:

Decide whether it is worth the sacrifice to start your own business. Evaluate the trade-offs—the time, the commitment, the security—versus doing it on your own. It is a very individual choice and one to be made with much thought.

REFERENCES

DeCarlo, J., and P.R. Lyons. December 1979. A comparison of selected personal characteristics of minority and nonminority female entrepreneurs. *Journal of Small Business*, 22-29.

Hisrich, R.D., and C.G. Brush. April 1983. The woman entrepreneur: Implications of family, educational, and occupational experience. Proceedings of the 1983 Conference on Entrepreneurship, 255-270.

Hisrich, R.D., and C.G. Brush. 1986. *The woman entrepreneur: Starting, managing, and financing a successful new business.* Lexington, MA: Lexington Books.

Hisrich, R.D., and C.G. Brush. April 1987. Women entrepreneurs: A longitudinal study. *Proceedings of the 1987 Conference on Entrepreneurship*, 187-199.

Hisrich, R.D., and M. O'Brien. June 1981. The woman entrepreneur from a business and sociological perspective. Proceedings of the 1981 Conference on Entrepreneurship, 21-39.

Hisrich, R.D., and M. O'Brien. June 1982. The woman entrepreneur as a reflection of the type of business. Proceedings of the 1982 Conference on Entrepreneurship, 54-67.

Schwartz, E.B. Winter 1979. Entrepreneurship: A new female frontier. *Journal of Contemporary Business,* 47-76.

Wortman, M.S., Jr. 1986. A unified framework, research typologies, and research prospectus for the interface between entrepreneurship and small business. In D.L. Sexton and R.W. Smilor (Eds.), *The art and science of entrepreneurship.* (pp. 273-332). Cambridge, MA: Ballinger.

General References

Adams, J., R.W. Rice, and D. Instone. 1984. Follower attitudes toward women and judgments concerning performance by male and female leaders. *Academy of Management Journal, 27*, 636–643.

Barnett, R.C., and G.K. Baruch. 1985. Women's involvement in multiple roles and psychological distress. *Journal of Personality and Social Psychology, 49*, 135–145.

Baruch, G.K., L. Biener, and R.C. Barnett. 1987. Women and gender in research on work and family stress. *American Psychologist, 42*, 130–136.

Benjamin, L. 1982. Black women achievers: An isolated elite. *Sociological Inquiry, 52*, 141–151.

Bergmann, B.R. 1986. *The economic emergence of women*. New York: Basic Books.

Bodine, A. 1975. Sex differentiation in language. In B. Thorne and N. Henley (Eds.), *Language and sex: Difference and dominance*. Rowley, MA: Newbury House.

Beutell, N.J., and J.H. Greenhaus. 1983. Balancing acts: Work-family conflict and the dual-career couple. In L.L. Moore (Ed.), *Not as far as you think*. (pp. 149–162). Lexington, MA: Lexington Books.

Boardman, S.K., C.C. Harrington, and S.V. Horowitz. 1987. Successful women: A psychological investigation of family class and education origins. In B.A. Gutek and L. Larwood (Eds.), *Women's career development*, (pp. 66–86). Newbury Park, CA: Sage.

Borjas, G.J. 1983. The measurement of race and gender wage differentials: Evidence from the federal sector. *Industrial and Labor Relations Review, 37*, 79–91.

Bowen, D.D. 1985. Were men meant to be mentors? *Training and Development Journal, 39*, 30–42.

Burke, R.J. 1984. Mentors in organizations. *Group and Organization Studies, 9*, 353–372.

Burlew, A.K. 1982. The experience of black females in traditional and nontraditional professions. *Psychology of Women Quarterly, 6*, 312–326.

Collins, E.G., and T. Blodgett. 1981. Sexual harassment . . . some see it . . . some won't. *Harvard Business Review. 59*, 76–95.

Collins, E., and P. Scott. 1978. Everyone who makes it has a mentor. *Harvard Business Review*, July–August, 89–101.

Davis, G., and W. Glegg. 1982. *Black life in corporate America*. Garden City, NY: Anchor Press.

Dickens, F., and J.G. Dickens. 1982. *Black managers: Making it in the corporate world*. New York: The American Management Association.

Farley, J. 1982. *Academic women and employment discrimination*. Ithaca, NY: Cornell University Press.

Farmer, H. 1985. Model of career and achievement motivation for women and men. *Journal of Counseling Psychology, 32*, 363–390.

Fernandez, J. 1981. *Racism and sexism in corporate life*. Lexington, MA: D.C. Heath.

Fishman, P.M. 1983. Interaction: The work women do. In B. Thorne, C. Kramarae, and N. Henley (Eds.), *Language, gender, and society.* (pp. 89–102). Rowley, MA: Newbury House.

Fulbright, K. 1985. The myth of the double advantage: Black female managers. *Review of Black Political Economy, 14*, 33–45.

Gerstel, N., and H. Gross. 1984. *Commuter marriage*. New York: The Guilford Press.

Gutek, B.A. 1985. *Sex and the workplace*. San Francisco: Jossey-Bass.

Hall, D.T. 1986. *Career development in organizations*. San Francisco: Jossey-Bass.

Hardesty, S.A., and N.E. Betz. 1981. The relationships of career salience, attitudes toward women, and demographic and family characteristics to marital adjustment in dual-career couples. *Journal of Vocational Behavior, 17*, 242–250.

Heilman, M.E., and K.E. Kram. 1983. Male and female assumptions about colleagues' views of their competence. *Psychology of Women Quarterly, 7*, 329–337.

Hisrich, R.D., and C.G. Brush. 1986. *The woman entrepreneur: Starting, managing, and financing a successful new business*. Lexington, MA: Lexington.

Kelly, R.F., and P. Voydanoff. 1985. Work/family role strain among employed parents. *Family Relations, 34*, 367–374.

Kraiger, K., and J.K. Ford. 1985. A meta-analysis of ratee race effects in performance ratings. *Journal of Applied Psychology, 70*, 56–65.

Kram, K.E. 1985. *Mentoring at work*. Glenview, IL: Scott, Foresman.

Kramarae, C. 1981. *Women and men speaking*. Rowley, MA: Newbury House.

Locksley, A. 1980. On the effects of wives' employment on marital adjustment and companionship. *Journal of Marriage and the Family, 42*, 337–346.

Malveaux, J. In press. Between a rock and a hard place: Integration, structural change, and the status of black women in typically female professions. In B. Gutek, A.H. Stromberg, and L. Larwood, (Eds.), *Women and Work.* (Vol. 3), Newbury Park, CA: Sage.

Markham, W.T. 1987. Sex, relocation, and occupational advancement: The "real cruncher" for women. In A.H. Stromberg, L. Larwood, and B.A. Gutek (Eds.), *Women and work.* (Vol. 2, pp. 207–232). Newbury Park, CA: Sage.

Marshall, J. 1984. *Women managers: Travellers in a male world*. New York: Wiley.

MacKinnon, C.A. 1979. *Sexual harassment of working women*. New Haven, CT: Yale University Press.

Misserian, A.K. 1982. *The corporate connection: Why executive women need mentors to help them reach the top.* Englewood Cliffs, NJ: Prentice-Hall.

Nieva, V.F. 1985. Work and family linkages. In L. Larwood, A.H. Stromberg, and B.A. Gutek (Eds.), *Women and work: An annual review.* (Vol. 1, pp. 162–190). Beverly Hills, CA: Sage.

Nieva, V.F., and B.A. Gutek. 1981. *Women and work: A psychological perspective.* New York: Praeger.

O'Neill, J. 1985. The trend in the male-female wage gap in the United States. *Journal of Labor Economics, 3,* S91–S116.

Pfeffer, J., and J. Ross. 1982. The effects of marriage and a working wife on occupational and wage attainment. *Administrative Science Quarterly, 27,* 66–80.

Rice, R.W., D. Instone, and J. Adams. 1984. Leader sex, leader success, and leadership process: Two field studies. *Journal of Applied Psychology, 69,* 12–31.

Rose, S. (Ed.) 1986. *Career guide for women scholars.* New York: Springer-Verlag.

Shann, M.H. 1983. Career plans of men and women in gender-dominant professions. *Journal of Vocational Behavior, 22,* 343–356.

Schein, V.E. 1973. The relationship between sex role stereotypes and requisite management characteristics. *Journal of Applied Psychology, 57,* 95–100.

Schwartz, E.B. 1979. Enterpreneurship: A new female frontier, *Journal of Contemporary Business,* 47–76.

Smith, A., and A. Stewart. 1983. Approaches to studying racism and sexism in black women's lives. *Journal of Social Issues. 39,* 1–15.

Staines, G.L., K.J. Pittick, and D.A. Fudge. 1986. Wives' employment and husbands' attitudes toward work and life. *Journal of Applied Psychology, 71,* 118–128.

Valdez, R.L., and B.A. Gutek. 1987. Family roles: A help or a hindrance for working women? In B.A. Gutek and L. Larwood (Eds.), *Women's career development.* (pp. 157–169). Beverly Hills, CA: Sage.

Wexley, K.N., and E.D. Pulakos. 1983. The effects of perceptual congruence and sex on subordinates' performance appraisals of their managers. *Academy of Management Journal, 26,* 666–676.

Wiley, M.G., and A. Eskelson. 1982. The interaction of sex and power base on perceptions of managerial effectiveness. *Academy of Management Journal, 25,* 671–677.

Wolf, W., and N. Fligstein. 1979. Sex and authority in the workplace. *American Sociological Review, 44,* 235–252.

Zey, M.G. 1984. *The mentor connection.* Homewood, IL: Dow Jones-Irwin.

Index

About the Editors and Contributors

SUZANNA ROSE, Ph.D., is an Associate Professor of Psychology and Director of the Women's Studies Program at the University of Missouri-St. Louis. She received her doctorate from the University of Pittsburgh in 1979. Her research is on women's professional networks, friendships, and romantic relationships. She edited *Career Guide for Women Scholars* and currently is on the editorial board of *Group and Organization Studies*. She also is a member of the governing body of the Association for Women in Psychology.

LAURIE LARWOOD, Ph.D., is Dean of the School of Business at the State University of New York at Albany. Dr. Larwood has published extensively in the field of women and work. She is editor or author of 11 books, including *Women and Work: An Annual Review*, vols. 1, 2, & 3; *Women's Career Development*; and *Strategies . . . Success . . . Senior Executives Speak Out* (forthcoming, Harper & Row). She also is editor of *Group and Organization Studies* and formerly was chair of the Women and Management Division of the Academy of Management.

CANDIDA G. BRUSH is presently a Ph.D. candidate in Management Policy at Boston University. She received a Master's in Business Administration from Boston College, where she was awarded the Dean's Letter of Commendation for Special Achievement in working with the Small Business Development Center. Ms. Brush is the co-author (with Robert Hisrich) of *The Woman Entrepreneur: Starting, Financing, and Managing a Successful New Business*. She is also a partner in Brush & Coogan Associates, a consulting business offering assistance to entrepreneurs, and runs a land sales and development business with her husband.

SUSAN SCHICK CASE received her Ph.D. in Organization Studies at State University of New York at Buffalo. She is an Assistant Professor of Management at the University of Texas at El Paso. Her research interests are in managerial language, patterns of managerial influence, and the management of cultural differences. Current projects include an examination of gender differences and similarities in how managers speak, analyses of changing language patterns over time in decision-making groups, self-portraits on career experiences of Mexican-American women executives, and work of the management of cultural differences with Maquila workers in Mexican factories.

GEORGIA T. CHAO is an Assistant Professor of Management at Michigan State University. She received her Ph.D. degree in industrial and organizational psychology at Pennsylvania State University. Her current research interests are in the areas of career development and organizational socialization.

LILLIAN WILSON CLARKE, Associate Professor, is Chairperson of the Department of Office Management at Southern University at New Orleans. She received her Master's degree from the University of New Orleans and her Ph.D. from the University of Southern Mississippi. Dr. Clarke has published 27 articles in professional journals such as the *Journal of Business Education, Business Education Forum*, and *Delta Pi Epsilon Journal*. Her biographical sketch appears in the *U.S. Register of American Writers of 1986*. She was nominated as business teacher of the year by the Louisiana Association of Business Educators, and she was awarded the Mayor's Award for outstanding community service in 1986. Current research interests include communication theory and gender-related issues.

CHESTER C. COTTON, Ph.D., (University of Oregon) is Professor of Management in the College of Business at California State University, Chico. During the 1985–1986 academic year he was Visiting Professor of Management in the College of Business and Public Administration at the University of Guam. Articles by Dr. Cotton have appeared in *Administrative Sciences Quarterly, Academy of Management Review, Group and Organization Studies, Journal of Applied Behavioral Science, Personnel Journal*, and *Training and Development Journal*.

DALLAS CULLEN, who received her Ph.D. from Ohio State University, is an Associate Professor in the Department of Organization Analysis at the

University of Alberta. She teaches courses in gender issues in organizations and does research on various aspects of women's labor force participation.

IRENE DEVINE, Ph.D. (Organizational Behavior, Case Western Reserve University) is Associate Dean of Administrative Affairs and Assistant Professor, Department of Management, Concordia University. Her consulting and training experience in Canada and the United States includes business and industry as well as educational, social service, health, and government organizations. Her research interests are in the areas of organizational change and development and professional women in organizations.

LINDA DYER, Ph.D. (Carnegie-Mellon University), is Assistant Professor of Management at Concordia University and is a Fellow at the Simone de Beauvoir Institute (Women's Studies). She is interested in how women have survived and prospered in diverse organizations such as business firms, universities, and convents, both today and in the past.

ROBIN J. ELY is a doctoral candidate in Organizational Behavior at Yale University. Her dissertation examines how the proportional distribution of women in positions of organizational authority affects hierarchical and peer relations. Her research interests focus on gender-related issues in organizational behavior and depression and social cognition. Ms. Ely also has been involved in a number of statistical and organizational consulting projects for government and private industry.

DANA L. FARROW, Ph.D., is Chair and Associate Professor of the Department of Management and International Business at Florida International University. Dr. Farrow's work experience includes employment as an industrial engineer. He has published extensively in the areas of human relations, management, and drug addiction. His work includes the book *Using Applied Psychology in Personnel Management*. Dr. Farrow also does consulting in areas such as effective management skills and equal employment opportunity issues.

ROBERT D. HISRICH is the Bovaird Chair Professor of Entrepreneurial Studies and Private Enterprise and Professor of Marketing at The University of Tulsa and is also President of H & P Associates, a marketing and management consultant firm he founded. Dr. Hisrich is the author of *Marketing a New Product: It's Planning, Development, and Management; The MBA Career; Marketing Decisons for New and Mature Products; The Women*

Entrepreneur; and *Entrepreneurship, Intrapreneurship, and Venture Capital.* He has published widely, as well, in business and management journals. Dr. Hisrich formerly held management positions with Proctor and Gamble and Ford Motor Co., has acted as a consultant to several corporations, and has designed management programs for U.S. and foreign businesses and governments.

MARSHA KATZ has been an Assistant Professor of Management at Loyola University of Chicago since 1981. She is a principal in the consulting firm, M & M Associates of Schaumburg, Inc. Her specialty is management training and leading seminars on role conflict resolution for women. She has published in a variety of professional journals, including *Academy of Management Review, Organizational Behavior Teaching Review, College Student Journal, Journal of Conflict Resolution, Public Personnel Management,* and *Compensation and Benefits Review.*

S.D. MALIK is a Ph.D. candidate in Organizational Behavior and Personnel at Michigan State University. Currently, Ms. Malik is a Visiting Lecturer in the Department of Organization and Human Relations at the State University of New York in Buffalo. Ms. Malik's research interests are centered in the areas of decision making and management development.

JOHN F. McKENNA (Ph.D., University of California, Irvine) is Professsor of Management in the College of Business at California State University, Chico. Articles by Dr. McKenna have appeared in the *Academy of Management Journal, Human Relations,* and *Business Horizons.* He is coauthor, with Andrew Sikula, of *The Management of Human Resources: Personnel Text and Current Issues.*

ALICE NAKAMURA (Ph.D., Johns Hopkins University) is Professor in the Department of Finance and Management Science at the University of Alberta. Her research interests are labor economics and econometric methods.

MASAO NAKAMURA received his Ph.D. from Johns Hopkins University and currently is Professor in the Department of Finance and Management Science. His research focuses on models and theories of economic behavior among firms and households.

STELLA M. NKOMO is an Assistant Professor in Personnel/Human Resource Management in the College of Business and Economics at the

University of North Carolina at Charlotte. She earned her Ph.D. in business administration from the University of Massachusetts at Amherst. Her current research interests include career experience of black managers, women in management, and nonability factors in performance assessment. She has published articles in *Personnel Administrator; Group and Organization Studies; Strategic Management Journal* and is currently co-authoring a text of cases and exercises for personnel/human resource management.

GLORIA L. SHAPIRO, Ph.D., is currently a Visiting Professor in the College of Business at the University of North Florida, where she teaches courses in management science and women and management. She has presented papers at many national and international conferences and authored several articles. Dr. Shapiro was on the national executive board of the Women and Management Division of the Academy of Management for four years and served as the division's first historian. She is a consultant to industry, a frequent guest on television and radio talk shows and conducts seminars on negotiating, delegating, superwomen, time management, mentoring, and networking.